Marija Wakounig, Markus Peter Beham (Eds.)

Mind and Memory in Discourse

EUROPA ORIENTALIS

herausgegeben vom

Institut für Osteuropäische Geschichte
an der Universität Wien

Band 15

LIT

Mind and Memory in Discourse

Critical Concepts and Constructions

edited by

Marija Wakounig and Markus Peter Beham

editorial support by
Ferdinand Kühnel

LIT

Cover image:
http://ndtponton.files.wordpress.com/2013/08/2013-07-11-3109.jpg

Gedruckt mit Unterstützung des Bundesministeriums für Wissenschaft, Forschung und Wirtschaft in Wien.

Bibliographic information published by the Deutsche Nationalbibliothek
The Deutsche Nationalbibliothek lists this publication in the Deutsche Nationalbibliografie; detailed bibliographic data are available in the Internet at http://dnb.d-nb.de.

ISBN 978-3-643-90622-9

A catalogue record for this book is available from the British Library

Klosbachstr. 107
CH-8032 Zürich
Tel. +41 (0) 44-251 75 05
Fax +41 (0) 44-251 75 06
E-Mail: zuerich@lit-verlag.ch
http://www.lit-verlag.ch

LIT VERLAG Dr. W. Hopf
Berlin 2014
Fresnostr. 2
D-48159 Münster
Tel. +49 (0) 2 51-62 03 20
Fax +49 (0) 2 51-23 19 72
E-Mail: lit@lit-verlag.de
http://www.lit-verlag.de

Distribution:
In the UK: Global Book Marketing, e-mail: mo@centralbooks.com
In North America: International Specialized Book Services, e-mail: orders@isbs.com
In Germany: LIT Verlag Fresnostr. 2, D-48159 Münster
Tel. +49 (0) 2 51-620 32 22, Fax +49 (0) 2 51-922 60 99,
E-mail: vertrieb@lit-verlag.de

In Austria: Medienlogistik Pichler-ÖBZ, e-mail: mlo@medien-logistik.at
e-books are available at www.litwebshop.de

Contents

Center Reports

Articles

I. (Collective) Mind and Memory

Preface

The seventh special volume of the Europa Orientalis series contains reports and papers from the VII Annual Convention of the Centers for Austrian and Central European Studies, held in Leiden (The Netherlands) on October 23–27, 2013. These Centers were established, to improve the Cooperation between the host nations and Austria. They are also an opportunity for young researchers to connect with colleagues and to strengthen their international perspective during the scientific career.

This special volume covers a wide range of topics compiled by current Ph.D. students of the eight Centers for Austrian and Central European Studies. The focus of the contributions is on cultural, political and modern Central European history. The annual reports of the Center Directors provide a vast overview of the activities of these institutions during the Academic Year 2013/2014.

It is one of the most important aims of the Austrian Federal Ministry of Science, Research and Economy not only to supply young scholars with research grants and scholarships, but also to encourage them to establish themselves in the international scientific community. While senior scholars usually benefit from their connections with partners all over the globe, the younger generation often has trouble getting in touch with their colleagues abroad. For this reason, in 2007, the then Austrian Federal Ministry of Science and Research decided to bring together the best and most promising Ph.D. students conducting their research at the various Centers for Austrian and Central European Studies. The present volume shows how important it was to implement the idea of the annual meetings and to support it financially. International experience and exchange will be more important for future scientists. Therefore events like the VII Annual Convention of the Centers for Austrian and Central European Studies are a significant contribution to reach these targets.

Dr. Reinhold Mitterlehner

Vice Chancellor and Austrian Federal Minister of Science, Research and Economy

Preface

The seventh special volume of the Europa Orientalis series contains reports and papers from the VII Annual Convention of the Centers for Austrian and Central European Studies, held in Leiden (The Netherlands) on October 23–27, 2013. These Centers were established, to improve the Cooperation between the host nations and Austria. They are also an opportunity for young researchers to connect with colleagues and to strengthen their international perspective during the scientific career.

This special volume covers a wide range of topics compiled by current Ph.D. students of the eight Centers for Austrian and Central European Studies. The focus of the contributions is on cultural, political and modern Central European history. The annual reports of the Center Directors provide a vast overview of the activities of these institutions during the Academic Year 2013/2014.

It is one of the most important aims of the Austrian Federal Ministry of Science, Research and Economy not only to supply young scholars with research grants and scholarships, but also to encourage them to establish themselves in the international scientific community. While senior scholars usually benefit from their connections with partners all over the globe, the younger generation often has trouble getting in touch with their colleagues abroad. For this reason, in 2007, the then Austrian Federal Ministry of Science and Research decided to bring together the best and most promising Ph.D. students conducting their research at the various Centers for Austrian and Central European Studies. The present volume shows how important it was to implement the idea of the annual meetings and to support it financially. International experience and exchange will be more important for future scientists. Therefore events like the VII Annual Convention of the Centers for Austrian and Central European Studies are a significant contribution to reach these targets.

Dr. Reinhold Mitterlehner

Vice Chancellor and Austrian Federal Minister of Science, Research and Economy

Editorial

Once more, the work of the Austrian Centers has culminated in a volume presenting the wide range of activities this international network is engaged in, in particular the working papers of the Center's current Ph.D. students, which lie at the heart of the present publication. It is an invaluable tool for the interested reader to get a concise overview of current research interests and projects undertaken across the field of humanities and beyond. The disciplines thereby covered are range from history over cultural studies to law and pedagogy. In particular, the present volume includes a number of highly valuable biographical studies, set to cover a number of desiderata of the current research landscape. The title 'Mind and Memory in Discourse' refers not just to the topics of the respective papers, but also to the innovative methodology applied thereto. Thereby, the volume has been structured according to the broader framework of collective and individual memory (biographical research), legal aspects and novel methodological approaches to analysis of mind and memory.

Each Center's director respectively the thesis' supervisors were obliged to advise their Ph.D. students in drafting their papers before these were sent to the editors. This has surely resulted in an even higher quality output of the research work presented within this volume. Particular effort was made by both authors and editors in consistently translating foreign language titles within the text and in footnotes into the English language to make the volume even more accessible for the English speaking scientific community. These are included in square brackets, either within the text or – with regard to longer passages – in the footnotes. Foreign language terms used within the text, in particular Latin, German and French technical terms are held in italics. Abbreviations within the text are usually spelt out at their first mention. While the individual articles were formally streamlined following the guidelines of the Europa Orientalis series and put into American English, the editors have tried to limit changes to the character of a text only where it served readability. Therefore, each text remains an expression of style and method of the individual author.

The editors would especially like to thank the Austrian Federal Ministry of Science, Research and Economy (Bundesministerium für Wissenschaft, Forschung und Wirtschaft, BMWFW) and the Austrian Agency for International Cooperation in Education and Research (Österreichischer Austauschdienst, OeAD) for their support. Ferdinand Kühnel of the University of Vienna has proven an invaluable help and addition to the editing process.

Vienna, July 2014

Marija Wakounig, Markus Beham

Center Reports

Marija Wakounig

Times of Fluctuation and Changes – The Academic Year 2013/2014

University of Vienna

Personnel

The Academic Year 2013/2014 offered a lot of opportunities for presenting the capacities of the staff of the Institute of East European History. This was connoted with the highest change and fluctuation in the personnel matters in the Institute's long history. At the moment, eleven scholars are employed at the Institute, among whom seven have a permanent contract: three full professors, three extraordinary professors, and one assistant professor. The two post-doc assistants and the two prae-doc assistants have temporary contracts. Emilia Hrabovec, our colleague since 1995, quitted her post at the end of September 2013 due to a professorship in Bratislava, after having been discharged on unpaid leave since 2005. For Hans-Ulrich Lempert and Sarah Lemmen, who were the last 'stakeholders' during the temporary leave of Hrabovec, the employment ended in January/March 2014. The 'credit points' of this vacant post will be hopefully used for the professorship for East European History/Russian History, which was previously held by Andreas Kappeler and which is vacant since his retirement in 2011. This is also the reason why the Institute is forced to apply for a guest professor each term. Russian/Soviet History was taught by Francine-Dominique Liechtenhan (Paris), Angela Rustemeyer (Köln), and Wolfgang Mueller (Wien) during the Academic Year 2013/2014. In addition, we got new colleagues, who are reinforcing the staff's capacities since April/September 2013: Elisabeth Haid and Ulrich Hofmeister became prae-docs for two years and Konrad Petrovszky, who moved from Berlin to Vienna, was appointed to a newly created post-doc position, temporarily limited to a four year contract period. Machteld Venken and Dean Vuletic are our research fellows for five/three years, which means that the number of project collaborators has not changed. Also, the personnel and numerical structure of the administration has remained unchanged.

Conferences

The Institute's staff organized and hosted – mainly also as participants – international conferences, symposia, workshops, and other events. Among the most moving and surprising meetings was the international symposium 'Verbunden und Verflochten. Geschichte und Legenden', in honor of the seventieth birthday of our former colleague *emeritus* Andreas Kappeler. The event took place in Vienna on September 18–20, 2013. The opening remarks and the *laudatio* were given at the Center for International Development; the conference was hosted by the Viennese Slovenian Research Institute (Slovenski znanstveni inštitut Dunaj, SZI). The organizers Christoph Augustynowicz, Alojz Ivanišević, and Marija Wakounig were able to invite fourteen international friends and colleagues of Kappeler as a surprise, to present papers, which corresponded to the *histoire croisée* and entangled and shared history. The funds were provided by the Fritz Thyssen Stiftung and the Viennese Austrian and Central European Center via the Bundesministerium für Wissenschaft, Forschung und Wirtschaft.

From 13 to the 15 November 2013, Marija Wakounig organized and, as director of the Viennese Austrian and Central European Center in cooperation with Vincenc Rajšp, director of the Viennese Slovenian Research Institute, funded the international symposium 'Ordenshäuser und Ordensprovinzen als Verbindungs- und Kreuzungsfaktoren von geographischen Räumen'. Nineteen researchers provided new insights into the diverse, 'colorful' and trans-regional relations between the various congregations and monasteries, monks, and nuns through the ages.

The conference 'Heilige und Heiligkeit. Transkulturelle Verehrungskulte in epochenübergreifender Perspektive', organized by our colleague Kerstin S. Jobst and Dietlind Hüchtker from Leizpig (GWO), was held from 27 February to 1 March 2014. While the welcome and opening remarks and the keynote speech (Waltraud Pulz, München) were given at the Old Chapel (Alte Kapelle) on the University Campus, the conference venue was at the Institute's lecture hall.

The Institute hosted the conference 'Urban Space and Multilingualism in the Late Habsburg Monarchy', which was prepared in cooperation with the University of Tübingen and the Ludwig Boltzmann-Institut für Historische Sozialwissenschaft and held from 13–15 March 2014. This meeting was organized by our colleague Markian Prokopovych as well as Tamara Scheer (Boltzmann-Institut) and Carl Bethke (Tübingen).

Our Institute held the international conference 'Cities as Cultural Spaces' in cooperation with the neighborhood Institute of Slavonic Studies, which was devoted to a very difficult region 'Ukraine: History, Legacy, Literature', from 3–5 April 2014. The conference was organized within the frame of the research project 'Region, Nation and Beyond. An Interdisciplinary and Transcultural Reconceptualization of Ukraine'; it was financed by German, Swiss, and Austrian Research Funds.

From 15 to 17 May 2014, the Institute hosted the international conference 'Autocracy and Market Economy. The Transformation in Eastern Europe and East Asia in Comparison'. The event was a result of a cooperation between our Institute and the Departments of Political Sciences and East Asia Studies at the University of Vienna, and was financially supported by the University's research platform 'Wiener Osteuropaforum' and the City of Vienna. The opening public lecture was held at the Österreichische Nationalbank, the conference in our Institute's lecture hall.

Just at the beginning of the summer vacation, the Institute hosted the young-researcher-conference 'Ethno-political Conflicts Between the Adriatic and the Aegean in the 1940s. The Long-term Impact on Diplomacy and Cultures of Memory', from 3–4 July 2014. The conference was organized and supported by young researchers of the research platform 'Wiener Osteuropaforum' as well as the Institutes of Byzantine and Modern Greek Studies and Contemporary History at the University of Vienna. The principal aim of this meeting was to connect young researchers with distinguished scholars.

Book Presentations, Public Lectures, Events, Activities

As we have seen so far, the academic staff of the Institute of East European History was apparently occupied with preparing, organizing, hosting, and also participating in international scientific meetings. Therefore, it is not surprising that other events were rather scarce. *Inter alia*, a mixture between book presentation and round-table at the Institute in cooperation with the Institut für Neuzeit- und Zeitgeschichtsforschung (Austrian Academy of Sciences) should be mentioned, which was held on 28 March 2014. The presentation of anthologies edited by Michael Gehler and Robert Rollinger (Imperien und Reich in der Weltgeschichte. Epochenübergreifende und globalhistorische Vergleiche) and Stephan Wendehorst (Die Anatomie frühneuzeitlicher Imperien. Herrschaftsmanagement jenseits von Staat und Nation) were attended by comments and statements, among others by Andreas Kappeler.

On the occasion of the 100th anniversary commemoration of the outbreak of the First World War, a recital of song and verse was held at the Institute on Mai 12, 2014. Under the motto 'Draußen in Schönbrunn. Triumph und Tragik', Magdalena Bruckmüller sang war songs, accompanied on piano by Walter Bass and inter-narrated by Ernst Bruckmüller, professor in retirement. Welcoming remarks to this special and very well attended concert were held by Marija Wakounig, who arranged a reception with the support of the Viennese Austrian and Central European Center.

Andreas Kappeler was – despite his retirement (2011) – one of the most prolific and sought-after researchers in the Academic Year 2013/2014. His two-weeks U.S.-lecture tour led him to Harvard, the Universities of Illinois and Arizona, and finally to Stanford in April 2014. During the current Ukraine crisis he is a wanted discussant, speaker, interviewee, and columnist for national and international newspapers. It is a great pity that this vacant professorship (2011) has not been re-announced to date. Further vacancies and mere substitutions by visiting professorships bear the threat of a loss of relevance and importance, because the students will probably look for re-orientation elsewhere.

The Institute's academic staff has participated in a number of national and international symposia and has hosted a number of guest lecturers. But, without trying to satisfy any vanities, the high effort by Christoph Augustynowicz, who has attended and spoken at nine international conferences between 20 September 2013 and 28 June 2014, must be mentioned with recognition. In context with the Crimea and Ukraine crisis, Kerstin S. Jobst also had several performances.

Teaching

Teaching complemented the mentioned activities of the Institute's academic staff. The teaching-offer is attractive to students thanks to a good choice of courses and lectures, but the substitution by visiting professors of the mentioned vacant professorship have meanwhile become noticeable. The BA-introductory lectures on Eastern Europe were held by Kerstin S. Jobst during the winter term 2013/2014 and by Christoph Augustynowicz, Alojz Ivanišević, and Marija Wakounig as team teachers during the summer term 2014. In the Academic Year 2013/2014 Alojz Ivanišević also offered BA-lectures on Modern History, which were attended by more than 700 students, who also took their exams. The commemoration of the 100th anniversary of the outbreak of the First World War and Christopher Clark's much discussed monograph, 'The Sleepwalkers. How Europe Went to War in 1914', inspired Oliver Jens Schmitt to the lecture series '1914 und das östliche Europa' during the summer term 2014. Almost the whole Institute's teaching staff as well as foreign colleagues took part, so that the interested students were given a well-rounded and in-depth look into the first year of the war in Eastern Europe. The lecture was concluded with a speech by Włodzimierz Borodziej (University of Warszaw), as a presentation of the book 'Nasza wojna. Imperia, 1914–1916' [Our War. Empires, 1914–1916, co-edited with Maciej Górny (DHI Warszawa)] and a convivial reception. This event was subsidized by our Institute and the Viennese Polish Institute.

The Institute hosted the GRAINES summer school 'The European City in Transformation. From the Early Modern Period to the Present' on 11 June 2014. In the course of this event, one round-table-discussion and two keynote lectures were held.

Our students had the opportunity to attend two field trips: Oliver Jens Schmitt organized a trip to Venice together with Claudia Märtel (München) (special topic: Venedig im späten Mittelalter. Lektüre von Schlüsselquellen) in November 2013. The second Institute's excursion, also organized by Oliver Jens Schmitt and Iskra Schwarzc, led the students to Bulgaria for twelve days in May 2014.

The so-called 'unique selling propositions' of the several individual master curricula didn't convince the person in charge in the rectorate. This means that our Master of East European History – metaphorically speaking – only had a few active years and will be studied in a short version as 'Schwerpunkt' (focus) within the Master for History beginning with autumn 2014.

Publications

The active scholars and *emeriti* of the Institute published the following anthologies and monographs between October 2013 and June 2014:

- Christoph Augustynowicz, Geschichte Ostmitteleuropas. Ein Abriss, Basistexte Wirtschafts- und Sozialgeschichte 2, Budapest [2]2014;
- Robert Born – Sarah Lemmen (Eds.), Orientalismen in Ostmitteleuropa. Diskurse, Akteure und Disziplinen vom 19. Jahrhundert bis zum Zweiten Weltkrieg, Postcolonial Studies 19, Bielefeld 2014;
- Armin Heinen – Oliver Jens Schmitt (Eds.), Inszenierte Gegenmacht von rechts. Die 'Legion Erzengel Michael' in Rumänien 1918–1938, Südosteuropäische Arbeiten 150, München 2013;
- Andreas Helmendach – Markus Koller – Konrad Petrovszky – Stefan Rohdewald (Eds.), Das osmanische Europa. Methoden und Perspektiven der Frühneuzeitforschung zu Südosteuropa, Leipzig 2013;
- Konrad Petrovszky, Geschichte schreiben im osmanischen Südosteuropa. Eine Kulturgeschichte orthodoxer Historiographie des 16. und 17. Jahrhunderts, Balkanologische Veröffentlichungen 60, Wiesbaden 2013;
- Philipp Ther, Center Stage. Operatic Culture and Nation Building in Nineteenth-Century Central Europe, Central European Studies, West Lafayette 2014;
- Arnold Suppan, Hitler – Beneš – Tito, Wien 2013;
- Marija Wakounig – Markus Peter Beham (Eds.), Transgressing Boundaries. Humanities in Flux, Europa Orientalis 14, Wien/Berlin 2013.

Postscript

Last but not least, a message on one's own account: Markus Peter Beham, the coeditor of this anthology, and Florian Gerhardus, our well appreciated 'general-servant' of the OeAD (Österreichischer Austauschdienst, Austrian Agency for International Cooperation in Education and Research), both happened to marry on the same day, on summer solstice (21 June 2014). All the best and a lifelong, respectful, and cheerful wedlock!

Joseph F. Patrouch

The Wirth Institute for Austrian and Central European Studies: Fifteen Years and Counting

University of Alberta

The most important development of the year was the renewal of the Memorandum of Understanding with the Bundesministerium für Wissenschaft, Forschung und Wirtschaft (BMWFW, Federal Ministry for Science, Research and Economy) which funds the Wirth Institute's visiting Austrian doctoral researcher and the Faculty of Arts' Visiting Professorship in Austrian Studies currently held by Dr. Helga Mitterbauer in the University of Alberta's Department of Modern Languages and Cultural Studies.[1] The BMWFW also provides a grant to help cover the Institute's operational expenses. This agreement, originally signed in 1998, has now been renewed for an additional five years. Sektionschef Barbara Weitgruber and Christoph Ramoser of the BMWFW visited Edmonton in October 2013 for the official signing ceremony.

Each year the Wirth Institute hosts advanced doctoral students from Central Europe for year-long research and writing stays as part of five separate fellowship programs administered for students from Austria, Croatia, Czech Republic, Hungary, and Poland. During 2013/2014 five such students were on staff at the institute: Carl-Johannes Rokitansky of the University of Innsbruck, Iva Drozdek of the University of Osijek, Stanislav Štěpánik of the Charles University, Henriett Dinók of the Hungarian Academy of Sciences, and Olga Cielemęcka of the University of Warsaw. (Drozdek and Dinok participated in the annual convention of the Austrian Centres in Leiden: see their contributions elsewhere in this volume.) During Academic Year 2013/2014, three additional scholars have been in residence at various times at the Institute. These scholars were the historian Dr. Michael Chisholm (Canada), the social anthropologist Dr. Jaro Stacul (Italy), and the immigration researcher Adam Chrobak (Hungary). Chisholm is pursuing research on a book project dealing with the early modern Habsburg empire, Stacul is working on a project titled 'The Making and Unmaking of Political Subjectivi-

1 For more on Professor Mitterbauer and her activities, see Eva Maria Müller, Crossing the Atlantic, Crossing the Disciplines. An Interview with Helga Mitterbauer, in: Austrian Studies Newsmagazine 25/2, Minneapolis 2013, 3–31.

ties in Post-Socialist Poland', and Chrobak is studying the immigration of Hungarians to Edmonton.

Klára Pinerová of the Charles University, an alumna of the Wirth Czech Doctoral Research Fellowship Program who participated in the 2011 annual convention of the Austrian Centers which was held in Budapest, visited the Wirth Institute in September, 2013 and donated a copy of the 2011 film 'Documentary Portrait of K. Ch.' to the institute library. Her colleague Anna Windisch of the University of Vienna, who also was resident at the Wirth Institute in 2011–2012 and participated in the same conference in Budapest, recently was awarded a multi-year DOC fellowship (Doktorand(inn)enprogramm der Österreichischen Akademie der Wissenschaften) for her research project 'Cultural Exchanges and Transnational Encounters. A Comparative Study of Audiovisual Performance Practices in Austria and the United States during the Silent Film Era'. Dr. Jana Stejskalikova, a 2012/2013 Wirth Czech Doctoral Research Fellow and participant in the 2012 Austrian Centers convention held in Vienna, recently was awarded her doctorate by the Department of History of the Faculty of Education at the Masaryk University in Brno. Dr. Stejskalikova now works for the new European Union Center of Excellence (EUCE) located at the University of Alberta, one of five such centers in Canada funded by the European Commission. Wirth Institute Director Joseph F. Patrouch sits on the Advisory Board of the center and serves as the Theme Leader for the EUCE activities on democratic development in the post-communist member states and the western Balkans. On 16 October, 2013 Her Excellency Marie-Anne Coninsx, Ambassador of the European Union to Canada, visited the Wirth Institute when she was in Alberta for the opening of the EUCE.

The Wirth Institute sponsored or co-sponsored over two dozen talks and public presentations over the last Academic Year. Highlights included the Wirth Institute's Annual Central European Art History Lecture on 5 September: 'NAME Readymade' by one of the Slovenian conceptual artists named Janez Janša. The endowed Toby and Saul Reichert Holocaust Lecture held on 3 October was titled 'The Vatican and the Holocaust in Italy'. It was delivered by the historian Susan S. Zuccotti. Wirth Institute alumnus Gregor Kokorz of Austria returned to Edmonton and on 13 November delivered the lecture 'Music, Space, and Nation in Central Europe: Music at the Borders of the Habsburg Empire'. Ulrike Butschek, the Director of the Austrian Cultural Forum in Ottawa and Deputy Chief of Mission of the Austrian Embassy there, delivered the talk 'OSCE: Co-operation in Europe, a No-Brainer?' on 4 December.

One of the most important events of the year at the Wirth Institute was the visit by Dr. Iveta Radičová, the former premier of Slovakia and professor at the Comenius University in Bratislava. Dr. Radičová delivered a well-attended public lecture titled 'The Common House of Europe: Integration of Diversity' on 7 May. She also met with the former Prime Minister of Canada, Kim Campbell, and discussed with her plans to establish a new leadership college at the University of Alberta. (Ms Campbell is the Founding Principal of the college.)

The Slovenian Embassy in Ottawa provided a documentary about the author Boris Pahor. On 1 April, selections from it were shown in conjunction with a discussion of the works of Pahor and his contexts in Trieste by the Slovenian linguist Professor Emeritus Tom Priestly and Wirth Research Associate Stacul. A member of the local Slovenian community read excerpts from Pahor's writings in the original language. The endowed Tova Yedlin Lecture was delivered on 9 April by Howard N. Lupovitch of Wayne State University (Detroit, USA). His lecture was titled 'Polish Jews and Hungarian Jews: Comparative Perspectives across the Carpathians'.

Cooperation with the Canadian Institute for Ukrainian Studies at the University of Alberta was deepened. The publication of Andriy Zayarnyuk, Framing the Ukrainian Peasantry in Habsburg Galicia, 1846–1914 was partially subsidized by the Wirth Institute.[2] This work was based on a doctoral dissertation written in the Department of History and Classics at the University of Alberta and supervised by long-time Wirth Institute Academic Advisory Board member Professor John Paul Himka. (Professor Himka retired from the University this year.)

The panel discussion 'Let's Riot: What we can learn from "events" in Central and Eastern Europe' held on 4 March included participants from a number of different disciplines who discussed the comparison between popular demonstrations in the Balkans with those in Ukraine. Also in cooperation with the CIUS, the Polish ethnographer Dr. Patrycja Trzeszczyńska-Demel of the Jagiellonian University presented a lecture titled 'The Lemko Land Remembered: Research on the Memory of the Lemkos in Poland and Ukraine' on 21 May.

A volume based on the proceedings of a conference sponsored by the Wirth Institute and held at the University of Victoria on the music of Béla Bartók is due to be released in July 2014. Titled 'The String Quartets of Béla Bartók', it will appear with Cambridge University Press.[3] To launch the book, and also to celebrate the renewal of the existing agreement structuring a scholarship program administered by the Wirth Institute and the University of Alberta for students to participate in the annual Franz Schubert Institut in Baden bei Wien, a concert and reading was held at the University of Alberta's Convocation Hall on 17 March. Titled 'Words, Songs, and Strings: the Visions of Schönberg, Berg and Bartók', this concert featured performances by alumni of the Schubert Institut and musicians affiliated with the University of Alberta. The Schubert Institut director, Dr. Deen Larsen, was in attendance and went on to hold master classes and deliver a lecture titled 'The Sensual Awakening of Viennese Modernism'. Dr. Larsen was ac-

2 Andriy Zayarnyuk, Framing the Ukrainian Peasantry in Habsburg Galicia, 1846–1914, Edmonton/Toronto 2013.

3 Daniel Peter Biro – Harald Krebs (Eds.), The String Quartets of Béla Bartók: Tradition and Legacy in Analytical Perspective, Cambridge 2014.

tive both at the main Edmonton campus of the university as well as at the Liberal Arts-centered Augustana Campus in Camrose, Alberta. There, Wirth Institute Academic Advisory Board member Professor Alexander Carpenter directed performances of student compositions inspired by Schönberg's music and presented a recorded production of Schönberg's opera 'Lulu'. Dr. Larsen had delivered a lecture 'Eros and Pathos in the Songs of Schubert' when he visited the Edmonton campus for master classes and auditions on October.

Other musical performances sponsored by the Wirth Institute in Academic Year 2013/2014 were held at various locations on the University of Alberta campus as well as at other concert venues across the city of Edmonton. A concert by the Czech pianist Boris Krajny was held at Grant MacEwan University's concert hall on 29 October. Wirth Institute Director Patrouch collaborated with Professor Marnie Giesbrecht of the Department of Music on a commented concert on 19 January at Convocation Hall titled 'On the Path to Bach: Windows into the Times, Teachings, and Traditions'. The Wirth Institute continued its sponsorship of the Alberta Baroque Ensemble by supporting their performance '18th Century Music from Central Europe' at the Robertson-Wesley United Church in downtown Edmonton on 16 March.

The concert 'Moravian Composers: Ernst and Janáček' held in Convocation Hall on 8 February featured a Czech poetry reading by the Wirth Fellow Stanislav Stěpáník. The 39th Annual Johann Strauss Ball to raise money to support music scholarships for Albertan students to study music in Austria was held at the Chateau Lacombe Hotel on 15 February. It featured performances by this year's Strauss Scholarship winners. One came from the University of Alberta and one from King's University College in Edmonton. On 15 January in the Art Gallery of Alberta, Wirth Institute Founding Director Franz A.J. Szabo and current Director Patrouch participated in a panel discussion held in conjunction with the Edmonton Opera's performance of 'Die Fledermaus'. The Institute also helped to fund the CD: 'In a New Light' by the group Trio Voce (including pianist Professor Patricia Tao of the Department of Music of the University of Alberta). It was released by Con Brio Publishing, 2013 and is related to the Wirth Institute-sponsored concert of the music of Schubert, Zemlinsky, and Suk which had been held in Convocation Hall in March, 2013.

Each year the Wirth Institute hosts a Christmas concert featuring music from Central Europe. Benefits from the concert support the Student Food Bank at the University of Alberta. This year's concert, held on 8 December, featured performers from various local groups representing Central European immigrants to Canada from Austria, the Czech and Slovak Republics, Hungary, and Poland. A children's choir from the local Hungarian language school stole the show! Two days earlier, 'St. Nikolaus' visited the Wirth Institute to participate in a discussion of Central European holiday practices and traditions.

'Central European Cafes' continued to be held on one Friday each month. These informal gatherings allow community and university members to come together to hear presentations on Central European topics followed by discussion over coffee and cakes. Topics included a local Polish-Canadian's reminiscences about life in Poland during and after World War II, presentations of term research projects by students in Political Science Professor Lori Thorlakson's course on the EU and Central Europe, and presentations of research by Professor Piet Defraeye's (Department of Drama) students on the contemporary Romanian playwright Matei Visniec. (Both Professor Thorlakson and Defraeye are members of the Wirth Institute's Academic Advisory Board.) Founding Director Szabo talked about evidence from his recent research in Vienna's Haus-, Hof- und Staatsarchiv. A representative of the Edmonton Opera attended a 'Central European Café' and gave some behind-the-scenes information about their production of 'Die Fledermaus'.

The Wirth Institute helped to sponsor an exhibition of contemporary Austrian printmaking which was held in the university's art gallery from 25 February to 22 March. Works by artists Josef Danner, Wojciech Krzywoblocki, Margret Kohler-Heilingsetzer, Georg Lebzelter, Henriette Leinfellner, Darina Peeva, Elli Schnitzer, and Michael Wegerer were shown. Krzywoblocki, Kohler-Heilingsetzer, and Lebzelter attended and consulted with University of Alberta printmaking students. The exhibition was titled 'Printed Matter: Current Positions in Austrian Printmaking' and was co-sponsored by the Künstlerhaus Wien.

As part of the Institute's plans to preserve and better utilize its oral history collection on Austrian immigration to Canada, the Austrian oral historian Andrea Strutz of the University of Graz visited Edmonton to consult on this project. She delivered a lecture titled 'They Came as "Enemy Aliens": Memories of Internment and the Subsequent Lives of Austrian Jews in Post-45 Canada' on 17 September. Dr. Strutz reviewed the holdings of the immigration collection and prepared a detailed report of her findings. She also consulted with the project's original organizer, Founding Director Szabo.

Professor Jeroen Duindam, a historian at Leiden University, visited Edmonton in January and participated in a seminar on the Early Modern Habsburg Empire led by Founding Director Szabo and in a second seminar, on Comparative Early Modern Empires, led by Director Patrouch. Professor Duindam also delivered a public lecture on 23 January: 'Vienna and Versailles 1660 and Beyond: Reputations, Reforms, Results'.

As part of the ongoing faculty exchange program with the University of Innsbruck, Dr. Kurt Scharr from that institution was in residence at the University of Alberta for one month, from 28 February through 30 March. While in Edmonton, Dr. Scharr consulted with the Canadian Mountain Studies Initiative organizers about future cooperation and delivered three public lectures: 'The Historical Geography of the Oetztal Valley' (11 March), 'State, National Idea, and Confession in the Nineteenth Century Habsburg Empire: the Case of Transylvania' (13 March), and 'The Bukovina Greek-Oriental Religious Fund, 1783–1949: Institution and Modernisation of the Periphery' (27 March). University of Alberta professor Waclaw Osadnik, a Polish language and translation specialist, visited the University of Innsbruck in May and participated in courses and delivered lectures.

The Wirth Institute administers various awards, including the Strauss Foundation Music Awards and the Schubert Institute Awards, which provide funds to enable students from the Province and the University of Alberta to study music in Austria. In summer 2014 five students are benefiting from these music scholarships. The Hungarian Studies Award was given to a graduate student in the Department of History, Ernest Gyidel, who is working on a research project dealing with a Hungarian POW's during World War II. In addition, a modest student stipend was awarded to assist an undergraduate University of Alberta student, Emma Rose Nelson from the Department of English and Film Studies, to enable her participation in the 'IWitness' Holocaust memory program in Poland and Austria.

Director Patrouch taught two History courses (one undergraduate lecture course on the histories of the Habsburgs' empires with 35 students and one mixed graduate-undergraduate seminar on comparative early modern empires with 10) in Winter Term, 2014. He also served on the thesis evaluation committee of one MA student, Alexander Loschberger. In fall, 2013 Mr. Loschberger of the Department of History and Classics successfully defended his thesis 'Flashpoints of Austrian Memory: A Critical Analysis of the Controversial Veterans Meetings on the Ulrichsberg'. The thesis was directed by Professor Dennis Sweeney. Visiting Professor Helga Mitterbauer taught an undergraduate course on Austrian Literature and Culture in Fall Term 2013.

Director Patrouch serves as one of the three primary editors of the online discussion group HABSBURG affiliated with H-Net: Humanities and Social Sciences Online, an umbrella organization of over a hundred such groups focusing on various historical topics and hosted by the Department of History at Michigan State University in East Lansing, Michigan (USA). He was named to the editorial board of the online journals Musicologica Austriaca and East/West: Journal of Ukrainian Studies. He published an introductory essay in the new collection Early Modern Habsburg Women released in 2013.[4]

The mandate of the Wirth Institute is national. For example, as mentioned above, the Institute sponsored a musicology conference on Bartók which was held in British Columbia. Ongoing collaboration with the ethnomusicologist Professor Marcia Ostashewski at Cape Breton University resulted in the Wirth Institute's participation in the nationally-funded research project 'East Central European Communities and Cultures in Cape Breton, Nova Scotia'. As part of this project, the Croatian ethnomusicologist Jelka Vukobratović pursued fieldwork relating to the Croatian immigrants in eastern Canada with the financial support of the

4 Joseph F. Patrouch, '*Bella gerant alii.*' Laodamia's Sisters/Habsburg Brides. Leaving Home for the Sake of the House, in: Anne J. Cruz – Maria Galli Stampino (Eds.), Early Modern Habsburg Women. Transnational Contexts, Cultural Conflicts, Dynastic Continuities, Women and Gender in the Early Modern World, Burlington/Farnham 2013, 25–38.

Wirth Institute. The Institute also sponsored a film screening and roundtable 'Living History: Documenting Gerda Lerner's Life and Work' at the Berkshire Conference on the History of Women hosted by the University of Toronto on 22 May. Gerda Lerner was an important Austro-American historian who grew up in Vienna before being forced to emigrate in the 1930s. The well-attended roundtable was chaired by Professor Franca Iacovetta of the University of Toronto, President of the Berkshire Conference of Women Historians.

Future plans include the biannual meeting of the Wirth Alumni Network (WAN), the organization of one-time Wirth Fellows, which will be held in Prague in June, 2014. A conference dealing with the internment of Austro-Hungarian citizens and others in Canada during World War I and a second one discussing the Austrian School of Economics are planned for October, 2014. Activities relating to the anniversary of the Congress of Vienna of 1814/1815 are also being organized, and collaboration with the European Union Centre of Excellence and the Canadian Mountain Studies Initiative will continue.

Georg Kastner

Report on the Academic Year 2013/2014: Faculty of Central European Studies

Andrássy University Budapest

After getting the accreditation of a new degree programme in Cultural Diplomacy in July 2013 the Faculty's activities focused on its implementation during the Academic Year 2013/2014. The new degree is offered as an interfaculty programme, and comprises courses in political science and law in addition to its cultural studies components. As a unique selling point, it includes a mandatory internship at a cultural diplomacy institute in another country during the programme's third semester. Preliminary plans for the new programme go back to the year 2010, after the degree programme in Central European History had been established as a First Master at Andrássy University, the first of its kind in the university's humanities programme. After the framework accreditation required in Hungary had been prepared by ELTE (Eötvös Loránd Tudományegyetem, Eötvös Loránd University Budapest), a process in which we were involved in a consultative capacity, the actual submission process began in autumn 2012. The Hungarian Accreditation Committee (HAC) granted its approval in July 2013, which enables us to start the new programme in the Academic Year 2014/2015. As the personnel situation continues to be difficult, we will not move forward with the other degree programmes made possible by the framework accreditation – Minority Studies, Central European Economy and Central European Cultural Studies – for the time being. We launched new contacts to cultural diplomacy institutes, e.g., the Polish "Lengyel Intézet Budapest". After the admission procedure was held during June and July we will start in September with 10 new students. The main future activities will cover establishing contacts to universities in Germany, Austria and other central European countries, mainly during the Erasmus network.

With these developments, our academic teaching has been put on as broad a basis as appears feasible for the moment, given the staffing and premises available. After we intended an open discussion on the pre-existing postgraduate Master's programme in Central European Studies, which was renamed in Danube Studies suggested two possible programmes – the first one as two semester programme with focusing on history and cultural studies, and a second one as four semester programme still including lectures form the faculties of law and economic.

After a break in summer 2013 the doctoral college has invited applications for a new class, which is now the fifth one. After giving two scholarships – one to Béla Teleky a young Austrian historian, who graduated at Vienna University and one to Reka Szentinvany, german native who graduated at our university, two more scholarships shall be awarded in late fall. During fall 2014 we will also have an international evaluation.

Two of our staff-members got invitations for a visiting professorship. Marcel Martonffy went from October to January to Berlin's University and Ursula Mindler stayed between January and June at Arizona State University. So for 2013/2014 we have welcomed on our parts three new visiting professors: Frank Stern, professor of contemporary history at the University of Vienna, is one of the most internationally renowned specialists on 20th century cultural history in Central Europe, especially the history of film; Ibolya Murber, university lecturer at Főiskola Szombathely, is a particularly accomplished young colleague who recently qualified as a professor at ELTE. Last but not least Christoph Augustynowicz, who is professor for east central European history at the University of Vienna, who hold a course during fall semester.

Among the many events organized by the Faculty, first mention should go to the series of debates on resurgent anti-Semitism organized by Ursula Mindler. A first evening debate took place on 16 May 2013, and two more in autumn.

In February 2014 we started with a series of lectures as a kind of prequel for a big conference, which will take place in November 2014 dealing with the development of Austria and Hungary between 1914 and 2014.

During spring semester we were able to invite two visiting fellows: Oswald Ueberegger, who is head of the new established institute for local history in Bozen and Gerald Lamprecht, member of the Center for Jewish Studies at the University of Graz.

During October the first volume of the new Yearbook for Central European Studies will be published. Among the many publications published by members and associates of the Faculty, special mention should be made of volume 5, 6 and 7 of the Central European Studies series:

- Christopher Walsch (Ed.), 'Einhundertfünfzig Jahre Rückständigkeit? Wirtschaft und Wohlstand in Mitteleuropa von 1867 bis zur Gegenwart' [One Hundred and Fifty Years Bachwardness? Economy and Wealth in Central Europe from 1867 to the Present], Herne 2013;
- Béla Matthias Teleky, 'Westungarische Magnaten und die Reformation' [West-Hungarian Magnates and the Reformation], Herne 2014;
- Andra Octavia Drăghiciu – Fabienne Gouverneur – Sebastian Sparwasser (Eds.), 'Bewegtes Mitteleuropa' [Moving Central Europe], Herne 2014;
- Ursula Mindler's 'Die jüdische Gemeinde in Oberwart/Felsöör' [The Jewish Community in Oberwart/Felsöör], Oberwart 2013.

Ruth Fine

Center for Austrian Studies: Activities Report 2012/2013

Hebrew University of Jerusalem

The following annual report (2012/2013) introduces the activities of the Center for Austrian Studies at the Hebrew University of Jerusalem.

A. Research Grants

The Center for Austrian Studies provides various individual research grants so as to encourage young scholars and students to actively participate in research projects. After a call for papers was issued, the scholarship committee of the center assessed the research proposals. The research-grant recipients are required to submit the results of their year-long work in a paper to be published in the Working Paper Series of the European Forum.

One research scholarship of 10,000 ILS was awarded by the Center for Austrian Studies and the Aaron Menczer Fund:

Nir Cohen, MA student, Department of Musicology
'Gideon Klein: Life and Music'

Three research grants were provided by the City of Vienna:

- Nir Barak, Ph.D. candidate, Department of Political Science
  'Hundertwasser's Contribution to Urban Ecologism: How Could Ecologism be Manifested in Social and Political Urban Institutions?';
- Dr. Daniel Reiser, post-doctoral fellow, Department of Jewish Thought
  'Mesmerism, Hypnosis and Jewish Mystics in Vienna in the Early Twentieth Century'
- Prof. Yoav Rinon, Department of German Language and Literature
  'Karl Kraus: Translation and Publication of Selected Writings'.

One research grant was granted jointly by the Center for Austrian Studies and the IWM:

- Moran Pearl, MA student at the European Forum at the Hebrew University
  'Books and Libraries as Witnesses of the Holocaust: Monuments in Vienna, Berlin and Jerusalem'

Books and archives contain knowledge and signify the human desire to preserve the past for future generations. My project deals with monuments that use books and libraries as symbols to commemorate the Second World War and the Holocaust. As I am especially interested in the connections between politics, society and visual culture these monuments will be examined in the context of local memory culture and placement, artistic relations and agency.

B. Student Stipends

- Omri Ben-Yehuda, Ph.D. studies at the European Forum at the Hebrew University
  Research topic: 'Analysis of Voice and Voices: Kafka and Agnon'
  Supervisors: Prof. Hanan Hever, Department of Hebrew Literature, The Hebrew University of Jerusalem and Prof. Galili Shahar, Department of Comparative Literature, Tel Aviv University;
- Dr. Susi Cohen-Weisz, post-doctoral fellow at the European Forum
  Research topic: 'Strengthening Jewish Group Identity and European-Jewish Identity in Germany and Vienna'
  Supervisor: Prof. Peter Medding, Department of History of the Jewish People and Contemporary Jewry;
- Moran Pearl, MA studies at the European Forum at the Hebrew University
  Research topic: 'Books and Libraries as Agents of Memory'
  Supervisor: Prof. Bianca Kühnel, Department of the History of Art;
- Shimrit Shriki, MA studies at the European Forum at the Hebrew University
  Research topic: 'Calvaries, Viae Crucis, Copies of the Holy Sepulchre, Lent and Christmas Scenes in German Speaking Countries'
  Supervisor: Galit Noga-Banai, Department of the History of Art;
- András Sziklai, Ph.D. studies at the European Forum
  Research topic: 'Shaping Jewish Public Opinion in Hungary at the Turn of the Twentieth Century: the Weekly Egyenlőség (Equality) and Its Editor Miksa Szabolcsi'
  Supervisor: Dr. Michael K. Silber, Department of History of the Jewish People;
- Ofer Waldman, MA studies at the European Forum
  Research topic: 'The Binding Fracture: the Czech-German "Searching for Traces" Project in the Former Sudetenland'
  Supervisor: Prof. Yfaat Weiss, School of History;
- Sara Yanovsky, post-doctoral fellow at the European Forum
  Research topic: 'Facing the Challenge of Jewish Education in the Metropolis: a Comparative Study of the Jewish Communal Organizations of Budapest and Vienna, from 1867 until World War II'
  Supervisor: Dr. Michael K. Silber, Department of History of the Jewish People.

C. Travel Scholarships

Omri Ben Yehuda, Ph.D. candidate, European Studies
'Hiding Oneself in Psalms: Agnon and Zionism'
29th Annual AIS Conference (Association for Israel Studies), University Of California, Los Angeles (22–24 June 2013).

D. Language Scholarships

The Center for Austrian Studies grants thirty students from the Hebrew University scholarships for a two-month intensive language course at the University of Vienna. These scholarships include flight cost as well as dormitory and tuition fees. The scholarships are funded by the Austrian Foreign Ministry, the Austrian Ministry of Science and Research, the Austrian Friends of the Hebrew University and the Center for Austrian Studies, the Helmut Zilk Fonds für internationale Beziehungen Wiens, and the University of Vienna.

In addition, the Center grants fifteen students from the Hebrew University scholarships for two- or three-week intensive language courses at different Austrian universities: Graz, Klagenfurt, Salzburg, Innsbruck, and Linz. Theses scholarships are funded by the hosting universities and the Austrian Friends of the Hebrew University and the Center for Austrian Studies, and cover the dormitory and tuition fees. The language scholarships are granted to students from different faculties and departments of the Hebrew University who need an extensive knowledge of German for their academic work. Many of these students also deal directly with Austria or the Austrian legacy in Central Europe.

E. Conferences, Workshops and Guest Lectures

'Education in Migrant and Minority Families: Explorations in Religious Faith, Societal Integration, and Civic Education'
International Symposium, 9–11 October 2012, In cooperation with the Melton Center, School of Education
Cross-national migratory flows and internal migrations involving millions of people from diverse social statuses, and from heterogeneous ethno-cultural and religious backgrounds, have rapidly intensified under the ascendancy of globalization.

Modern education systems were established in order to build social cohesion through homogenization and maintain social control, whether through decentralized and varied school systems as in the United States or in highly unified and centralized systems as in France.

Migratory flows pose challenges to some of the constitutive principles of education systems in highly developed and developing countries (*i.e.* Western and Eastern Europe and the Middle East) where social cohesion is viewed as being endangered by cultural and religious differences (*e.g.* involving Muslims). In recent decades the problem has been aggravated to the extent that modern societies seem to have set constraints on their culture of political debate and reached their limits in terms of their capacity to integrate migratory/minority groups. Furthermore, public opinion has come often to view the project and ideals of multiculturalism as a failure. Within this context, certain cultures and religions are perceived as a danger to democracy.

Since 2000, Pisa studies have shown highly diversified education systems in European countries (*e.g.* Austria, Germany) to have a negative impact on the education of migrants. The socialization and education of migrant/minority youth is suspected of not supporting civic and democratic attitudes and practices, and migrant/minority families have become a focus of public interest. It is the migrant/minority families and their associated social networks that are seen as the main factor responsible for the present failures of the education systems.

The symposium focused on the intersection between education, religion, and citizenship within socio-political contexts, as well as tensions related to the presence of varied migrant/minority populations in a selection of countries.

The countries chosen for the first stage of what will hopefully evolve into a larger international comparative study – Austria, Germany, Croatia, Romania, Serbia, and Israel – all confront such situations and have developed or are developing different approaches to the perceived problems.

The symposium offered a first opportunity for a rather small group of researchers representing these countries to get acquainted with each other's socio-political contexts, the societal and educational approaches developed within them to manage cultural differences, and the existing academic work on these issues, with the aim of starting a dialogue that could lead to the submission of a proposal to a competitive research foundation.

'Annual Convention of the Austrian and Central European Centers'

Vienna, 24–28 October 2012

This year's annual convention, organized by the Austrian Ministry for Science and Research was held in Vienna.

The Center for Austrian Studies at the European Forum was represented by its academic director, Prof. Ruth Fine, and two students, Shimrit Shriki and Moran Pearl, who presented their research:

- Shimrit Shriki, MA student at the European Forum at the Hebrew University
  'Modern Conflicts, Historical Context: the Relation between Representations of the Way of the Cross and Commemoration of Modern Conflicts in Austria'
- Moran Pearl, MA student at the European Forum at the Hebrew University
  'Books and Libraries as Witnesses of the Holocaust: Monuments in Vienna and Jerusalem'

'Simulation Workshop: Security Cooperation in the EU' (17 January 2013)

The workshop started with a lecture that focused on the organisation of EU foreign policy, its possibilities and limitations. The Common Foreign and Security Policy (CFSP)/Common Security and Defence Policy (CSDP) structures after the entry into force of the Lisbon Treaty was explained as well as the rules governing the conduct of EU foreign policy after the establishment of the European External Action Service.

Since the EU has acquired the capability to conduct both civilian and military operations abroad only 10 years ago, part of the workshop consisted of explaining the EU crisis management procedures to give an idea of the different stages of the planning process for an operation from the initial stages until the elaboration of the operation plan which are the binding guidelines for the operation commander, sometimes going into hundreds of pages.

The aim was to give participants an idea about the complexities of EU decision-making in the area of foreign policy and the possibilities for EU member states and third countries to influence it.

The second part was dedicated to a simulation conducted by the students themselves (meeting of the Political and Security Committee of the EU) against a given scenario, concerning a fictitious non-EU country – Alisia, which is suffering from an on-going inner ethnic conflict. Each participant played a role (EU member state, Chairman). We faced the dilemma how to formulate an EU response to the mounting crisis in Alisia.

'Europe Day' (13 May 2013)

In cooperation with the Delegation of the European Union to the State of Israel, Issta and the Student Union at the Hebrew University.

Celebrating Europe Day at the Hebrew University is a well established tradition initiated and organized by the European Forum. Throughout the years, Europe Day was commemorated with a strong emphasis on reaching to the general public, bringing key speakers from academia and the policy arena to speak and debate at different central places in the city of Jerusalem. Europe Day 2013 furthered this tradition by blending together academic excellence with a festive celebration of the European spirit. Europe Day comprised of two events: an academic conference and a Eurofest, featuring Café Europe, Prize winning contest, live music and more. All events were free and open for students and the general public.

F. Publications

Lily Arad, The Crown of Jerusalem: Franz Joseph's Dream of an Ideal Empire, Jerusalem 2012.

Eyal Ginio – Karl Kaser (Eds.), Ottoman Legacies in the Contemporary Mediterranean. The Balkans and the Middle East Compared, Jerusalem 2013.

G. Teaching

Visiting Lecturers

During the previous academic year, the Center for Austrian Studies hosted three guest lecturers from different Austrian institutions, each of whom taught a brief course.

Prof. Anton Pelinka, Central European University, Budapest
Comparative Politics: Central and Eastern Europe (12–23 May 2013)
The seminar focused on the part of Europe which was dominated – until 1990 – by political systems of the Soviet type. It described and explained the reasons for the transformation and the existing political systems.

The following topics were discussed:

- Conceptual and historical definition: what is Central, what is Eastern Europe? Geography and civilization;
- Historical framework: the implosion of empires, the birth of nation states, the rise of the Soviet Union and the post-1945 order;
- Historical framework: transformation – from communism to liberal democracy, the center and the periphery;
- Westernization: towards NATO- and EU- membership – economic and political incentives;
- The Visegrad group: Poland, the Czech Republic, Slovakia, Hungary – the most "Western" among the post-communist countries;
- The western Balkan: Yugoslavia's successor states plus Albania – violent transformation and the consequences;
- The eastern Balkan: Romania, Bulgaria – late-comers to westernization;
- The Baltic states: darlings of the West – plus ethnic problems;
- Ukraine, Moldova, Belarus: EU and NATO – still an option?;
- The Russian Federation: democracy in the making – or a failing state?

Long-term Guest
Dr. Christian Gerbel, Austria
From Fin de siècle Vienna to Red Vienna
First and second semester

Fin de Siècle Vienna is one of the classic focal points within the formation of Modernity. The course negotiated the worldviews established by the most influential political forces, which arose to challenge Liberalism in the last third of the 19th century. Parallel to this transformation of the political public sphere, path-breaking projects were developed in the fields of literature, art, science, and architecture.

Questions that were discussed are: what forms and modes of 'Austrian self-understanding' were involved in these projects and competed with each other in the dynamically expanding metropolis? How were 'Austrian' identities shaped and defined in the crucible of conflicting demands put forward by the different nationalities? What consequences did some of these Fin de Siècle projects have on the 'self-understanding' of Red Vienna and the First Republic? The discussion of questions was underpinned by constant references to political actors, events, movements, cultural practices and art works from the last quarter of the 19th century until the mid-1930s.

Dr. Christian Gerbel, Austrian Lector at the Center for Austrian Studies
European Cultures of Remembrance from 1945
First and second semester

Influential strands of 'post foundational' political thought argue that the connection between the 'recognition of the other' and the 'recognition of one's own self-alienation' has to be regarded as a prime mover for establishing democratic solidarity. To a certain extent, mnemohistorical concepts have taken up this impulse of post foundational political thought; on a programmatic level this means that incriminating historical events of one's own nation become points of departure for a 'shattering of one's own complacency' and occasion critical societal reflexion. Consequently, mnemohistorical approaches amount to a critique of traditional national history, focusing on its self-celebrating function and its pronounced monologic orientation. Along the lines of different national cultures of remembrance the transformation of European post war narratives, their patterns and functions since 1945 were discussed and examined for the impact they have on current democratic developments.

H. Austrian Film Forum

The Center for Austrian Studies, in cooperation with the Austrian Library at the Hebrew University, has established the Austrian Film Forum, which offers the opportunity to view a selection of Austrian movies at the university. This is an open and accessible forum for the general public at the Hebrew University and beyond, in which viewers can get acquainted with various aspects of Austrian history, society, and culture, in addition to several courses at the university, which deal specifically with those issues.

This year's Austrian Film Forum presented a series of movies under the heading 'Aspects of Austrianness'. The focus was on certain concepts that have shaped Austrian identity, as well as the changing perceptions of 'Austrianness' by Austrian filmmakers in the late 20th and early 21st centuries.

Films produced in early postwar Austria after 1945 often celebrated the idea of the 'good old days' of the Habsburg monarchy, portraying the pre-1918 era as one of peace and happiness, contrasting supposedly 'typical Austrian' funny, quaint, old-fashioned harmlessness with supposedly 'typical German' efficient, humorless ambition, and militarism. This simultaneously helped propagate an Austrian national identity separate from a German one and the 'victim theory' of Nazi crimes having been committed by Germans, not by Austrians. However, since the 1980s more skeptical, critical views of the Habsburg monarchy entered Austrian public discourse, as it was discovered as a historical source of problematic ideas, conflicts, and patterns of behavior such as authoritarianism, traditionalism, deep-rooted anti-Semitism, and racist attitudes towards Slavs. Similarly, denazification, and *Vergangenheitsbewältigung* (coping with the past) regarding Austrian participation in National Socialism gained pace in Austria after the Waldheim affair of 1986, leading to an intense political, cultural, and societal debate which lasted throughout the 1990s and 2000s. Dissenting intellectuals now characterized negatively connotated concepts as supposedly 'typically Austrian', criticizing Austria's notoriously complicated, sometimes corrupt bureaucracy, the widespread obsession with hierarchy and titles, popular provincialism, and a growing xenophobia rooted in a general unwillingness to accept social and cultural change fostered by immigration from southeastern Europe and Turkey.

Austrian documentary and feature filmmakers dealt with these topics in various ways. They also mixed them with an Austrian tradition of political stand-up comedy, a form of cabaret called Kabarett. This led to the production of some very successful Austrian Kabarett movies combining controversial social and political issues with elements of tragedy, horror, and dark humor.

The seven movies selected for our film program this year were intended as a sample showing the multitude of ways in which Austrian filmmakers have dealt with all these different issues and supposedly 'typical' concepts as 'Aspects of Austrianness'. The program encompassed such diverse formats as historical dramas, documentaries, interview features, and Kabarett movies produced between 1985 and 2009. Each screening included a brief introduction by Andreas Rathberger, this year's Austrian research fellow at the European Forum, providing some historical, social, and political context. At the end of each movie there was an optional debate on questions raised by the films.These are the movies that were shown:

- Oberst Redl (Colonel Redl) (1985)
  Director: István Szabó (10 March 2013);
- Hafners Paradies (Hafners Paradise) (2007)
  Director: Günter Schwaiger (17 March 2013);
- Angeschwemmt (Washed Up) (2007)
  Director: Nikolaus Geyrhalter (7 April 2013);
- Indien (India) (1994)
  Director: Paul Harather (28 April 2013);
- Die Kronenzeitung (2002)
  Director: Nathalie Borgers (5 May 2013);

- Der Knochenmann (2009)
  Director: Wolfgang Murnberger (26 May 2013);
- Import/Export (2007)
  Director: Ulrich Seidl (2 June 2013).

I. Austrian Library

The Austrian Library, incorporated into the Bloomfiled Library for the Humanities and Social Sciences, contained in 2009 3687 books. Since it is a reference library, it is not easy to estimate how often and how many of these books are used. However, 520 of these books have been borrowed in 2009.

The Center for Austrian Studies has organized its own reference library for students and scholars and has set up working space for its students and research fellows. With these steps, the Center became a vivid point of intellectual exchange.

Jeroen Duindam

Leiden University: Venue of the 2013 Annual Convention

Leiden University

In 2013 Leiden's relatively recent status as 'Austria Center' was confirmed by the organization of the 2013 Annual Convention. This was accomplished by the Foundation for Austrian Studies ('Stichting Oostenrijkse Studiën') and the Leiden History Department, with the constant and invaluable support of our Viennese colleagues Dr. Christoph Ramoser and Florian Gerhardus. Other highlights of this year included the visiting professorship of Prof. Dr. Marie-Agnes Dittrich (Universität für Musik und darstellende Kunst Wien). Also, the Foundation for Austrian Studies has initiated an evaluation to redefine its key activities for the coming years, preparing among other things a more intensive co-operation with colleagues from other Dutch universities dealing with Central European history and culture.

The Annual Convention took place from 23 October to 26 October 2013. During the festive opening in the Leiden Faculty Club, where the director of the History Institute Prof. Dr. Leo Lucassen and our own Chairman Dr. Hugo Weiland addressed the participants, it immediately became clear that this again was to be a great meeting in social as well as intellectual terms. Young researchers from Budapest, Edmonton, Jerusalem, Minneapolis, Vienna, Leiden, and New Orleans presented brief and coherent papers. Their presentations, in the historic venue of the Leiden Gravensteen, were followed by lively discussions, in which the directors and former directors took a characteristically active role – soon joined by a gradually growing number of other participants. A tour through the old center of Leiden and a visit to several sites in The Hague including the Peace Palace, and a boat trip through Amsterdam formed part of the program. A classic Indonesian dinner ('Rijsttafel') showed one of the traditional – yet not very Dutch – highlights of local cuisine. A festive reception and dinner was hosted at the Austrian embassy by the ambassador, Dr. Werner Druml. While the academic section was mainly organized by Dr. Patrick Dassen in consultation with me, all other activities were planned by a committee including Dr. Hugo Weiland, Dr. Ida van Veldhuijzen, Mr. Jaap Kool, and Dr. Reinildis van Ditzhuyzen as well as Patrick Dassen. I use this opportunity to thank them for their work. The only disappointment of the meeting was the absence of our friend and colleague Prof. Dr. Marija Wakounig, director of the Vienna center, who was forced to cancel her visit because of illness.

The activities of the Leiden History Institute related to Central Europe can be summarized by the names of several researchers: Dr. Felicia Rosu works on Polish and Transylvanian elective monarchies, Jovan Pesalj, who is preparing a dissertation on borders, migration and state control in the eighteenth-century Habsburg monarchy in consultation with Leiden and Vienna colleagues. During this year, a major new study on Germany and the First World War was completed by Dr. Patrick Dassen: 'Sprong in het Duister. Duitsland en de Eerste Wereldoorlog' will be published by van Oorschot in 2014. While I have been working on Vienna and the Holy Roman Empire, and hope to return to this theme, I have devoted this year largely to comparative studies of dynasty and empire.[1] In the summer semester, I had the privilege of writing a book at the Netherlands Institute of Advanced Studies in Wassenaar. This book, 'Dynasty. A Global History 1300–1800', will be published by Cambridge University Press in 2015. In January 2013, I gave a guest lecture at the Wirth Institute of the University of Alberta (Canada) on the invitation of fellow director Prof. Dr. Joseph Patrouch and former director Prof. Dr. Franz Szabo, using the opportunity to take part in several seminars. This visit showed to me how effectively this center operates, with its professional and friendly staff, talented research-fellows from Central European countries, and a profound connection with the local Edmonton community.

During the second semester of 2012/2013, the foundation's visiting professorship was held by the Vienna musicologist Prof. Dr. Marie-Agnes Dittrich who taught a lecture class on 'Musical compositions as documents of Austrian history' as well as a seminar on 'Alterity-Studies: Othering Austrian Music'. Not only was Prof. Dittrich highly appreciated by her students, she also confirmed our previous exceptionally positive experiences by being a great colleague and friend. We can now announce that Prof. Dr. Georg Kastner, known to all of us as director of the Budapest Austria Center based at the Andrássy University, will come to Leiden in the summer semester of 2014/2015. We are sure he will be a worthy successor. The introduction of the new Austrian 'Universitätsgesetz 2002', will gradually make it more difficult to invite professors from Austria to Leiden on the current financial basis, providing no financial compensation to the institutes who gracefully allow their colleagues to teach at Leiden. In the last years this caused several problems, which we could luckily solve in an ideal way. There is no guarantee that we will be as lucky every time. This can have an impact on our procedures for selecting and inviting candidates and in the longer run may change the priorities of the foundation.

1 See, *e.g.*, Jeroen Duindam, The Habsburg Court in Vienna. Kaiserhof or Reichshof?, in: Robert Evans – Peter H. Wilson (Eds.), The Holy Roman Empire 1495–1806. A European Perspective, Boston/Leiden 2012; Brill's Companions to European History I; comparative work in volumes edited for my Brill series 'Rulers and Elites' published in 2013–2014: with co-editors Jill Harries, Caroline Humfress, Nimrod Hurvitz, Law and Empire: Ideas, Practices, Actors, Leiden/Boston 2013; with co-editor Sabine Dabringhaus, Agents and Interactions. The Early Modern Dynastic Court and the Provinces, Leiden/Boston 2014.

The renewal of the special chair for Central European Studies, temporarily left vacant upon the retirement of Prof. Dr. Nicolette Mout, occupies an important position among the plans of the board of the foundation. Within 1–3 years we hope to convince the university board that renewal of this special chair will provide a better foundation for the Austrian and Central European connections at Leiden University. However, this is contingent upon the availability of an excellent candidate within comfortable traveling distance of Leiden. At the same time, we have established contacts with colleagues from Leiden (Social Sciences, The Hague Campus), Amsterdam, and Groningen, asking them to participate in a network of researchers interested in Central Europe. If we succeed in bringing together this group, ideally under the aegis of the special chair, this could also entail a change in responsibilities, allowing our venerable chair Hugo Weiland to gradually leave some of his responsibilities to others.

A final word of thanks should be devoted to our Viennese friends and sponsors Florian Gerhardus and Dr. Christoph Ramoser, as well as to the Austrian ambassador Dr. Werner Druml, whose cordial support and jovial presence remains a cornerstone of our activities.

Kevin Mummey

2013/2014: Transition and Tradition at The Center for Austrian Studies

University of Minnesota

The Academic Year 2013/2014 was a year of positive transition for the Center for Austrian Studies. We remodeled our space, organized new offices for the editorial and administrative staff, and generally made room for the twenty-first century. The Center has also become part of the Institute for Global Studies administrative hub, which connects us to the personnel, resources, and energy of related centers, whose briefs include a variety of European Studies, Human Rights, Genocide and Holocaust Studies, and community outreach. The 'hub' makes it much easier for the Center to plan, coordinate, and co-sponsor events, and we are collaborating with these centers on bigger and better events in the coming year. A highlight of the transition was the success of our international search for a faculty director. This had become almost an annual, and admittedly sometimes frustrating, tradition, but the third time was a charm. We brought three outstanding finalists to campus in the fall semester for scholarly research lectures and presentations about their vision for the Center. In addition to the input of faculty colleagues in the future academic home department, the Search Committee solicited input from all stakeholders in the Center's programs, both intra- and extramural. At the end of that process, Dean Duvall extended an offer to Dr. Howard Louthan, professor of history at the University of Florida. Dr. Louthan is an internationally renowned historian of Central Europe, who has the scholarly acumen and vision to make the Center a premiere American research facility for Austrian and Central European Studies for years to come. We are looking forward to welcoming Howard Louthan to the Center. As many of you know from our press release, we will have to wait one more year for Dr. Louthan to take charge of the Center. We are delighted that Gary Cohen, former director, has agreed to bring his expertise and experience back to the Center for the interim year.

As stimulating as the reorganization of our offices and the acquisition of a new director was, the Center's lecture series, scholar support, and publishing activity remained at the core of its mission. In October, our own Gary Cohen, Professor of History at the University of Minnesota, delivered the 2013 Robert A. Kann Memorial Lecture, 'Cultural Crossings in Prague, 1900: Scenes from Late Imperial Austria', to a large and enthusiastic audience. A week later, Vahram Shemmassian, director of the Aremenian Studies Program at the California State University, Northridge, gave the 2013 Ohanessian Chair Lecture. Shemmassian shared his work on 'The Musa Dagh Resistance to the Armenian Genocide and Its Impact through Franz Werfel's Historical Novel The Forty Days of Musa Dagh'.

The Center has made a commitment to highlight issues facing Austria and the new Central Europe, and our lecture series reflected that commitment. Austrian Ambassador to the United States Hans Peter Manz outlined the challenges and opportunities of trans-Atlantic relations, while EU Ambassador to the US João Vale de Almeida spoke to the future of EU-US relations. A number of emerging Austrian scholars were also brought to the Center, speaking on topics ranging from Somali immigration to Austria, the Kurdish para-state in war-torn Syria, and the relationship between religion and Austria's extremist right.

A variety of fascinating culturally-oriented events complemented an impressive list of historical and political presentations. Kalani Michell, a University of Minnesota doctoral candidate illuminated the later-period work of Austrian avant-garde artist VALIE EXPORT. Visiting Fulbright Professor Rainer Köppl decorated our Halloween with a hilarious and thought-provoking study of the Austrian Vampire Princess. The highlight of the season was a visit by Lisa Peschel from the University of York. A troupe of actors and musicians performed sketches and songs unearthed by Peschel that were originally performed at the Theresienstadt concentration camp. Peschel interwove the music of 'Laughter in the Dark' with the context behind this unique world of creativity and sorrow.

Peschel's performance was part of a series of outreach events that the Center organized around the theme of the 75th anniversary of Kristallnacht in November 1938. In collaboration with our colleagues at the Center for Holocaust and Genocide Studies we organized the public screening of several internationally acclaimed films relevant to the theme. We also hosted a symposium entitled 'Antisemitism: Then and Now'. The symposium brought together five renowned scholars in the field of anti-Semitism, reviewing its long-term aftereffects and contemporary manifestations in Europe and the United States.

In addition to promoting lectures, symposia, and cultural events the Center offered financial support to scholars on both sides of the Atlantic. In addition to Fulbright Professor Köppl, the Center hosted bilingual poet and literary translator Renee von Paschen. Our offices were brightened by our BMWFW Fellow Verena Stern, who spent the year working on issues of Somali migration to the US. Matthias Falter, last year's Fellow, stayed on in an unofficial capacity, contributing to our lecture series and providing us with invaluable linguistic and cultural expertise. The Center also continued its tradition of supporting graduate student research, granting summer stipends and the Voices of Vienna scholarship. Transatlantic relations were bolstered by our faculty research grants, aimed at fostering collaboration between Austrian and American scholars.

The Center's publications continue to reach an international audience. The 'Austrian Studies Newsmagazine' (ASN), edited by Daniel Pinkerton since 1992, continues as a clearinghouse for information about the Center's activities and the people who participate in them. The ASN plays an international service role by carrying columns featuring news from the Wirth Institute, CenterAustria, and the Society for Austrian and Habsburg History. It publishes news about the Austrian Cultural Forum in New York, and has recently expanded to cover news, events, and artistic and literary topics relevant to the New Central Europe. Pinkerton was assisted in 2013 by copyeditors Dr. Kevin Mummey, Mollie Madden, and Sharon Park. Madden and Park also edited the 'Austrian History Yearbook' (AHY). Founded in 1965 by John R. Rath, the Yearbook remains the only English language journal devoted to the history of the Habsburg monarchy, modern Austria, and the Central European lands with a common Habsburg heritage. The Center supports the work of the AHY by offering the Rath Prize for the best article in the AHY. This year, four prizes were awarded for the 2012 and 2103 issues. 2012's first prize went to Madalina-Valeria Veres for her thought-provoking work on Habsburg Cartography, and the top 2013 award went to Werner Telesko, Richard Kurdiovsky, and Dagmar Sachsenhofer for their investigation of the Vienna Hofburg in the nineteenth century. The Center is also proud to announce the publication of 'Understanding Multiculturalism: The Habsburg Central European Experience', in Berghahn Books Austrian and Habsburg Studies series. The volume, edited by Gary Cohen and Johannes Feichtinger, was copyedited by a series of graduate students at the Center.

The Center is only as strong as those who support it with their time, energy, and financial support. As always, we thank individual donors, including members of the Kann family, the Botstiber Foundation, the Horst Rechelbacher Foundation, the Austrian Cultural Forum, the Austrian Federal Ministry for Science, Research and Economy (BMWFW), and the people of Austria, who provided the initial endowment that created the Center for Austrian Studies. We would also like to recognize the efforts of Emily Janisch, Rachel Wolf, Barbara London, Evelyn Davidheiser, and Jeff Nelson of the Institute for Global Studies, and to Sharon Park, Mollie Madden, Dr. Kevin Mummey, and Daniel Pinkerton, who continue to give the Center devotion and attention far beyond their job descriptions. Lastly, we want to thank Klaas van der Sanden, our interim director for the last three years. As we recognize this transition in our leadership, we look forward to the coming years, and to continuing our tradition of support for the dynamic world of Austrian and Central European studies.

Further details of our year can be found in the Austrian Studies Newsmagazine and the CAS Annual Report. You can also follow us on Facebook and Twitter, or on our website: www.cas.umn.edu

Günter Bischof

CenterAustria: Faculty Exchanges

University of New Orleans

'Incoming' and 'outgoing' student exchange programs with the University of Innsbruck continued unabatedly. 'Incoming' to UNO were 92 Innsbruck students taking courses at UNO, most of them for a semester (45 in the spring, 47 in the fall), a few stayed the entire Academic Year of 2012/2013. Three students spent a year at UNO on scholarships. Christian Riml, a chemistry/biology major from the University of Innsbruck held the CenterAustria fellowship and contributed to our regular office work. Theresa Maierhofer, a Ph.D. candidate in the Department of Education at the University of Innsbruck, was the 2012/2013 Nick Mueller Fellow. She worked on her dissertation 'Trust: A Phenomenological Study of Educational Learning Experiences' and observed classes and conducted interviews with students and principals in a few New Orleans public schools for her research. Dominik Hoffman-Wellenhof, a Ph.D. candidate in German Studies from the University of Graz, was the Austrian Ministry of Science Fellow. He worked on his Graz dissertation on the topic of 'Autobiographische Darstellungen von Identitätskrisen im Exil: Frederic Mortons und Ruth Klügers Suche nach Brücken in einer neuen Heimat' [Identity Crises in Austrian Jewish Refugees' Autobiographies]. He conducted long personal interviews with Morton in New York and Klüger in Los Angeles.

18 students from universities all over Austria (including Graz and Vienna) participated in the 'Austrian Student Program' – a *Schnupperstudium* at an American

St. Niklaus/Christmas Party for Innsbruck Students, Dec. 2013

university during their semester break in February and took 'American Studies' courses in History, Political Science, Sociology, and Economics. The many UNO students in Austria some years ago formed a UNO-Austrian Alumni Association Chapter Innsbruck and have organized regular reunions in Innsbruck, usually in late June before the UNO-Innsbruck Summer School Program begins its session.

'Outgoing' to Innsbruck were 275 American students and 25 faculty members from more than 20 universities from all over the South, attending the 38th annual UNO International Summer School in Innsbruck in from beginning of July to mid-August 2012. A dozen students attended our 'Academic Year Abroad' semester/year-long program in Innsbruck.

Conferences/Workshops

Center Austria organized with the University of Innsbruck Department of German Studies the Annual UNO – Innsbruck Conference, in cooperation with Austrian Literature Archives in the National Library, Vienna. The March 2013 meeting was on the topic of 'The Life and Work of Günther Anders: Émigré, Iconoclast, Philosopher, Literateur'. The Polish born Heidegger student Anders was the first husband of Hannah Arendt, a refugee from Hitler's persecutions he found a haven in the U.S. during the Nazi period; as a philosopher and public intellectual critical of technology, he came to Vienna in 1950 and became one of the world's premier critics of nuclear weapons. An international group of scholars led by the University of Vienna's Konrad Paul Liessmann and Stanford's Jean-Pierre Dupuy explored the many sides of one of the twentieth century's leading intellectuals.

(From left to right): Franz Roessler (Austrian Trade Commission, Chicago), Ronald Hall (European Commission, Brussels), Ambassador Wolfgang Petritsch (Chairman of Board of Austrian Marshall Plan Foundation & Harvard Unviersity), Elisabeth Springler (University of Applied Science bfi Vienna), Günter Bischof, Martin Heintel (University of Vienna), Jodok Regional Economic Development Workshop, Oct. 2013. Schäffler (Alpla, Altanta) Regional Economic Development Workshop, Oct. 2013 Schäffler (Alpla, Altanta)

In October 2013 CenterAustria organized a one-day workshop that was co-sponsored by the Austrian Marshall Plan Foundation. The topic was 'Regional Economic Development in Europe and the United States: Development in the European Union and the American South Compared'. Ronald Hall from the European Commission office in Brussels and University of Georgia historian James Cobb delivered key note addresses. Austrian and American economists discussed issues of regional economic development strategies with practitioners of public policy and industry.

German Instruction

In a unique cooperation between UNO's CenterAustria, Benjamin Franklin High School, Deutsches Haus of New Orleans, Tulane University, and Louisiana State University the 'Deutsche Samstagsschule' was continued in the spring of 2013. This new initiative of a German School in New Orleans teaching Saturday morning classes for adults and German immersion instruction for kids ages 4+ comes out of the American Association for German Teachers, Louisiana Chapter. During their regular fall meeting at UNO's CenterAustria, the idea was born to enhance the instruction in the German language in the City of New Orleans with the *Samstagsschule* and to promote German language instruction in area high schools. CenterAustria also hosted again the annual fall meeting of the Louisiana Chapter of the American Association for German Teachers. The noted Austrian journalist and blogger Robert Misik served as the keynote speaker for the meeting.

Cooperations

Next to its partnerships with the Universities of Innsbruck and Graz, CenterAustria continued its cooperations with the Austrian Marshall Plan Foundation, the Ludwig Boltzmann Institut fűr Kriegsfolgenforschung in Graz, the Botstiber Foundation in Media, PA. The cooperation with the Universities of Innsbruck and Graz covers the routine of regular administrative organization meetings (UNO and UI have bi-annual 'Business Meetings' – one in New Orleans in February, and one in Innsbruck in July of every year), student exchanges, faculty contacts, symposia, and guest lectures. Roberta Maierhofer, a former Vice Rektor from the University of Graz, gave a guest lecture in the fall of 2013 on 'Let's Talk about Age: Traces of Time and Experience: An Introduction to Cultural Gerontology'.

UNO administers the Marshall Plan Chair of Austrian and European Studies in cooperation with the Austrian Marshall Plan Foundation. The 2011/2012 chairholder was Dr. Bertold Molden, an adjunct lecturer in the Department of History at the University of Vienna. He taught a course in the History Department on Central America in the Twentieth Century, the Holocaust, and Comparative European Fascism. The Marshall Plan Foundation also administers a scholarship program for Austrian and American students for mid-term research visits.

University of Innsbruck students Christian Riml in biology and Bernhard Köhl in geology were recipients of such MP grants in the fall of 2013. In October 2013 the Marshall Plan Foundation co-sponsored a one day workshop on 'Regional Economic Development' with CenterAustria (see above).

CenterAustria continued its work in the 'Quiet Invaders Project', funded by the Botstiber Foundation. This project works on the prosopography (collective biography) of Austrian immigrants to the United States in the 20th Century from the Burgenländers to Schwarzenegger. Günter Bischof revised and republished a chapter on Schwarzenegger in his essay collection on US – Austrian relations and also published a chapter on the expulsion of the Viennese Jews after the Anschluss of 1938 in the same volume. Dominik Hoffman-Wellenhof conducted research on his Graz dissertation on 'Identity Crises in Austrian Jewish Refugees' Autobiographies' under the auspices of Botstiber Foundation – his travel to conduct interviews was funded by Botstiber. Eva Maltschnig is continuing her dissertation research on 'Austrian War Brides' and conducting interviews with Austrian war brides across the United States for her Vienna dissertation. Günter Bischof continues to sit on the board of the Botstiber Institute for Austrian-American Studies, which has become a major funding agency for research in the field of Austrian – American Relations.

CenterAustria also continued its unofficial cooperation with the Wirtschaftsunversität Wien and Günter Bischof has been giving special seminars and lectures there.

CenterAustria's cooperation with the Ludwig Boltzmann Institut für Kriegsfolgenforschung (BIK) in Graz is expanded in the new joint project 'The End of the Cold War in Eastern Europe'. BIK has become a premier platform in Cold War Studies in Europe with its vast network of scholars in Eastern and Western Europe built since its 'Red Army in Austria' and 'Prague Spring 1968' research projects. BIK has become a premier bridge builder within the Cold War scholarly community in the Russian Federation and Eastern East/Central Europe, building and promoting a network of scholars working on the international history of the Cold War. This has allowed access to Russian and Eastern European/East Central European archives and has richly informed our knowledge of 'the other' side in the Cold War. A smaller English version of the massive volume on the Vienna Summit of 1961, which appeared in German in 2012, was published late in 2013: Günter Bischof/Stefan Karner/Barbara Stelzl-Marx, eds., The Vienna Summit and Its Importance in International History (The Harvard Cold War Studies Book Series, ed. Mark Kramer) with Lexington Books. Next to Dr. Mark Kramer of Harvard University's Project of Cold War Studies in the Davis Center of Russian and Eurasian Studies, CenterAustria serves as the American node in this '1989: The End of the Cold War in Eastern Europe' research collaborative project. BIK's Peter Ruggenthaler is coordinator of the ambitious 1989 project. On the occasion of the 25th anniversary of the 'End of the Cold War' in 2014, three volumes of essays are planned on the sea changes taking place from 1989

Bischof Festschrift Presentation, Vienna, Oct. 2013. (From left to right): Peter Ruggenthaler (BIK), Ambassador Martin Eichtinger, Stefan Karner (BIK), Angelika (sister in her native Bregenzerwälder dress), Bischof and wife Melanie Boulet, Josef (brother), Mark Kramer (Harvard University)

to 1991: volumes each on Russia and Eastern Europe, Germany, and the West and 1989, next to documentary volumes in German and Russian on the 1989–91 Revolutions. The BIK, in cooperation with Mark Kramer organized a one-day workshop on 'The Fate of Communist Regimes, 1989–1991' at Harvard's Davis Center on November 20, 2013. Bischof delivered a paper on 'U.S. Policy and the Collapse of East European Communism'. BIK also organized a one-day conference at Vienna's Diplomatic Academy on the occasion of the 70th anniversary of the 1943 Moscow Declaration on October 29, 2013 with Bischof giving a paper on 'The Moscow Declaration and Austrian Politics of History'. This conference ended with a surprise celebration of Bischof's 60th birthday and the transfer of a *Festschrift*, organized by his BIK colleagues and friends with Gertraud Griessner of CenterAustria: Martin Eichtinger, Stefan Karner, Mark Kramer, Peter Ruggenthaler, eds., Reassessing History from Two Continents: Festschrift Günter Bischof (Innsbruck University Press 2013).

Prizes

CenterAustria initiated and sponsored a new scholarly prize in conjunction with the American Friends of the Dokumentationsarchiv des Österreichischen Widerstandes (DÖW), on whose board Bischof sits. This major new prize in studies related to Austria and Czechoslovakia in the World War II Era is dedicated to the scholarly work and legacy of Radomir Luža, the late scholar of Central Europe who taught at Tulane University in New Orleans for three decades. Luža published major works on Czechoslovakia, Austro-German relations in the Anschluss Era, as well as the Austrian and the Czech resistance during World War II. Luža was a refugee from Communist Czechoslovakia (he slipped across the border into Austria during the Czech Coup of February 1948). The prize is organized by the American Friends of DÖW and is sponsored by CenterAustria. The second prize went to Dr. Leslie Marie Waters for her 2012 UCLA dissertation 'Resurrecting the Nation: Felvidék and the Hungarian Territorial Revisionist Project, 1938–1945'. The 2013 Luža Prize was announced during the reception of the Austrian Cultural Forum at the annual meeting of the German Studies Association in Denver, CO, in October. Dr. Waters was not able to attend.

Art Exhibitions and Film Series

As part of the art exchange program between the Cultural Office of the City of Innsbruck and the Department of Fine Arts at UNO, two art exhibits were organized. UNO fine arts students Ryn Wilson and Kevin Baer exhibited their work in the Andechs Gallery in Innsbruck's old city in July 2013. Innsbruck artists Daniela Span and Charlotte Simon presented their work in an exhibit entitled **OSMOSIS-identity quest** at UNO St. Claude Gallery in New Orleans in October 2013. These exhibits allow young artists to display their work for the first time overseas and visit and get to know the art world in these cities (the Innsbruck artists also visit New York City for a few days and stayed at the Austrian Cultural Forum). The quality of the art displayed in these exhibits is getting a growing amount of attention in both venues. The artists were present during the openings of both shows.

For the first time CenterAustria organized a Central European Film Series, with the help of Lazslo Fülop, a faculty member from UNO's Department of Film and Theatre. The following films were shown with brief introductions: 'The White Ribbon' (2009), dir. Michael Haneke; 'Love' (1971); dir. Károly Makk; 'The Lives of Others' (2006), dir. Florian Henckel von Donnersmarck.

Publications

CenterAustria Book Series

Contemporary Austrian Studies Series (UNO Press/innsbruck university press):

Günter Bischof – Ferdinand Karlhofer (Eds.), Austria's International Position after the End of the Cold War, Contemporary Austrian Studies Series 22, New Orleans/Innsbruck 2013.

TRANSATLANTICA:

Günter Bischof, Relationships/Beziehungsgeschichten. Austria and the United States in the Twentieth Century, TRANSATLANTICA 4, Innsbruck 2013;

Berndt Ostendorf, New Orleans. Creolization and all that Jazz, TRANSATLANTICA 7, Innsbruck 2013.

Books

Günter Bischof – Stefan Karner – Barbara Stelzl-Marx (Eds.), The Vienna Summit and Its Importance in International History, in: Mark Kramer (Ed.), The Harvard Cold War Studies Book Series, Lanham 2013;

Poster Central European Film Series, Spring 2013

Cover, Contemporary Austrian Studies 22

Andreas Exenberger – Philipp Strobl – Günter Bischof – James Mokhiber (Eds.), Globalization and the City. Two Connected Phenomena in Past and Present, Innsbruck 2013.

Networking and Research Platform

Günter Bischof is regularly providing leads to American and Austrian researchers from the worlds of media and academia who work on topics of 20th century Austrian history, U.S. – Austrian relations, and/or contemporary New Orleans. CenterAustria hosted the following short-term research fellows in the spring of 2013: David Mayer, a historian from the University of Vienna working on intellectual Marxist networks in Latin America; Nicole Melanie Goll and Georg Hoffmann, Ph.D. students at the University of Graz working on their project 'The Lynching of Downed Allied Airmen in 1944/1945'. Meyer lectured at CenterAustria, while Goll and Hoffmann participated on a panel in the National World War II Museum in New Orleans and were panelists in a session on oral history techniques at UNO; both went on to interview American veterans throughout the U.S. Bischof gave interviews to the Wall Street Journal Europe and the Austrian Press Agency. Bischof also consulted with many scholars individually on their research projects. This kind of 'service' to the international research and media communities is increasingly becoming a function of Austrian Centers in the U.S. and elsewhere.

Summary

I. Lectures – Spring 2013

- Thomas Vieregge, U.S. Correspondent, Die Presse, Washington, D.C.: 'Obama's Times from a European Perspective'
- Günter Bischof, Director, CenterAustria, UNO: 'From Cold War Mediator to Bad Boy of Europe: Austrian and the U.S. in the Transatlantic Arena (1990–2010)'
- Anton Pelinka, Central European University, Budapest: 'Obama's Victory – Lessons for Europe'
- Center Austria and Austrian Students Program Special Lecture: Dr. Anton Pelinka, Central European University, Budapest; Dr. Molden's HIST 2991 Class on 'European Fascism': 'Dollfuß – Schuschnigg: The Lesser Evil? Austrofascism in a Comparative Perspective'
- Nikki Brown, Black History Month: Exhibit with Introductory Talk: 'After Katrina: A Visual History of African-American Men, 2010–2012'

Annual Lecture of the Marshall Plan Chair in Austrian and European Studies

- Berthold Molden, Marshall Plan Chair 2012–2013, Department of History: 'Can Anticommunism Be Neutral? Austria's Media during the Cold War'
- Dr. David Mayer, University of Leipzig & CA Visiting Research Fellow: 'Debates, Intellectuals and Activists: Current Perspectives on the Transnational History of 20th Century Marxism'

Center Austria – National World War II Museum Panel Presentation

- James Weingartner, Nicole-Melanie Goll, Georg Hoffmann, Tyler Bridges: 'The Lynching of Allied Airmen in the Third Reich during the Final Months of WWII'
- Oral History Workshop – with UNO History Department with Connie Atkinson, Berthold Molden, Georg Hoffmann, Nicole-Melanie Goll, Seth Paridon.

CenterAustria Fellows Present Their Research

- Theresa Mairhofer, City of Innsbruck/Land Tirol Nick Mueller Fellow 2012–2013: 'Trust: A Phenomenological Study of Educational Learning Experiences – What Does It Mean to Learn? What Experiences Do Children Undergo at School?'
- Dominik Hofmann-Wellenhof, Austrian Ministry of Science Fellow 2012–2013: 'Frederic Morton & Ruth Klűger: Analyzing the Lives of Austrian Émigré Writers'

2013 Marshall Plan Lecture: Berthold Molden, Günter Bischof

- Margarethe Szeless, Botstiber Research Fellow & University of Vienna: 'Okamoto's Vienna. Austrian-American Relations in Press Photography after WWII'

II. Lectures – Fall 2013

- Book Talk on Contemporary Austrian Studies vol. 22: 'Austria's International Position after the End of the Cold War (2013)'
- Thomas Schnoell, Consul General of Austria in Chicago/Ambassador in Albania: 'Austria and the Western Balkans'
- Hermann Kaufmann, Technical University of Munich: 'Modern Wood Architecture in Europe'
- Oliver Kühschelm, University of Vienna: 'Patriotic Shopping: A Comparative Perspective on the Call to "Buy National" in the 20th Century'
- Election panel on German and Austrian Elections: Chair: Günter Bischof; Discussants: Berthold Molden, Christina Kiel, Markus Habermann
- Mariam Tazi-Preve, University of Vienna: 'Motherhood in Patriarchy: Empirical Situation, Politics, and Theory'
- Marty Manor, University of Washington/New Orleans: 'Košice, Slovakia: Distinct Ways the "European Capital of Culture 2013" experienced the Czechoslovak Revolutions of 1948, 1968 and 1989'
- Roberta Maierhofer, University of Graz: 'Let's Talk about Age: Traces of Time and Experience'

Ingeborg Fialová

Austrian Center Olomouc

Palacký University Olomouc

The Research Center for German Moravian Literature in Olomouc was appointed to be an Austrian Center as recently as February 2013. The activities of the previous year are thus to be classified as preparatory arrangements dedicated mainly to the establishment of organizational structures. It was also important to introduce the Austrian Center to the local academic circles and to the broader public:

An 'inventory' was taken – a summary of all former activities of the German Department in Olomouc and the Research Center which somehow concerned Austria. An information brochure intended for promotion was printed, the website of the Austria Center was launched (www.oezentrum.cz) and multiple articles about the establishment of the Center and about its plans and framework of tasks were published in the university press. A team of co-workers was put together which consists of three 'constant co-workers' (the leader, the manager, student assistant) and four 'associated team members' (the manager of the Research Center/Arbeitsstelle für deutschmährische Literatur, the librarian of the Austrian Library, the Austrian lecturer, the Endowed Professor of the Federal Republic of Germany). There are also other lecturers and students of the department who take part in the activities of the Center.

Furthermore, previously on-going and recently initiated activities have been continued – now under the aegis of the Austrian Center:

A. Research and Presentation of Research Findings

In the Research Center for German Moravian Literature/Arbeitsstelle, research was conducted as usual, the archive of the Research Center was being filled and its collection was gradually stored and secured electronically. In 2013, a new interactive and user-friendly database was developed, into which data about German Moravian literature will be transferred starting in May 2014.

In the autumn of 2013, half of the staff of the German Department in Olomouc participated in the VIII Convention of Young Germanist from Central Europe in Bad Kissingen, and they delivered speeches on topics of German Moravian/Austrian literature. Enriched through/by the presentations of colleagues from Praha, Brno, München, Münster, Weimar, Dresden, and Köln, the speeches are going to be published in a collective volume of this convention as the first volume of the e-book edition of the Austrian Center in the autumn of 2014. The meeting could be used for further discussions of the publishers of the planned handbook of German Bohemian literature as well. The handbook should be published under the title 'German Literature from Prague. A New Definition' by the Metzler publishing house in 2016.

In 2013, two books from the edition 'Contributions to German Moravian Literature' were published by the Palacký University Publishing House:

- Milan Horňáček – Sabine Voda Eschgfaeller, Kulturgeschichtliche Daten zur deutschmährischen Literatur. Beiträge 24 [Cultural-Historical Data on German Moravian Literature], Olomouc 2013;
- Tereza Pavlíčková, Die Entwicklung des Nationalitätenkonflikts in der Znaimer deutschen Presse 1850–1938. Beiträge 26 [The Development of the Ethnic Conflict in the German Press in Znojmo 1850–1938], Olomouc 2013.

An entire issue of *Germanoslavica* (a journal for German-Slavic Studies published by the Academy of Sciences of the Czech Republic, year of issue 24, Praha 2013) was filled with articles about German Moravian literature submitted by researchers from Olomouc.

B. Teaching and Scientific Work of Students

In the winter and summer semesters of 2013/2014 five courses (lectures and seminars) dealing with Austrian history and literature were offered. Four Master's theses on Austrian topics were submitted, and eight dissertations focusing on Austrian history and literature are being elaborated upon, *i.e.* they are being supervised and consulted. A dissertation about Richard von Schaukal (by Libor Marek) was successfully defended in December 2013.

C. Public Relations Work/Cultural Activities for the Broader Public

Two books for the broader public (in the edition 'poetica moraviae') are being prepared: a bilingual anthology of texts of German Moravian literature as well as one bilingual version of Roman Karl Scholz's work. Both books will be published in 2014.

In cooperation with radio, ten programs were created in the cycle Toulky krajem/Landschaftswanderungen/Wanderings through the landscape. A program about the German Šternberk was awarded the media prize 'Prix Non Pereant'.

The members of the Research Center held several public speeches about German Moravian literature (*e.g.*, in the lecture series of the association of professors 'Societas cognitorum', in diverse cultural organizations of the city and the region). Furthermore, active contacts with homeland associations (Jägerndorf, Schönbeg,

Römerstadt) were maintained, articles were written for the press and published by homeland associations and for regional press (*Olmützer Blätter*, *Rýmařovský horizont*, *Krok*, *Olomoucký deník*, *Listy*, *Hlubočky zpravodaj*, *Týdeník Rozhlas*). As support for the publishing of the work of Roman Karl Scholz, a native of Šternberk, the Research Center was awarded the Viktor-Dostal-Prize of the city Šternberk.

Various guest lectures and readings by authors took place, and the announcements and reports were/are available on the website.

D. Plans for 2014/2015

- Entering data into the new database
- Basic research on the topic of 'Romantic literature in Bohemia and Moravia in the context of Austrian literary history'
- Conference about Franz Spunda
- Conference 'Cultural transfer in the case of (Post-)Kakanien (1848–1939)'
- Publications:
    - Selection from the work of Roman Karl Scholz (bilingual edition)
    - Publication of the correspondence between Friedrich Torberg and Hugo Haas
    - Bilingual anthology of German Moravian literature
    - Monograph about Kurt Gröger
    - Contributions from the conference in Bad Kissingen
- Assignment and supervision of Master's and doctoral theses on Austrian topics
- Offer of at least four courses on Austrian topics
- Compilation of a list of 'Austrian activities' at the Palacký University, interconnection of individual representatives (the Research Center, the Austrian Center, the Endowed Professor of the Federal Republic of Germany), workshop
- Supervision of scholarship students intending to apply for an Austrian scholarship
- Guest lectures of Austrian scientists and/or readings of authors
- Translation services for authors from the Palacký University who wish to publish their articles/books in German

Articles

I. (Collective) Mind and Memory

Thomas Rohringer

Spaces and Emotional Styles. War Victims in Czechoslovakia and Austria 1918–1938

University of Vienna

1. Introduction

This article primarily deals with an outline of the research project 'Spaces and Emotional Styles', which aims at analyzing the role emotional styles played in the formation of war victims' organizations. The research project therefore investigates which values and emotions were (re-)produced, fostered, denied or dismissed in the organizations' periodicals and how (or if) individual war victims adopted these emotional standards. To this end, the 'official' and public discourse in the organizations' periodicals shall be compared with war victims' ego-documents. The latter consist of letters addressed to bureaucratic institutions, letters published in gazettes and newspapers as well as private letters and diaries. The project will then analyze how individual (male and female) war victims reacted to these (gendered) emotional styles and the normative processes actualized by them. The analysis therefore looks for correlations (or disparities) between the organizations' periodicals and individual war victims' petitions when it comes to topics and tropes, language and style. By not presupposing that the latter are set by the war victims' organizations and then adopted by the war victims, the goal is to investigate these organizations as arenas where war victims' place in society is negotiated.[1] At the same time this provides insight into the formation of social groups and gendered identities. These two processes (group formation and gendered identities) are intimately linked with emotions[2] as is negotiating war vic-

1 Such an approach is for example suggested by Benjamin Ziemann, in: *idem*, Republikanische Kriegserinnerung in einer polarisierten Öffentlichkeit. Das Reichsbanner Schwarz-Rot-Gold als Veteranenverband der sozialistischen Arbeiterschaft [Republican War Memory in a Polarized Public. The Black-Red-Gold Banner of the Realm as Socialist Labor's Veteran Organization], in: Historische Zeitschrift 267/2, Frankfurt am Main 1998, 357–398.

2 For emotions and group formations see for example Benno Gammerl, Emotional Styles – Concepts and Challenges, in: Rethinking History 16/2, London 2012, 161–175; Barbara Rosenwein, Emotional Communities in the Early Middle Ages, Ithaca 2006; for the connection between emotions and masculinity see Manuel Borutta – Nina Verheyen (Eds.), Die Präsenz der Gefühle. Männlichkeit und Emotion in der Moderne [The Presence of Feelings. Masculinity and Emotions in Modernity], Bielefeld 2010.

tims' place in society, which will be shown in the author's Ph.D. project through adopting a history of emotions perspective.

Since the topic of emotions requires a complex, multilayered theoretical and methodological framework, the following contribution will give an overview of those concepts developed in the research on the history of emotions that will be adapted in the author's Ph.D. project.

2. History of Emotions

In recent years, there has been a growing interest in the role of emotions in history.[3] In line with the focus of this newfound research on the history of emotions, this project aims at analyzing the relevance of emotions for human agency. Scholars of the history of emotions have engaged critically with the grand narrative of Western/European modernization, challenging the notion of regarding it as a process of continuous rationalization and growing emotional control[4], as prominently portrayed in the works of Max Weber (1864–1920) or Norbert Elias (1897–1990).[5] The new research in the history of emotions distinguishes itself from the field's forerunners, including Lucien Febvre (1878–1956) and Johan Huizinga (1872–1945)[6], in the way feelings are conceptualized. The understanding of emotions utilized by Febvre, Elias or Huizinga has been called the 'hydraulic model' of feelings by Barbara Rosenwein.[7] It considers emotions to be something natural and inherent, surfacing in times of great pressure. Rather than considering them to be purely biological, the history of emotions considers feelings as historically changing and culturally formed. Consequently, present-day research also strives for an analysis of the emotional knowledge and vocabulary of a specific historical context.[8]

---

3 See Susan J. Matt, Current Emotion Research in History. Or, Doing History from the Inside Out, in: Emotion Review 3/1, Thousand Oaks 2011, 117–124; Bettina Hitzer, Emotionsgeschichte – Ein Anfang mit Folgen [History of Emotions – A Beginning with Consequences], http://hsozkult.geschichte.hu-berlin.de/forum/2011-11-001.pdf, 23 November 2011.

4 See Barbara Rosenwein, Problems and Methods in the History of Emotions, in: Passions in Context 1, Potsdam 2010, http://www.passionsincontext.de/uploads/media/01_Rosenwein.pdf, 23 November 2011; Eva Illouz, Gefühle in Zeiten des Kapitalismus [Feelings in the Time of Capitalism], Adorno-Vorlesungen 2004, Institut für Sozialforschung an der Johann-Wolfgang-Goethe-Universität, Frankfurt am Main 2004, 7–9.

5 See Max Weber, The Protestant Ethic and the Spirit of Capitalism, New York 1958; Norbert Elias, The Civilizing Process 2: Sociogenetic and Psychogenetic Investigations, 2 vols., Oxford 1982.

6 See Lucien Febvre, Sensibility and History. How to Reconstitute the Emotional Life of the Past, in: *idem.*, A New Kind of History and other Essays, New York 1973, 12–26; Johan Huizinga, The Waning of the Middle Ages. A Study of the Forms of Life, Thought and Art in France and The Netherlands in the 14th and 15th Centuries, London 1950.

7 See Rosenwein, Problems.

8 See Jan Plamper, Geschichte und Gefühl. Grundlagen der Emotionsgeschichte [History and Feeling. Principles of a History of Emotions], München 2012, 85.

The adaptation of recent theoretical concepts on emotions in history will provide the epistemological tools to fulfill this project's objective of analyzing emotions as social practices. As such, they are conceived of as being learnt during the socialization process and adopted in a 'subjectivation process'.[9] For this conception it is essential to take into account the 'emotionologies'[10] – that is, the knowledge and discourse on emotions and the emotional standards – of a specific time and place. However, research in the history of emotions should not limit itself to analyzing only the normative level, but should rather strive to examine the latter's relevance for social interactions. As sociologist Arlie Hochschild has pointed out, individuals not only seek to express their emotions in congruence with emotional standards, but to feel the required emotions – she refers to that effort as 'emotion work'.[11]

William Reddy insists in his critique of (radical) social constructivism that emotions cannot be constructed – in the sense of created – by society, that in fact it can only shape their expressions and the ways in which they are experienced. With the concept of 'emotives', Reddy makes a crucial methodological proposition.[12] Drawing on speech act theory, he defines 'emotives' as being neither merely 'constative', nor 'performative' utterances, but rather as being 'a third type of communicative utterance'[13], because any attempt to represent one's emotions is 'necessar[ily]'[14] bound to fail. However, this failure is not due to the lack of an 'inner dimension' of emotions, but is rather based on the fact that emotives can only be 'effort[s] by the speaker to offer an interpretation of something that is observable to no other actor [which corresponds exactly with this 'inner' experience of emotions].'[15] The emotive's difference from the self-referential performative act arises from the way in which it refers 'to something close to its origin, to its own world-anchor.'[16] Emotives therefore have a communicative quality, but at the same time serve to explore and alter one's self, insofar as the effects of this self-

---

9 See Andreas Reckwitz, Umkämpfte Maskulinität. Zur Historischen Kultursoziologie männlicher Subjektformen und ihrer Affektivitäten vom Zeitalter der Empfindsamkeit bis zur Postmoderne [Contested Masculinity. On a Historical Sociology of Culture Concerning Forms of Masculine Subjects and their Affectivities from Sentimentalism to Postmodernism], in: Manuel Borutta – Nina Verheyen (Eds.), Die Präsenz der Gefühle. Männlichkeit und Emotion in der Moderne [The Presence of Feelings. Masculinity and Emotions in Modernity], Bielefeld 2010, 57–77.

10 Peter N. Stearns – Carol Z. Stearns, Emotionology. Clarifying the History of Emotions and Emotional Standards, in: The American Historical Review 4/90, Oxford 1985, 813–836.

11 See Arlie R. Hochschild, Emotion Work, Feeling Rules, and Social Structure, in: The American Journal of Sociology 85, Chicago 1979, 551–575; *idem.*, The Managed Heart. Commercialization of Human Feeling, Berkeley/Los Angeles/London 1983.

12 See William M. Reddy, Against Constructionism. The Historical Ethnography of Emotions, in: Current Anthropology 38/3, Chicago 1997, 327–351.

13 *Ibid.*, 327.

14 *Ibid.*, 331.

15 *Ibid.*

16 *Ibid.*

examination are not determined by the emotive itself. Finally, Reddy proposes a basis for political struggle and moral judgments – the way in which social constructivism seems to render such struggles impossible being at the heart of his critique – with his concept of 'emotional liberty'. With this notion he distinguishes between 'emotional regimes' that grant 'the freedom to change goals in response to bewildering, ambivalent thought activations that exceed the capacity of attention and challenge the reign of high-level goals currently guiding emotional management'[17] and those with a more rigid set of emotional norms and practices.[18]

Monique Scheer follows a different approach, adapting praxeology to analyze emotions and integrating Reddy's notion of the emotive into her concept, thereby making the notion more fruitful for the current research project. For her, it is crucial to understand 'emotional practices as things people do *in order to* [italics in the original] have emotions, [...] in a performative sense'.[19] She points out four interrelated fields of emotional practice:

1) Mobilizing: Viewing emotional practices not as expressions of emotions that are or are not there *a priori*, but 'as means of achieving an embodied experience of [them]'[20];
2) Naming: Integrating Reddy's emotives, Scheer stresses the performative act of naming emotions, but also highlights the importance of taking into account discursive practices, the habitus and the more concrete framework of the social interaction in which the practice is performed, as well as of the re-experiencing and re-interpreting of emotions through remembrance[21];
3) Communicating: Stressing that the performative expression of emotions is only half the story and that the success of such practices is as much dependent on the interpretative patterns, skills, and habits of the recipient actors[22];
4) Regulating: Analyzing the role which emotional norms and rules ('emotionologies') play in forming a habitus or 'emotional style'.[23]

Scheer also stresses the relevance of the 'knowing body' concept for 'emotions-as-practice', a culturally formed and performed bodily experience drawing on Bourdieu's habitus concept.[24]

---

17 William M. Reddy, The Navigation of Feeling. A Framework for the History of Emotions, Cambridge 2001, 129.

18 See *ibid.*

19 Monique Scheer, Are Emotions a Kind of Practice (and Is That What Makes Them Have a History)? A Bourdieuian Approach to Understanding Emotion, in: History and Theory 51/2, Middletown 2012, 193–220, here 194.

20 *Ibid.*, 209.

21 See *ibid.*, 212–214.

22 See *ibid.*, 214f.

23 *Ibid.*, 215–217.

24 See *ibid.*, 204–209; Pierre Bourdieu, The Logic of Practice. Cambridge 1990, 52–66; Pierre Bourdieu, Masculine Domination, Stanford 2001.

Since individuals are not socialized in society as a whole, but rather in particular social institutions – the family, the military or the working place – and participate in groups sharing certain emotional standards and emotional styles, looking at these institutions and groups is particularly fruitful for a history of emotions. Barbara Rosenwein has called these groups 'emotional communities'.[25] The question then arises as to whether war victims constituted an emotional community or not. War victims make up a very heterogeneous group comprised of men and women from different social backgrounds, with different war-disabilities or none at all (for example, widows and orphans).[26] For this reason, the project will analyze the homogenizing effect of the shared military drill, war experiences and, in particular, the role of the organizations as intermediaries between individual war experiences and social interpretations of the war.[27] Here, the concept of 'emotional styles' comes into play, defined by Benno Gammerl as 'encompass[ing] the experience, fostering, and display of emotions, and [as] oscillat[ing] between discursive patterns and embodied practices [...]'.[28] Located at the intersection of social norms and individual action, this concept allows for a better understanding of how emotional standards were adopted and subjectivized.

3. State of the Art and Scientific Relevance

The First World War brought new challenges to social policy, especially due to the unprecedented number of war-disabled veterans, widows, and orphans. As Michael Geyer highlights in his seminal essay on British, French and German welfare policy towards war victims after the First World War, governmental responses bore on the one hand certain similarities in fundamental principles, for example in the assessment and definition of disability based on non-military criteria, such as the reduction in earning capacity. On the other hand, these responses also differed greatly, for example, in regard to the roles ascribed to the state and private welfare organizations in the welfare system.[29] Geyer also points out that war victims are not only a product of the war, but also of contemporary political,

25 See Rosenwein, Communities, 20–25, 199–201.

26 See for example: Verena Pawlowsky – Harald Wendelin, Die Verwaltung des Leides. Kriegsbeschädigtenfürsorge in Niederösterreich [The Administration of Suffering. Government Care for War-disabled Veterans in Lower Austria], in: Peter Melichar – Ernst Langthaler – Stefan Eminger (Eds.), Niederösterreich im 20. Jahrhundert 2: Wirtschaft, 3 vols., Wien/Köln/Weimar 2008, 507–536, here 528f.

27 See Ziemann, Kriegserinnerung, 357–398.

28 See Benno Gammerl, Emotional Styles – Concepts and Challenges, in: Rethinking History 16/2, London 2012, 161–175, here 163.

29 See Michael Geyer, Ein Vorbote des Wohlfahrtsstaates. Die Kriegsopferversorgung in Frankreich, Deutschland und Großbritannien nach dem Ersten Weltkrieg [Precursor to the Welfare State. War Victims' Policy in France, Germany and Great Britain after the First World War], in: Geschichte und Gesellschaft 9/2, Göttingen 1983, 230–277, here 234–237.

scientific and juridical discourses[30], rendering the analysis of the various welfare policies and the attitude of the war victims' organizations towards society and state particularly promising. David A. Gerber delivered a classification of the various types of war veterans' and war victims' organizations in his comparative essay on veterans' and war victims' organizations in North America and Western Europe from 1914 to 1950.[31]

Sabine Kienitz has written extensively on the social and cultural history of war victims in Germany, combining a wide variety of sources and perspectives on the topic.[32]

The Czechoslovak Republic's foundation, its political and institutional history[33], its military system and the legionary tradition[34] are well researched. The Republic's social policies, and particularly its policy on war victims, have been explored in Natali Stegmann's work 'Kriegsdeutungen – Staatsgründungen – Sozialpolitik'[35]. She focuses on the discourses of heroism and victimization in Czechoslovakia from 1918 to 1948. Furthermore, the author's project draws on works dealing with the concept of 'loyalty', which has been employed particularly when dealing with the First Czechoslovak Republic as a multi-ethnic state.[36]

Verena Pawlowsky and Harald Wendelin published several articles on the juridical and social history of policy on war victims for the Austrian context after 1914.[37] Historical comparative studies of the situations of war victims in the in-

30 See *ibid.*, 233f.

31 David A. Gerber, Disabled Veterans, the State and the Experience of Disability in Western Societies 1914–1950, in: Journal of Social History 36/4, Oxford 2003, 899–916.

32 See for example: Sabine Kienitz, Beschädigte Helden. Kriegsinvalidität und Körperbilder 1914–1923 [Damaged Heroes. War-Disabled Veterans and Body Images 1914–1923], Paderborn/Wien 2008; Sabine Kienitz, Beschädigte Helden. Zur Politisierung des kriegsinvaliden Soldatenkörpers in der Weimarer Republik [Damaged Heroes. On the Politicization of the War-disabled Soldier's Body in the Weimar Republic], in: Jost Dülffer – Gerd Krumeich (Eds.), Der verlorene Frieden. Politik und Kriegskultur nach 1918 [The Lost Peace. Politics and War Culture after 1918], Essen 2002, 199–214.

33 See for example: Jörg K. Hoensch, Geschichte der Tschechoslowakei [History of Czechoslovakia], Stuttgart 1992; Jörg K. Hoensch, Studia Slovaca. Studien zur Geschichte der Slowaken und der Slowakei [Studies on the History of the Slovaks and Slovakia], München 2000; Josef Kalvoda, The Genesis of Czechoslovakia. East European Monographs 209, New York 1986.

34 Martin Zückert, Memory of War and National State Integration. Czech and German Veterans in Czechoslovakia after 1918, in: Central Europe 4/2, Leeds 2006, 111–121.

35 Natali Stegmann, Kriegsdeutungen – Staatsgründungen – Sozialpolitik. Der Helden- und Opferdiskurs in der Tschechoslowakei 1918–1948 [Interpretations of War – State Foundations – Social Policy. Discurses of Heroism and Victimhood in Czechoslovakia 1918–1948], München 2010.

36 See for example: Martin Schulze Wessel (Ed.), Loyalitäten in der Tschechoslowakischen Republik 1918–1938. Politische, nationale und kulturelle Zugehörigkeiten [Loyalties in the Czechoslovak Republic 1918–1938. Political, National and Cultural Affiliations], München 2004.

37 See for example: Verena Pawlowsky – Harald Wendelin, Government Care of War Widows and Disabled Veterans after World War I, in: Günter Bischof – Fritz Plasser – Peter Berger (Eds.), From Empire to Republic. Post-World War I Austria, Contemporary Austrian Studies 19, New Orleans/Innsbruck 2010, 171–191; *idem.*, Die normative Konstruktion des Opfers. Die Versorgung der Invaliden des Ersten Weltkrieges [The Normative Construction of the Vic-

terwar period have been focused on Western Europe so far, primarily comparing Great Britain, France, and Germany.[38] In contrast, comparative studies of the Habsburg monarchy's successor states in East Central Europe are still in an early phase of development. The 2010 issue of 'Comparativ', entitled 'Veterans and War Victims in Eastern Europe during the 20th Century' and edited by Katrin Boeckh and Natali Stegmann, combined a number of nation-specific essays on war victims in East Central and Central Europe, opening up a large field for comparisons from both synchronic and diachronic perspectives.[39] Another anthology edited by Natali Stegmann, 'Die Weltkriege als symbolische Bezugspunkte', has a similar aim, comparing Czechoslovakia, Poland and Germany after the First and Second World War.[40] The author's Ph.D. project offers a thoroughly comparative and transnational perspective, not only dealing with Austrian and Czechoslovakian war victims within their respective national frameworks, but also highlighting the links and relations between the respective welfare systems and war victims' organizations.

4. War Victims Organizations

A brief overview of the history of Czechoslovakian and Austrian war victims' organizations shall serve as a preface to the outline of the four social spaces forming the center of the analysis. A comparison of Austrian and Czechoslovakian war victims' organizations reveals similarities and differences.

According to David A. Gerber's typology of war veterans' organizations, the four organizations outlined here fall into the category 'composite', described as organizations consisting of war-disabled veterans with all kinds of war-disabilities. Gerber distinguishes these from 'mixed' and 'singular population' organizations, of which the former also have able-bodied members and the latter consist only of members with the same form of war injury.[41] However, these categories are not

---

tim. Care for the War-disabled Veterans of the First World War], in: Laurence Cole – Christa Hämmerle – Martin Scheutz (Eds.), Glanz – Gewalt – Gehorsam. Militär und Gesellschaft in der Habsburgermonarchie (1800 bis 1918) [Glamor – Violence – Obedience. The Military and Society in the Habsburg Monarchy (1800–1918)], Frieden und Krieg, Beiträge zur Historischen Friedensforschung 18, Essen 2011, 359–383.

38 See for example: Geyer, Vorbote; Deborah Cohen, The War Come Home. Disabled Veterans in Britain and Germany 1914–1939, Berkeley/Los Angeles/London 2001; *idem.*, The War's Returns. Disabled Veterans in Britain and Germany 1914–1939, in: Roger Chickering – Stig Förster (Eds.), The Shadows of Total War. Europe, East Asia, and the United States 1919–1939, Cambridge 2003, 113–128.

39 Katrin Boeckh – Natali Stegmann (Eds.), Veterans and War Victims in Eastern Europe during the 20th Century. A Comparison, Comparativ 20/5, Leipzig 2011.

40 Natali Stegmann (Ed.), Die Weltkriege als symbolische Bezugspunkte. Polen, die Tschechoslowakei und Deutschland nach dem Ersten und Zweiten Weltkrieg [The World Wars as Symbolic Points of Reference. Poland, Czechoslovakia and Germany after the First and Second World War], Prag 2009.

41 See Gerber, Veterans, 902f.

mutually exclusive: in the course of their formation, organizations might start as 'mixed' and then develop into 'composite' organizations. Members of 'composite' organizations in turn might form a 'singular population' branch or an independent organization, while remaining affiliated with the larger 'composite' organization.[42] Furthermore, and although often not in their initial phases, both Austrian and Czechoslovakian war victims' organizations included surviving dependents, following the legal development of a joint regulation of both groups' entitlement to compensation.[43]

The precise number of members for each organization is hard to determine. In part, this has to do with the problem of assessing the number of war victims in general, which itself is due to the fact that reliable statistical data for the numbers of war victims are only available from the late 1920s onwards. The first reason for this is the time it took to establish the necessary bureaucratic apparatus. That apparatus then had to catch up with the number of applications received up to that point, constantly working on a backlog up until the early 1920s. This was further complicated by the fact that the final boundary lines of Czechoslovakia and Austria were drawn only in 1919/1920 and 1921, respectively.[44] Beyond that, the number of war victims was constantly shifting, on the one hand due to changes in the legal criteria regulating entitlements, on the other hand due to natural causes, for example death or attaining majority.[45] Additionally, the organizations themselves faced double memberships[46] and belated payment of membership fees[47], which were the primary means of assessing membership numbers. Finally, the data published by the organizations were continually contested by the other organizations themselves, since they were also used to affirm each organization's importance.[48]

---

42 See for example: Barbara Hoffmann, Kriegsblinde in Österreich 1914–1934. [Blindness as War Injury in Austria 1914–1934] Veröffentlichungen des Ludwig-Boltzmann-Instituts für Kriegsfolgen-Forschung 9, Graz/Wien/Klagenfurt 2006, 160.

43 See Verena Pawlowsky, Opfer und Akteure. Organisierung der Kriegsbeschädigten und Kriegerwitwen in der Ersten Republik [Victims and Actors. Organization of War-Disabled Veterans and Widows], in: Ingrid Böhler – Eva Pfanzelter – Thomas Spielbüchler – Rolf Steininger (Eds.), 1968 – Vorgeschichten – Folgen. Bestandsaufnahme der österreichischen Zeitgeschichte, 7. Österreichischer Zeitgeschichtetag 2008 [1968 – Preludes – Consequences. Survey of Austrian Contemporary History, 7th Day of Contemporary History in Austria], Innsbruck/Wien 2010, 801–807, here 802.

44 Karl Vocelka, Geschichte Österreichs. Kultur – Gesellschaft – Politik [History of Austria. Culture – Society – Politics], Graz/Wien/Köln 2002, 273–275; Hoensch, Geschichte, 30–38.

45 See *ibid.*, 801–803; Rainer Hudemann, Kriegsopferpolitik nach den beiden Weltkriegen [War Victims' Policy after the Two World Wars], in: Hans Pohl (Ed.), Staatliche, städtische, betriebliche und kirchliche Sozialpolitik vom Mittelalter bis zur Gegenwart. [Public, Municipal, Corporate and Ecclesiastical Social Policy from the Middle-Ages to the Present] Stuttgart 1991, 269–294.

46 See Stegmann, Kriegsdeutungen, 106.

47 See for example: Einzahlung und Abrechnung der Mitgliedsbeiträge [Payment and Accounting of Membership Fees], in: *Burgenländische Kriegsopferzeitung 1*, Wien 1927, 13f.

48 See for example: Die Zählung der Kriegsopfer [The Census of War Victims], in: *Burgenländische Kriegsopferzeitung 2*, Wien 1929, 16–18.

Although most Czechoslovakian and Austrian war victims' organizations were founded only right after the war, efforts to do so date back to the second half of the First World War. These were, however, faced with an often (seemingly purposefully) uncooperative bureaucracy, which ultimately hindered the formation of any organized development. This is the way Bernhard Leppin, founder and president of the 'Bund der Kriegsverletzten, Witwen und Waisen in der Tschechoslowakischen Republik' ['Association of War-Disabled Veterans, Widows, and Orphans in the Czechoslovak Republic'], portrayed the initial phase of his organization.[49] It is important to note, however, that even in this respect there were regional differences within the Habsburg Monarchy. The precursor of the 'Družina Československých Válečných Poškozenců' ['Retinue of Czechoslovak War-Disabled Veterans'], for example, the 'Družina Českých Invalidů ze Zemi Koruny Svatováclavské' ['Retinue of Czech Invalids of the Lands of the Crown of Saint Wenceslas'], was founded in 1917.[50] Thus, this project also aims at highlighting the connections between the different war victims' organizations by analyzing relations between the precursors or initial efforts for organizing war victims within the Habsburg Monarchy as well as contacts between individual organizations after its dissolution, for example via the CIAMAC (Conférence Internationale des Associations de Victimes de la Guerre [Mutilés, Veuves, Orphelins et Ascendants] et Anciens Combattants [International Committee of Organizations of War Victims (War-Disabled Veterans, Widows, Orphans and Parents) and of Veterans]).[51]

The Czechoslovakian and Austrian organizations served similar purposes as lobbying organizations, also offering legal advice and counsel to their respective members, organizing charity events and self-help activities. Furthermore, all of the four organizations presented below claimed to be politically and confessionally neutral (despite their more or less open political and religious affiliations) and expressed their pacifism.[52] All four war victims' organizations had their respective periodical: In Austria, the Central Organization published *Der Invalide* [The Invalid] and the Association of the Realm started publishing 'Österreichs Kriegsop-

49 See Bernhard Leppin, Etwas zur Geschichte über die Kriegsbeschädigtenbewegung im ehemaligen Österreich-Ungarn [On the History of the War-disabled Veterans' Movement in former Austria-Hungary], in: *Der Invalide 11*, Wien 1929, 18.

50 See Stegmann, Kriegsdeutungen, 100.

51 See Christian Weiß, 'Soldaten des Friedens'. Die pazifistischen Veteranen und Kriegsopfer des 'Reichsbundes' und ihre Kontakte zu den französischen anciens combattants 1919–1933 ['Soldiers of Peace'– The Pacifist Veterans and War Victims of the 'Association of the Realm' and their Contacts to the French anciens combattants 1919–1933], in: Wolfgang Hardtwig (Ed.), Politische Kulturgeschichte der Zwischenkriegszeit 1918–1939 [Political Cultural History of the Interwar Period 1918–1939], Geschichte und Gesellschaft Sonderheft 21, Göttingen 2005, 183–204.

52 See Stegmann, Kriegsdeutungen, 100, 105; Eine Versammlung der Schwerinvaliden im alten Rathause [A Gathering of the Severely Disabled Invalids in the Old Town Hall], in: *Österreichs Kriegsopfer 3*, Wien 1925, 4–5; Generalversammlung der Ortsgruppe und Bezirksstelle Gmunden [General Assembly of Gmunden's Local Group and District Office], in: *Der Invalide 11*, Wien 1919, 6.

fer' ['Austria's War Victims'] in 1925. The Družina's periodical was called *Nový Život* [New Life] and the Bund published *Der Kriegsverletzte* [The War-Disabled].[53]

4.1 Austrian War Victims' Associations

Founded on 11 November 1918 as an organization for Austrian war-disabled veterans 'Zentralverband der deutschösterreichischen Kriegsbeschädigten' ['Central Organization of German-Austrian War-Disabled Veterans'], the 'Central Organization' also accepted surviving dependents during the course of 1919. It soon established itself as the largest and most important Austrian war victims' organization, although there were competing war victims' organizations as well up until 1934.[54] It was affiliated with the Social Democratic Party and played a mediatory and pacifying role between government and war victims in the early years of the First Austrian Republic, which made it a useful partner for a government fearing a communist politicization of war victims.[55] In return, the government supported the Central Organization's organizational development.[56] Functionaries of the Central Organization were positioned in the bureaucratic institutions concerned with welfare provisions for war victims and were consulted during the development of the 'Invalidenentschädigungsgesetz' ['War Victims' Compensation Act']. This 'phase of professionalization'[57] established the Central Organization as an important lobbying organization.[58]

From the 1920s onwards, as the Social Democratic Party went into opposition and especially with the implementation of Ignaz Seipel's politics for financial recovery[59], more and more conflicts arose, with the government on the one hand, and on the other with the ascending 'Reichsverband der christlichen Kriegsbeschädigten Österreichs' ['Organization of the Realm of Austria's Christian War-

53 The full title of *Der Invalide* changed several times: 1918: *Der Invalide. Offizielles Organ des Zentralverbandes der deutsch-österreichischen Kriegsbeschädigten* [The Invalid. Official Gazette of the Central Organization of German-Austrian War-Disabled Veterans]; 1919: *Der Invalide. Offizielles Organ des Zentralverbandes der deutsch-österreichischen Kriegsbeschädigten, Kriegsbeschädigtenvereinigung der Invaliden, Witwen und Waisen* [The Invalid. Official Gazette of the Central Organization of German-Austrian War-Disabled Veterans, Organization of War-Disabled Veterans, Widows and Orphans]; 1922: *Der Invalide. Offizielles Organ des Landesverbandes Wien der Kriegsinvaliden und Kriegerhinterbliebenen Österreichs* [The Invalid. Official Gazette of the Regional Association of War-Disabled Veterans and Surviving Dependants in Vienna], Wien 1918–1934; *Österreichs Kriegsopfer*, Wien 1925–1936. For Czechoslovakia see: Stegmann, Kriegsdeutungen, 33.

54 See Pawlowsky – Wendelin, Care, 181f.

55 See Ke-chin Hsia, A Partnership of the Weak. War Victims and the State in the Early First Austrian Republic, in: Günter Bischof – Fritz Plasser – Peter Berger (Eds.), From Empire to Republic. Post-World War I Austria, Contemporary Austrian Studies 19, New Orleans/Innsbruck 2010, 192–221, here 193–199.

56 See *ibid.*

57 Pawlowsky, Opfer, 805.

58 See *ibid.*

59 See Vocelka, Geschichte, 278.

Disabled Veterans'].[60] This organization became the main opponent of the 'Central Organization of German-Austrian War-Disabled Veterans', especially after its re-organization and re-naming in 1924 as the 'Reichsbund der Kriegsopfer Österreichs' ['Association of the Realm of Austria's War Victims'].[61] Indeed, the 'Association of the Realm' had much closer ties to the Christian-Social Party than the Central Organization did to the Social-Democratic Party, since several of its members, among them the organization's president, Karl Drexel, were Christian-Social Members of Parliament.[62]

After the establishment of the Austrofascist *Ständestaat*[63] the Central Organization's leadership was first replaced in 1934, and in 1936 both organizations were integrated into the 'Einheitsverband der Kriegsopfer Österreichs' [Unified Organization of Austrian War Victims'].[64]

4.2 Czechoslovak War-Victims' Associations

The most important Czechoslovak war victims' organization, the 'Družina československých válečných poškozenců' ['Society of Czechoslovak War-Disabled Veterans'], emerged in 1919 out of a reform of its precursor, which was founded in 1917. Membership was open to all war-disabled Czechoslovakian citizens and surviving dependents. Official languages were Czech and Slovak, after 1931 also German and Hungarian. Ondřej Kypr, the Družina's president, was also a member of the National Assembly and director of the State Office for War-Victims' Policy.[65]

The other organization in the Czechoslovak Republic shaping the public discourse on war victims was the 'Bund der Kriegsverletzten, Witwen und Waisen in der tschechoslowakischen Republik' ['Association of War-Disabled Veterans, Widows and Orphans in the Czechoslovak Republic'], founded in 1918. Its president was Bernhard Leppin, its main office located in Liberec. The Bund's official language was German; it claimed to represent all German war victims in the Czechoslovak Republic. Via the CIAMAC, the Bund was connected with the Austrian Central Organization. Although the organizations' statutes did not contain any segregating regulations along ethnic lines, during the 1920s and especially during the 1930s conflicts between the two organizations and complaints of the Bund directed against the state increasingly featured ethnic-nationalist undertones.[66]

---

60 See Pawlowsky – Wendelin, Verwaltung, 529.

61 See *ibid.*

62 See Biography of Karl Drexel delivered by the Austrian Parliament: http://www.parlament.gv.at/WWER/PAD_00239/index.shtml, 20 January 2014.

63 See Vocelka, Geschichte, 286–296; Emmerich Tálos – Wolfgang Neugebauer (Eds.), Austrofaschismus. Politik – Ökonomie – Kultur [Austrofascism. Politics – Economy – Culture], Wien 2012.

64 See Pawlowsky, Opfer, 806.

65 See Stegmann, Kriegsdeutungen, 101.

66 See *ibid.*, 104–112.

5. Stepping Stones for a Comparison

This chapter provides an outline of the four social spaces that form the analytical focus of the research project. They were chosen because they seem to be focal points for the ways in which war victims positioned themselves in and were positioned by Czechoslovakian and Austrian interwar society. The brief description of the scope and aims of the analysis of each of these social spaces will be supplemented by illustrative examples and preliminary hypotheses.

5.1 Memories of the War

This section aims at analyzing how war victims' organizations played an important role in integrating individual experiences of veterans into social (and group specific) interpretations of the war. Furthermore, memorial culture is of importance, but the focus is not exclusively on its material aspects. Rather, this project focuses on how, for example, statues and monuments were used and acknowledged or debated and criticized by the war victims' organizations.[67]

Keeping the memory of the war alive was a crucial goal of war victims' organizations, because their claim to pensions was fundamentally based on the war.[68] In Austrian war victims' periodicals, war-disabled veterans were portrayed in two conflicting but intertwined roles: On the one hand, they were depicted as 'heroes' who had endured the war's hardships in defending their home, families and country, had sacrificed their health and who were now expecting the 'Dank des Vaterlandes'[69] ['thanks of the fatherland'] promised during the war. This very sacrifice, however, also turned them into victims of the war.[70] Consequently, on the level of the individual soldier, both Austrian organizations conveyed a heroic image of the war.[71]

But differences between the Central Organization and the Association of the Realm become apparent on the level of their positions on international reconciliation, which featured prominently in the Central Organization's articles.[72] The Central Organization's goal therefore was to create an interpretation of the war that was both pacifist and did not devalue the individual's war experiences.[73] In

---

67 Ziemann, Kriegserinnerung, 384.

68 See Kienitz, Politisierung, 201–204.

69 Maximilian Brandeisz, Einer besseren Zukunft entgegen [Towards a Better Future], in: *Der Invalide 9*, Wien 1927, 1. See also: Kienitz, Helden, 74–77.

70 The ambiguity of sacrifice is explored in detail by Sabine Kienitz. See Kienitz, Helden, 94–96.

71 See Thomas Rohringer, Opferhelden. Analyse österreichischer Kriegsopfer-Zeitschriften 1918–1929 aus geschlechtergeschichtlicher Perspektive [Victim-heroes. Analysis of Austrian War Victims' Gazettes 1918–1929 from a Gender History Perspective], unpublished master thesis University of Vienna 2013, 80–103.

72 See for example: Die Kriegsinvaliden wenden sich an die Soldaten der ehemaligen feindlichen Mächte [The War-Disabled Veterans Address the Soldiers of the Former Hostile Powers], in: *Der Invalide 14*, Wien 1919, 3.

73 See also: Ziemann, Kriegserinnerung, 376f.

the late 1920s the Central Organization also linked the war victims' sacrifice to the foundation of the Austrian Republic.[74]

In Czechoslovakia, the First World War was a constitutive element of the First Republic's founding myth. Difficulties arose from the fact that most Czech and Slovak soldiers had fought in the former Austro-Hungarian army and only a smaller portion in the so-called 'legion'[75], a military formation founded in the Russian Empire and accepted as the military branch of Masaryk's independence movement. These legionnaires played an important role in the national narrative, in particular their deployment in the battle of Zborov in 1917. After 1918 they benefited from certain laws granting them a privileged position, for example on the job market.[76] Consequently, Ondřej Kypr sought to integrate the war victims into this national narrative by emphasizing their detached and even destructive role within the Habsburg army while fighting for it.[77] This trope also played an important role in Czechoslovak veterans' organizations' narratives.[78] Ironically, although in a totally different interpretational framework, Czech soldiers were thereby assigned the very same role the non-German peoples supposedly played in the Austrian 'stab-in-the-back myth'[79], namely, that they caused the defeat by undermining the Austro-Hungarian army.

The hypothesis is that in the newly formed successor states the narrative link between the war and the nation-state's foundation was crucial, but fragile and contested. Different interpretations of the war emerged, revolving around different values. These values were in turn attached to and supported by a network of emotional bonds and moral judgments. For example, the Central Organization's pacifism was embedded in a narrative detesting the Habsburg monarchy and welcoming the republic.[80] It relied upon the horrors faced and the fears overcome during the war[81] – never to occur again – and the hope for a better future.[82] The former were the objects of commemorative practices, the latter was performed in acts of solidarity (also informed by the notion of comradeship) and self-help. Both

74 See Zehn Jahre Invalidenentschädigungskommission [10th Anniversary of the Commission for Invalids' Compensation], in: *Der Invalide 5*, Wien 1929, 1f, here 1.

75 See Zückert, Memory, 111; Richard Lein, Pflichterfüllung oder Hochverrat? Die tschechischen Soldaten Österreich-Ungarns im Ersten Weltkrieg [Performance of Duties or High Treason? Austria-Hungary's Czech Soldiers in the First World War], Europa Orientalis 9, Wien/Berlin/Münster 2011, 11–14, 39–51.

76 See Stegmann, Kriegsdeutungen, 77–80; Lein, Pflichterfüllung, 203–344, 379–421.

77 See *ibid.*, 102f.

78 See Zückert, Memory, 117.

79 See Oswald Überegger, Erinnerungskriege. Der Erste Weltkrieg, Österreich und die Tiroler Kriegserinnerung in der Zwischenkriegszeit [Wars of Memory. The First World War, Austria and the Tyrolean War Memory in the Interwar Period], Tirol im Ersten Weltkrieg 9, Innsbruck 2011, 32–34; Ivan Šedivý, Češi, českе země a velká válka [The Czechs, the Bohemian Lands and the Great War], Praha 2001.

80 See Rohringer, Opferhelden, 90.

81 See for example: Karl Grundei, Ein Jahr! [One Year!], in: *Der Invalide 22*, Wien 1919, 1f.

82 Brandeisz, Zukunft, 1.

aspects intersect with notions of masculinity and class and therefore resonate in the other social spaces as well.[83]

The Družina subscribed to the hegemonic narrative of national liberation and tried to integrate the war victims into it in order to dissolve the hierarchy between the privileged former legionnaires on the one hand and the former soldiers of the Austro-Hungarian army on the other. To this end, 'loyalty' was re-interpreted, its object of duty, obedience and honor being transferred from the Habsburg emperor to the Czechoslovak nation. This was achieved by discouraging practices invoking the former object of loyalty and replacing them with other commemorative rituals.[84]

5.2 Interaction with Bureaucratic Institutions

The hopes and also the fears the war victims associated with encountering the bureaucratic apparatus and the ways in which they subsequently interpreted their relation to the newly formed states make up the subject of this subsection of the Ph.D. project. The comparison of Czechoslovakian and Austrian war victims' organizations reveals similarities as well as differences. The hypothesis is that in Austria attitudes towards the state and its institutions more strongly alternated along political lines and changed over time, reflecting shifts in the government, whereas Czechoslovakian war victims' organizations more often referred to ethnic tensions in their interpretation of the relations between the state, its administration, and the war victims. This should neither imply, however, that Austrian war victims' organizations did not draw ethnic boundaries, nor that their Czechoslovakian counterparts did not invoke political differences. Rather, it serves to grasp the hegemonic interpretational frameworks in interpreting and representing the respective organization's relation to the state.

The following scene can be considered emblematic of how encounters with the bureaucracy were presented in Austria, especially in the Central Organization's periodical:

> 'Primarius Groag beschimpfte den Kriegsbeschädigten, indem er ihm vorwarf, daß er sich von seiner Frau erhalten lasse, und als der Kriegsbeschädigte sich mit Recht gegen diesen Vorwurf wehrte […].'[85]

Articles of the Central Organization usually described the commissions assessing the war-disabled veterans' eligibility as sites of humiliation and rigidity, with the medical expert as the main perpetrator. In other instances, this was additionally

83 See Rohringer, Opferhelden, 118–121.

84 See Zückert, Memory, 115–117.

85 Frechheiten des Primarius Groag [Insolences of Chief Physician Groag], in: *Der Invalide 6*, Wien 1929, 10. ['Chief physician Groag insulted the war-disabled veteran by accusing him of letting his wife provide for him, and when the war-disabled veteran righteously defended himself against this accusation […].'].

linked to medical science's problematic role in sustaining the war machine.[86] This argument is often supported by pointing out personal continuities and/or continuities in the medical experts' attitude towards 'common soldiers'.[87] Commemorative practices were therefore not essentially linked to the social space of memorial sites. Rather, the Central Organization's interpretation of the war and central aspects of its 'semantic field' permeated the presentation of other topics.

This incident also shows the multiple intersecting layers of the bureaucratic situation. In the article, Groag's actions are explained through his affiliation to the Association of the Realm and hence his ill intent towards any member of the Central Organization. Another explanation for such rigidity in assessing war victims' entitlement to pensions is also delivered and denounced by the Central Organization: that it was a way to accomplish spending cuts.[88] Neither of these explanations questions the offensive nature of being provided for by one's wife though, highlighting the gendered role model at the heart of the occupational (re-)integration efforts. Even if Groag's accusation is interpreted as being directed towards the veteran's unwillingness – rather than his inability – to act as breadwinner, the normative force of the argument still extends to (and questions) the morality and masculinity of those war-disabled veterans who fail to fulfill this role within their families.

At first glance, the Bund's interpretations of encounters with the Czechoslovakian bureaucracy show some striking similarities to those of the Central Organization, mainly in the use of the monarchy as a negative point of reference. It is used to denounce the supposedly anti-German chauvinism of the Czechoslovakian bureaucracy[89], which seems to be a recurring topic in the Bund's periodical.[90]

5.3 The Working Place

The third social space is related to the second, insofar as it is focused on the occupational (re-)integration of war disabled veterans in Austria and Czechoslovakia. Since legal measures introduced during the war shared this emphasis on occupational (re-)integration, the question arises as to whether – and if so, how – the succeeding Austrian and Czechoslovak welfare policies were shaped by these legal forerunners and which differences can be identified. It also leads to the question: what consequences did the depiction of the 'working citizen' as a role model have

86 See Brigitte Biwald, Vom Helden zum Krüppel. Das österreichisch-ungarische Militärsanitätswesen und dessen Auswirkungen auf die Gesellschaft im Ersten Weltkrieg [From Hero to Cripple. The Austro-Hungarian Military Medicine Service and its Social Consequences during the First World War], 1, 2 vols., Wien 2000, 169f.

87 See for example: K. Sch., Die Superarbitrierungskommissionen und wir Invaliden [The Commission for Assessing Soldiers' Able-Bodiedness and We Invalids], in: *Der Invalide 3*, Wien 1919, 5f., here 5.

88 Interessante Entscheidungen des Verwaltungsgerichtshofes [Interesting Decisions of the Supreme Administrative Court], in: *Der Invalide 10*, Wien 1929, 5f., here 5.

89 See for example: Auf dem Wege nach Aufwärts [On the Way Up], in: *Der Kriegsverletzte* 2, Reichenberg 1921, 1.

90 See Stegmann, Kriegsdeutungen, 106f.

for the social re-integration of the war-disabled veterans? There were highly varying answers to the question as to what the ideal working place for war disabled veterans might look like. Accordingly, there is the question as to what extent these answers corresponded with the experiences of individual war-disabled veterans in the workplace. For the Czechoslovak context, the topic of the legionnaires' privileged position also needs to be addressed.

The crucial role emotions played in the construction of the 'right' environment is revealed by the different answers to the question of what the ideal working place for war-disabled veterans would look like. It seems that there are two discernible positions: The first one, promoted for example by Dr. Emmerich Ferenczi[91], is that war-disabled veterans should not be separated from able-bodied workers, on the one hand because the constant presence of other war-disabled veterans would make them aware of their disability every day. On the other hand, the presence of able-bodied workers would support the war-disabled's (re-)integration, because they would have to adapt to the 'Bestrebungen, Freuden und Leiden der Gesunden'[92]. Furthermore, competition with the able-bodied workers would instill in them an inherent desire to work hard and to try to overcome their disability, rather than relying on welfare.[93]

The contrary position is represented by an article on a Berlin factory staffed by war-disabled veterans only. This time it is considered an asset. It is the reason why for the war-disabled manager 'Liebe und Verständnis für die ihm Unterstellten wohl ein Akt der Selbstverständlichkeit ist'[94] ['it goes without saying that he feels love and sympathy for his employees']. By contrast, working solely among able-bodied workers would instill a feeling of inferiority, resulting in 'seelische[m] Zusammenbruch und völlige[r] Arbeitsunfähigkeit'[95] ['mental breakdown and total inability to work']. However, inactivity and reliance on welfare are again considered to undermine self-esteem, whereas occupation raises it.[96]

5.4 The Family

The family is a milieu crucial to the veterans. For many war-disabled veterans, the idea of returning home was linked to fears and anxieties of being rejected by one's wife, mother or girlfriend, as Joanna Bourke pointed out for the British context.[97]

---

91 See Emmerich Ferenczi, Invalidenkolonien und Anstellungszwang [Settlements for Invalids and Compulsory Employment], in: *Der Invalide 2*, Wien 1919, 5f., here 5.

92 *Ibid.*, 5. ['aspirations, joys and maladies of the able-bodied workers'].

93 See *ibid.*

94 Wie Berlin für die Kriegsbeschädigten sorgt. Städtische Werkstätten für die Kriegsverletzten. Berlin als Zigarrenfabrikantin [How Berlin Cares for its War-Disabled Veterans. Municipial Workshops for the War-Disabled. Berlin as Cigar Manufacturer], in: *Österreichs Kriegsopfer 1*, Wien 1927, 4f., here 4.

95 *Ibid.*

96 See *ibid.*

97 See Joanna Bourke, Dismembering the Male. Men's Bodies, Britain and the Great War, London 1996, 73–75.

This anxiety has also been picked out as a theme in fictional texts.[98] It was considered to be the natural obligation of the wives and mothers to care for 'their' war-disabled veteran. However, the article addressing this topic also reveals frictions in this moral regime. The question as to which occupational roles were considered desirable for men and women in the household needs to be analyzed as well as how the gendering of care and nursing established emotional regimes in the family.

The example of chief physician Groag mentioned above has already shown that the conduct of war victims could be and was monitored by the police in order to assess their claims and entitlements to pensions.[99]

An example of the emotional and moral regime established in families of war-disabled veterans in respect to caring and nursing is provided by an article in *Der Invalide*, supposedly written by a war-disabled veteran's wife.[100] Her argument revolves around a notion of love imbued by patience and self-abandonment, epitomized in the term 'stille Heldin'[101] ['silent heroine']. At the same time, the article reveals the hard work necessary to sustain this ideal by describing these wives' fates with words such as 'Ausharren' ['endure'] and 'Märtyrium' ['martyrdom'].[102].

The objective of a more extensive investigation of this social space is to further relate the anxieties of rejection along with the normative role-model of the conduct of wives to the narratives and practices of the other social spaces. This allows for an analytical engagement with inherent tensions, when, for example, the relation between male hero/war victim and female 'silent heroine'/war victim begins to blur because of the war widows' liminal position in this gendered hierarchy.

Preliminary Concluding Remarks

As these examples show, a wide variety of emotions played quite different roles in the four social spaces analyzed. The examples presented here also point out fractures and contradictory aspects within these emotion-laden narratives. For example, as the horrors faced during the First World War demonstrate, emotional experience could simultaneously constitute the (narrative) basis both for international reconciliation and for a martial, heroic masculinity with its very specific notion of solidarity and belonging (namely comradeship).[103] It should not be ne-

98 See for example: Andreas Latzko, Menschen im Krieg, Zürich 1918, cited in: Monika Szczepaniak, Militärische Männlichkeiten in Deutschland und Österreich im Umfeld des großen Krieges. Konstruktionen und Dekonstruktionen [Military Masculinities in Germany and Austria in Relation to the Great War. Constructions and Deconstructions], Würzburg 2011.

99 See for example: Warum die Polizei? [Why the Police?], in: *Der Invalide 4*, Wien 1927, 4.

100 See F. Sch., Allen lieben Kameradinnen! [To All Beloved Female Comrades], in: *Der Invalide 8*, Wien 1927, 6, s.v. Ein Frauenherz [A Woman's Heart].

101 *Ibid.*

102 *Ibid.*

103 See Thomas Kühne, '... aus diesem Krieg werden nicht nur harte Männer heimkehren.' Kriegskameradschaft und Männlichkeit im 20. Jahrhundert ['... not only hard men will return from this war'. Military Comradeship and Masculinity in the 20th Century], in: *idem*. (Ed.), Män-

glected, however, that these (re-)interpretations of experiences always took place in a specific context and had a transformative quality. Both the war victims' organizations' promotion of (soldierly) comradeship and their invocation of a heroic narrative drew on military experience. However, both the promotion of comradeship and the invocation of a heroic narrative were always [strategically?] oriented towards positioning war victims vis-à-vis the state, either positively as negotiating partners or more negatively as parties opposed to one another in a struggle for war victims' rights, and helped guarantee the organizations' coherence. Furthermore, some aspects specific to the heroic narrative, specifically the demand to master one's body and emotions, re-emerged in the discourse on war-disabled veterans' occupational (re-)integration.

This close interconnection between past and present can also be observed in the interpretation of war victims' interactions with state bureaucracy. 'Stories' revolving around experiences of shame (as with chief physician Groag) and embarrassment (*e.g.*, because of police inspections of war victims' living conditions) often referred back to the monarchy's bureaucratic apparatus, while at the same time reinforcing the positioning of war victims and state as opposing parties. This itself demonstrates that these situations were interpreted in order to emphasize certain emotions. In doing so, they provided an emotional motivation for collective action, namely righteous anger.

This article could only offer a glimpse at emotions' various forms and functions from the perspective of the war victims' organizations themselves. In order to analyze how (or if) their interpretations and actions were adopted and adapted by individual war victims, an extensive study of archival material is necessary. Thus, the hypotheses presented here can only be seen as first steps towards more conclusive analytical results, which will be developed in the author's doctoral dissertation. These conclusions will provide insights into the dynamics of the construction of masculinity, group formations and emotional styles in the processes of (nation-)state formation in Austria and Czechoslovakia.

nergeschichte – Geschlechtergeschichte. Männlichkeiten im Wandel der Moderne [History of Masculinity – Gender History. Masculinities through the Changes of Modernity], Geschichte und Geschlechter 14, Frankfurt am Main/New York 1996, 174–192.

Patrick Jajko

Street Names and Place Names in Budapest and Vienna Between 1918 and 1933: An Interim Balance in Consideration of Unchanged Toponyms of the Inter-War-Period

Andrássy University Budapest

This paper is going to discuss the street name changes[1] in Budapest and Vienna[2] between 1918 and 1932–1933 as a general topic. This topic is an outtake of the ongoing Ph.D. research that is why this paper will only give a brief overview of the state of the work and is therewith a more extensive version of a presentation given at the Austrian Centers Meeting in Leiden in October 2013. First the paper will discuss the theoretical framework and methodology of the research, then it is followed by a historical introduction of Budapest and Vienna, finally some tendencies for the street name development in the cities are going to be presented. In this last part of the paper the focus is on particular thematic patterns along groups of examples. At last, the conclusion of the paper provides a comparison of the patterns.

Theoretical Framework

Regarding the approach above, the need of a definition of street names is fundamental. Therefore the aim of this part of the paper is to define the street names, which are a special kind of toponyms. Street names are a concrete form of media of power on the one hand and they do have another, not less meaningful role, as one of the forms of mass media for the long-term cultural memory as well as for the communicative memory of everyday life.

---

1 When it comes to the usage of toponyms, one has the possibility to use endonyms or exonyms. For this paper the author is going to use for all names of metropolises, states and federal parts of a country the exonym, if a distinguished English one is existing and provides a footnote with the corresponding endonym with the first appearance of the exonym. All street-names will appear as endonyms and a translation of the endonym's generic part will be provided in square brackets within the text. Cf. Peter Jordan, Criteria for the Use of Exonyms – A Next Approach, United Nations Group of Experts on Geographical Names, Working Paper 64, Vienna 20191, http://unstats.un.org/unsd/geoinfo/ungegn/docs/26th-gegn-docs/WP/WP64_Criteria.pdf, 3 May 2014.

2 German endonym: Wien.

Street names are mostly introduced or changed by official institutions such as the city council or the major of a city, seeing as they have the legal position for such action. Change of a street name is a major act, because the new name has to be used both in the official as well as in every-day communication. However, unofficial names such as former names of the streets are still being used in private communication. They might be used by the older generations or as a form of protest against the official names or the political power and for the commemoration of something special. During upheavals or revolutions, those names could become the new official ones or depending on the new politics, the new street names could be dominated by the new ideology and do not particularly have to have a connection to the unofficial names.[3] For those situations, it is important to say that, '[…] the act of naming is often a demonstration of authority that entails the notion of appropriation. Naming is not a mere linguistic gesture but often evinces specific power relations. Naming places is an aspect of exploration as well as of (re) settlement activities.'[4] This general thought is independent from the political system, the politicians in charge and the specific meaning of a name. All in all one can say, 'toponymy signifies the ideology which underlies and legitimates its use as a proper nomenclature'.[5]

This way, street names are an official mass media channel for the current dominating ideology. Based on this assumption, street names obey according to the sense of the mass media system, which is multi-layered and has a complementary logic.[6] That means, street names, as one kind of mass media, can be as legitimating as the other official media. Other examples for such media offers are schoolbooks, or monuments and their information signs. Beside this group of specific offers of media, there are other mass media layers, such as institutions like the city or state-administration or public organizations, which regulate and create mass media offers.[7]

---

3 Cf. Reuben Rose-Redwood – Derek Aldermann – Maoz Azaryahu, Collective Memory and the Politics of Urban Space. An Introduction, in: GeoJournal 73, Dordrecht 2008, 161–164, here 162; Maoz Azaryahu, Rabin's Road. The Politics of Toponymic Commemoration of Yitzhak Rabin in Israel, in: Political Geography 31, Amsterdam 2012, 73–82.

4 Maoz Azaryahu – Arnon Golan, (Re)naming the Landscape. The Formation of the Hebrew Map of Israel 1949–1960, in: Journal of Historical Geography 27, Amsterdam 2001, 178–195, here 181.

5 Azaryahu – Golan, (Re)naming, 181.

6 Cf. Siegfried J. Schmidt, Medien. Die Koppelung von Kommunikation und Kognition [Media. The Connection of Communication and Cognition], in: Sybille Krämer (Ed.), Medien – Computer – Realität. Wirklichkeitsvorstellungen und Neue Medien [Media – Computer – Reality. Ideas of Reality and New Media], Frankfurt am Main 1998, 55–72, here 57; Harold A. Innis, Die Eule der Minvera [Minerva's Owl], in: Karlheinz Barck (Ed.), Kreuzwege der Kommunikation. Ausgewählte Texte [The Bias of Communication. Selected Texts], Wien/New York 1997, 69–94, here 69.

7 Cf. Astrid Erll, Medium des kollektiven Gedächtnisses. Ein (erinnerungs-)kulturwissenschaftlicher Kompaktbegriff [Medium of the Collective Memory. A (Memory-)Culuturological Definition], in: Astrid Erll – Astrid Nünning (Eds.), Medien des kollektiven Gedächtnisses. Konstruktivität – Historizität – Kulturspezifizität, Berlin 2004, 3–24, here 4. Erll confers to

Eric Hobsbawn wrote in his 'Invention of Tradition' that 'state education, transformed people into citizens of a specific country'[8]. The education itself depends on the nature thereof, and street names are one possibility, how the state hands parts of history down. Especially in less open societies, schoolbooks, newspapers, or the communication style of the government are the reasons, why people actually know the names of the streets and their meaning according to the system's official version of the history.[9] In more open societies one can witness less knowledge of the meaning behind street names.[10] Keeping this in mind, 'in the nineteenth and twentieth centuries, the systematic construction of "national" toponymies was an aspect of nation-building and state-formation'[11]. The street names are appearing in everyday life as they are written on the street signs, city maps, or in public transport systems, they are very important for the memory of a society. Azarahyu writes that 'renamings of streets became a well-known feature of political upheavals and ruptures in hegemonic ideologies. [...] street-names [...] are a source in which to read the "historical memory" of a given society'[12] and until today street names embody a special form of memory. This shows how the memory of a society in general could work – as a compression of past based on social developments of the present.[13]

Those names, which become official in maps and on street signs, are a special part of the cultural memory of a society. This means, that this kind of memory is based on the knowledge of a group, which helps to say who the 'we' is. It is the (re) constructed past and it shows up in long-living forms such as maps or signs. This memory is institutionally organized, it is authoritative, and helps to communicate inside the group. This memory reflects itself for the continuous reconstruction of itself and the referring group[14], and in that context street names are 'marking

---

Siegfried J. Schmidt, Kalte Faszination. Medien, Kultur, Wissenschaft in der Mediengesellschaft [Cold Fascination. Media, Culture, Science in the Media Society], Velbrück 2000, 93f.

8 Eric Hobsbawn, Mass-Producing Traditions. Europe 1870–1914, in: Eric Hobsbawn – T. Ranger (Eds.), The Invention of Tradition, Cambridge 1983, 263–308, here 264, 282.

9 Cf. Aleida Assmann, Erinnerungsräume. Formen und Wandlungen des kulturellen Gedächtnisses [Spaces of Memory. Forms and Transitions of Cultural Memory], München [4]2004, 29; Niklas Luhmann, Die Politik der Gesellschaft [Politics of the Society], Frankfurt am Main 2000, 172; Erll, Medium, 4.

10 Cf. Owen J. Dwyer – Derek H. Aldermann, Memorial Landscapes. Analytic Questions and Metaphors; in: GeoJournal 73, Dordrecht 2008, 165–178, here 167.

11 Azaryahu – Golan, (Re)naming, 181.

12 Maoz Azaryahu, The Purge of Bismarck and Saladin. The Renaming of Streets in East Berlin and Haifa. A Comparative Study in Culture-Planning, in: Germanistische Linguistik 129–130. Reader zur Namenskunde III/1: Toponymie, Berlin/New York 1996, 801–814, here 802.

13 Assmann, Erinnerungsräume, 29; cf. Luhmann, Politik, 172; Erll, Medium, 4.

14 Cf. Jan Assmann, Kollektives Gedächtnis und kulturelle Identität [Collective Memory and Cultural Identity], in: Jan Assmann – Tonio Hölscher (Eds.), Kultur und Gedächtnis [Culture and Memory], Frankfurt am Main 1988, 9–19, here 13–15.

space and forming a public collective memory [...]'.[15] Additionally, street names are also a part of everyday life. That transforms them even more into an 'arena of political contestation [...]'.[16] One is forced to use the official street names in an official discourse but one might use older or previous names, or unofficial names in private communication, or sometimes even in official situations, too.[17] Finally, one might agree with the conclusion of Azaryahu, where he says that

> '[t]he power of commemorative place naming, for example, comes from the manner in which history is inscribed into our daily vocabulary, both verbal and visual. Appearing on road signs, addresses, advertising billboards, and maps, the past constantly made part of one's spatial and historical frame of reference, contributing to the creation of a larger "city-text".'[18]

The meaning of the street names and the easy way to change them, both make them vulnerable during revolutions or political changes. Street names are easily to change; the change itself is just a question of time and resources. If a local government has enough of both, it might change a lot of street names within the actual laws, ruling name changes, during its legislative period, if not so, the change could be limited to symbolically important places. '[P]ower-filled sites'[19] are the most important way to show the symbolic use. Therefore the main hypothesis of the research is that the authorities changed street names in order to consolidate their world-views through communicating it within the street names.

Based on this theoretical framework, it would now be appropriate to analyze newspapers and schoolbooks as well as general historical context to get a comprehensive view of the whole discourse in the society as well as of the dominating themes in the street names as the key-medium of the analysis. This paper takes the focus only on the street names as one zone of a broader conflict area, while further analyses are going to be part of the Ph.D. research.

Historical Context

Within this theoretical framework, the cases Budapest and Vienna were chosen because of their strong connection in time and space. Since the analysis is focused on the time between 1918 and 1933, the history as well as the relationship

---

15 Emilia Palonen, Politics of Memory; ECPR Working Paper, Edinburgh 2003, http://helsinki.academia.edu/EmiliaPalonen/Papers/384133/The_City-Text_In_Post-Communist_Budapest_Street_Names_Memorials_and_the_Politics_of_Commemoration, 24 January 2012, 1.

16 Palonen, Politics, 1.

17 Cf. Richard Coates, Endonymic Place-Name Alternants and Their Cultural Significances, in: Botolv Helleland – Christian-Emil Ore – Solveig Wikstrøm (Eds.), Names and Identities, Oslo Studies in Language 4/2, Oslo 2012, 61–70.

18 Dwyer – Aldermann, Landscapes, 167.

19 Dwyer – Aldermann, Landscapes, 168.

of the cities during the 19th century is meaningful. The most crucial treaty for the comparison of Budapest and Vienna is the Austro-Hungarian Compromise of 1867. By this law, the Kingdom of Hungary, *i.e.* the Lands of the Holy Hungarian Crown of St. István (St. Stephen)[20], attained a privileged position among all other kingdoms and ethnic groups, such as Bohemians or Croatians. Within this new position and because of the need of an official nominal Hungarian capital Budapest was founded in the process of the association of Buda, Pest and Obuda 1872, and became official royal seat of the Habsburgs besides Vienna in 1892. Neither Prague[21], nor Zagreb had such an important political position alongside Vienna in the last fifty years of the monarchy.[22]

First, a short historical introduction about the political and social development of Budapest before and after World War I should be given. With the Austro-Hungarian Compromise (1867), Budapest experienced important economic growth. Also, the industrialization led to an expansion of the light and heavy industry in the suburbs of Budapest. Nevertheless, until 1914, this sector constituted only one quarter of the national income, the biggest part – two thirds – still being made by agriculture.[23] The urbanization and economic growth differentiate the city society more and more during the 19th century and became stronger after the Compromise.[24] One of the most important movements beside the 'Szabadelvű Párt' ['Liberal Party'] was the working class movement, which was theoretically influenced by Karl Marx, Ferdinand Lassalle, Viktor Adler, and Friedrich Engels. In Hungary, the first workers movement was founded in 1880 as 'Magyarországi Általános Munkáspárt' ['General Hungarian Workers Party'], which became the 'Magyarországi Szociáldemokrata Párt' (MSZDP ['Hungarian Social Democratic Party']) in 1890.[25] Their main aim was to improve the social situation of the new social group by nationalization, because the dominating 'Szabadelvű Párt' was rather concentrated on the interests of the landowners and the entrepreneurs than

20 Hungarian Endonym: Szent István Koronájàk Országai.

21 Czech endonym: Praha, historical German endonym: Prag.

22 Cf. Zoltán Halász, Kurze Geschichte Ungarns [Short History of Hungary], Budapest 1974, 175; Robert Kann, Geschichte des Habsburgerreiches 1526 bis 1918 [History of the Habsburg Empire 1526 until 1918], Wien/Köln/Weimar 1993, 311–314; Janos Hauszmann, Kleine Geschichte Budapests [Short History of Budapest], Regensburg 2012, 108–112.

23 Cf. Halász, Geschichte, 184; Kann, Geschichte, 311–314; Jörg K. Hoensch, Ungarn. Geschichte – Politik – Wirtschaft [Hungary. History – Politics – Economics], Hannover 1991, 68.

24 Cf. Halász, Geschichte, 185; Janos Hauszmann, Bürgerlicher Radikalismus und demokratisches Denken im Ungarn des 20. Jahrhunderts. Der Jászi-Kreis um "Huszadik Század" (1900–1949) [Civil Radicalism and Democratic Thinking in Hungary in the 20th Century. The Jászi-Circle around "Huszadik Század"], European University Studies. History and Allied Studies 352, Bern/New York/Paris 1986, 18–31.

25 Cf. Adalbert Toth, Ungarn [Hungary], in: Frank Wende (Ed.), Lexikon zur Geschichte der Parteien in Europa [Encyclopedia of the History of Parties in Europe], Stuttgart 1981, 731–773, here 757–759; Tibor Süle, Sozialdemokratie in Ungarn. Zur Rolle der Intelligenz in der Arbeiterbewegung 1899–1910 [Social Democracy. About the Role of Intelligentsia in the Workers Movement 1899–1910], Köln/Graz 1967, 24–37.

the working class.[26] Despite the political pressure from low earners and peasants the government of the Hungarian Kingdom managed neither to democratize the country nor the local representation. As a result different political groups claimed an equal election-law.[27]

Another important political cleavage alongside the claims of the MSZDP was the fight between liberal laicism and the churches. The Hungarian government managed to introduce civil marriage and civil registration of births against the resistance of the Hungarian King Franz Joseph, the Pope and the catholic population in the Kingdom of Hungary.[28] Janos Hauszmann described this situation shortly before the World War I with the words 'tödlicher Kampf der Ideologien' ['deadly fight of ideologies'].[29]

This situation does not change until the end of the World War I. During the whole time, the Hungarian society as well as the political stage was estranged between extreme positions. There are a few examples of those polarities: first, the celebration of the 1000th anniversary of the Hungarian Kingdom in 1896 on the one hand and the social problems of everyday life on the other hand. Second, the different political positions towards the negotiations about the compromise with the Empire of Austria, *i.e.* the Kingdoms and Lands represented in the Imperial Council[30], or third, the anti-militaristic position of the MSZDP and other parties in 1916 in contrast to the government. This illustrates the political tensions in the society. Additionally, from 1903 different suggestions to stabilize the political system by reforming the election law based on the demands of different political parties existed.[31]

Even at the end of the World War I, the Hungarian government turned down a reform of the institutions of the state as well as social reforms because of fears of a communist revolution as it happened at the same time in the Russian Empire[32] in January 1917. This decline, in view of social problems and political tensions, led the King to impeach the Hungarian Prime Minister Tisza István[33] in

26 Cf. Halász, Geschichte, 187; Janos Hauszmann, Ungarn. Vom Mittelalter bis zur Gegenwart [Hungary. From the Middle Ages to the Present], Regensburg 2004, 199; Friedrich Gottas, Ungarn im Zeitalter des Hochliberalismus. Studien zur Tisza-Ära, Studien zur Geschichte der Österreichisch-Ungarischen Monarchie [Hungary at the Pique of Liberalism? Studies About the Tisza-Era and the History of the Austro-Hungarian Monarchy] 16, Wien 1976, 32f; Hoensch, Ungarn, 68.

27 Cf. Halász, Geschichte, 197; Gottas, Ungarn, 45–52.

28 Cf. Hauszmann, Ungarn, 198.

29 Hauszmann, Ungarn, 199.

30 German Endonym: Die im Reichsrat vertretenen Königreiche und Länder.

31 Cf. Hauszmann, Ungarn, 200–212; Hauszmann, Radikalismus, 53–64; Hauszmann, Geschichte, 107; Péter Hanák (Ed.), Die Geschichte Ungarns. Von den Anfängen bis zur Gegenwart [The History of Hungary. From the Beginning to the Present Times], Essen/Budapest 1988, 193f.

32 Russian endonym: Rossijskaâ Imperiâ.

33 The Hungarian order of personal names (surname + given name) contrasts with the English or German order of personal names (given name + surname). In this paper the author uses the

1917. The new one, Wekerle Sándor, tried to implement a new election law with the large 'Választójogi Blokk' ['Coalition for Election Law'], consisting of the MSZDP, the 'Függetlenségi és 48-as párt' ['Independence and 48 Party'], and the 'Nemzeti Demokrata Párt' (NDP ['National Democratic Party']). This though, did not manage to include the right to vote for the working class. Until the end of 1918 the population all over the country demonstrated for the end of war because of hunger and poverty in the cities as well as in the rural area. During the upcoming dissolution process of the Habsburg Monarchy the 'Magyar Nemzeti Tanács' ['Hungarian National Council'] was constituted as a provisional government of the state by the same parties as those of the 'Választójogi Blokk'. The provisional government was formed because the former government had already left Hungary. Earl Károlyi Mihály was now the leader of the new government and the central politician beside Jászy Oszkár. He did not become the new Prime Minister, but in 1918 after affiliation of the strong communistic workers', farmers' and soldiers' councils to the national council around Károlyi Mihaly in the 'öszirozsás forradalom', the peaceful 'Aster Revolution', the pressure of this formation made the representative of the Hungarian King Karl IV to introduce Károlyi in the function of the Prime Minister at the end of October 1918. The new government had some very successful steps in the domestic policy, which included the general right to vote for men and women of the age of 21, the freedom of speech, press, the association and assembly, and finally some social reforms as well.[34]

During this process the city of Budapest its mayor since 1906 Barczy István joined the council structure and the political movement. In January 1919 the seventh law disbanded the city council, as it had existed since the foundation of Budapest. As a result a metropolitan people's council from the 7 January 1919 governed Budapest. The council constituted itself of 44 members, of whom 22 were delegates of the bureaucracy and 22 were members of the national council itself. The new people's council began its work on the 25th of February under the rule of Barczy. At the same time, the radicalization of the political landscape became stronger.[35]

Based on the already constituted workers councils, Kun Béla, who emigrated from Russia after the revolution back to Hungary, founded the 'Kommunisták Magyarországi Pártja' (KMP ['Communist Party of Hungary']) together with the leftist social democrats. This new party forced the fight against parliamentary institutions and demanded the introduction of a Republic with a council structure similar to the young Russian Soviet Federative Socialist Republic.[36] When the attacks on the government around the Prime Minister Károlyi intensified from both

name order according to the language of origin.

34 Cf. Hanák, Geschichte, 195–198; Hauszmann, Ungarn, 212–217; Hauszmann, Radikalismus, 183–187; Toth, Ungarn, 762.

35 Cf. Hauszmann, Geschichte, 133f.

36 Russian endonym: Rossijskajâ Sovetskajâ Federativnajâ Socialističeskajâ Respublika.

sides, the rightist conservatives as well as the leftist communists, the government had to resign in January 1919. In the course of this resignation process Károlyi became President and let the politicians form a new government, which was now dominated by the MSZDP. At the same time the government tried to avoid the rise of the KMP by taking dominant communists into custody. The government had to resign again because of the workers' demonstrations, the policy of the French, the British, and the Americans shortly thereafter.[37] In spring 1919 the Social Democrats were the strongest Party in charge. They founded the new 'Magyar Szocialista Munkáspárt' (MSZMP) ['Hungarian Socialistic Workers-party'] together with the communist leaders. On 1 April the 133 days of the Hungarian Socialistic Soviet Republic[38] began with its end on 1 August 1919. During the first days of the Hungarian Socialistic Soviet Republic, the first free elections for the city council of Budapest as well as for every town, city and the whole state were held open for every person regardless of their income or social status. Following the new Revolutionary Workers'- and Soldiers' Council of Budapest constituted itself a few days later and had to deal with problems of provision of the population with resources, food and living accommodations.[39]

Since the beginning of 1919, count Bethlen István formed the 'Antibolsewista Comité' ['Anti-Bolshevist Committee'] in Vienna, while at the same time Horthy Miklós founded a rival government in Szeged together with other officers.[40] When the short period of 133 days was over, the conservative parts of the political elite came in charge and for them Budapest was in some way a 'vaterlose, verjudete und sündige Stadt' ['fatherless, overjewished and sinful city'][41], they had to recapture Budapest from the communists.[42] One internal reason for the success of Horthy and his movement might be the 'Red Terror', which was followed by the 'White Terror', which lasted until 1921. In the same year Horthy became regent of the Kingdom of Hungary.[43] Meanwhile the 'subsequent white terror', which is described by Rothschild strongly as

37 Cf. Hanák, Geschichte, 198f.; Hauszmann, Ungarn, 218; Hoensch, Ungarn, 76.

38 Hungarian endonym: Magyarországi Szocialista Tanácsköztársaság.

39 Cf. Halász, Geschichte, 209; Hauszmann, Geschichte, 131, 135; Hauszmann, Radikalismus, 190.

40 Cf. Hauszmann, Ungarn, 222.

41 Hauszmann, Geschichte, 138.

42 Cf. Robert Gerwarth, Rechte Gewaltgemeinschaften und die Stadt nach dem Ersten Weltkrieg. Berlin, Wien und Budapest im Schatten von Kriegsniederlage und Revolution [Right Wing Violence Communities and the City after the First World War. Berlin, Vienna and Budapest in the Shadow of the Defeat and Revolution], in: Friedrich Lenger (Ed.), Kollektive Gewalt in der Stadt. Europa 1890–1939 [Collective Violence in the City. Europe 1890–1939], Schriften des Historischen Kollegs, Kolloquien 89, München 2013, 103–121, here 105.

43 Cf. Bela Bodo, The White Terror in Hungary, 1919–1921. The Social Worlds of Paramilitary Groups, in: Austrian History Yearbook 42, Minnesota 2011, 133–163; Bela Bodo, Militia Violence and State Power in Hungary, 1919–1922, in: Hungarian Studies Review 33/1–2, Kingston 2006, 121–156; Gerwarth, Gewaltgemeinschaften, 112, 114; Hauszmann, Radikalismus, 194.

> 'a systematic, ferocious hunt, combining "spontaneous" pogromist bestialities with a deliberate assault on those strata and institutions that had recently challenged and might once again seek to challenge the traditional arrangements of Hungarian political life[,] [...] was a reaction against the Károlyi as well as the Kun episodes.'[44]

Especially the 'Red Terror' as a phenomenon of arbitrary persecution was a catalyst for that, what Rothschild called the 'final tragedy of the Kun episode', because

> 'by the manner of its [the socialism] rise and fall, it appeared to discredit by association the Károlyi experiment that had preceded and given birth to it, and hence allowed the counterrevolutionary white regime that followed it equate liberalism with Communism. Social and political democratization could thus be resisted henceforth as allegedly treasonable to the Hungarian way of life.'[45]

The original administration of Budapest was reinstated during the time of the traditional-authoritarian politics[46] and policy of the years between 1921 and 1934. In 1934 the city got a government commissioner, Sipőcz Jenő, who until this time was one of the mayors of the city, too. The Liberals, especially the NDP and its successor organizations together with the MSZDP, were very strong in the city while the government of the country was conservative. This situation lasted until 1934 when the law concerning the administration of Budapest was changed. From this year on, regent Hórthy appointed the mayor of the city. Beyond that there was at least one election-result on the level of city politics, in which the government of the Country had to interfere to have the desired 'government's candidate' get the function of mayor. That might be one of the reasons additionally to the economic policy of the Prime Minister Bethlen István, who was in charge from 1921 until 1931, why workers and low-earners took to the streets very often, as they did also in 1930 with one of the biggest demonstrations, in which more than 100,000 persons participated. All inequalities between the different political groups were almost left aside, as the main political focus lied on the revisionism of the peace treaty and on nationalism.[47]

---

44 Joseph Rothschild, East Central Europe between the Two World Wars, Seattle/London 1974, 153.

45 Rothschild, Europe, 151.

46 Cf. Dieter Segert, Die Grenzen Osteuropas. 1918, 1945, 1989 – Drei Versuche im Westen anzukommen [The Borders of Eastern Europe. 1918, 1945, 1989 – Three Attempts to Arrive in the West], Frankfurt am Main/New York 2002, 39, 59, 154.

47 Cf. Hauszmann, Geschichte, 138f.; Hanák, Geschichte, 212–223; Gabor Vermes, Hungarian Politics and Society on the Eve of Revolution, in: Pater Pastor (Ed.), Revolutions and Interventions in Hungary and its Neighbor States, 1918–1919, War and Society in East Central Europe 20, New York 1988, 107–122, here 108f.

While Budapest just started to become a political center in the 1870s, Vienna already was the political center and one of the economic centers of the whole Habsburg Empire for a long time before it became the capital of Austria in 1918. Vienna was strongly connected to other parts of the state and the industrialization started there much earlier than in Budapest. This led to a more integrated, multinational and socially differentiated population in the city society. Especially for the wealthy parts of society, Vienna became a very important center for political participation. Just as in Budapest, the liberal powers in Vienna dominated city politics until 1895. In this time the famous ring road around the city center was built and the World Fair was held but poverty was broadly spread across the population of the city.[48]

In Vienna a more democratic election law was introduced earlier, because of the pressure of the so-called anti-liberal opposition and the demands of the workers-movement in 1885. The only economic condition for the participation in the elections was paying at least five gulden for taxes. Karl Lueger's 'Christlichsozialer Verein' ['Christian-Social Association'], from 1891 'Christlichsoziale Partei' (CSP ['Christian-Social party']), as well as the antisemitic and the Greater-German movements, which affiliated themselves to the city parliamentary group of the 'Bürgerklub' ['Club of Citizens'] succeeded since 1889 and made it possible, that Lueger was in charge from this year one until 1910, when he died. During his time in charge he mostly used and expressed 'antiisms' as there were the anti-liberalism, anti-capitalism and the lowest common denominator the anti-Semitism.[49] A few years before the election law was reformed the 'Sozialdemokratische Arbeiterpartei in Österreich' (SDAP ['Social-Democratic Workers-Party in Austria']) consolidated itself in 1874 and spread all over the empire. In order to represent the population and influence the politics, they founded the 'Sozialdemokratische

48 Cf. Gerhard Melinz – Susan Zimmermann, Großstadtgeschichte und Modernisierung in der Habsburgmonarchie [History of Metropols and Modernization in the Habsburg Monarchy], in: Gerhard Melinz – Susan Zimmermann (Eds.), Wien – Prag – Budapest. Blütezeit der Habsburgmetropolen. Urbanisierung, Kommunalpolitik, gesellschaftliche Konflikte (1867–1918) [Vienna – Prague – Budapest. Blossoming of the Habsburg Metropols. Urbanization, Local Politics, Conflicts of Society (1867–1918), Wien 1996, 15–33, here 22–25; Maren Seliger – Karl Ucakar, Wien. Politische Geschichte 1740–1934. Entwicklung und Bestimmungskräfte großstädtischer Politik, Teil 2: 1896–1934 [Vienna. Political History 1740–1934. Developments and Deciding Factors of Metropolitan Policy, Part 2: 1896–1934], Wien/München 1985, 714–720; Wolfgang Maderthaner, Von der Zeit um 1860 bis zum Jahr 1945 [From the Time around 1860 to the Year 1945], in: Peter Csendes – Ferdinand Opll (Eds.), Wien. Geschichte einer Großstadt, Band 3: Von 1790 bis zur Gegenwart [Vienna. History of a City, Part 3: From 1790 until Present], Wien/Köln/Weimar 2006, 175–544, here 175–177.

49 Cf. Maren Seliger – Karl Ucakar, Wahlrecht und Wählerverhalten in Wien 1848–1932. Privilegien, Partizipationsdruck und Sozialstruktur [Election Law and Behavior of the Electorate in Vienna? 1848–1932. Privileges, Partizipations Pressure and Social Structure], Kommentare zum Historischen Atlas von Wien 3, Wien 1984, 41f., 89; Margareta Mommsen-Reindl, Österreich [Austria], in: Frank Wende (Ed.), Lexikon zur Geschichte der Parteien in Europa [Encyclopedia on the History of Parties in Europe], Stuttgart 1981, 441–470, here 447f; Maderthaner, Zeit, 193, 218; Seliger – Ucakar, Wien, 918–922, 925–929.

Partei Österreichs' ['Social-Democratic Party of Austria'] in 1888/89 In contrast to the 'Bürgerklub'-parties they were not as successful in elections, because of the election law admitted by the majority especially the 'Bürgerklub' until 1919 written against the SDAP.[50] Within the city government of Lueger, the policy became at least on a symbolic level more social because of a small increase of expenses for welfare services.[51] Building new public schools[52] and reinvesting in public infrastructure, prepared during the liberal era, consisted of investing in water supplies[53] or buying back, *e.g.*, the public transportation[54] are only a few examples of those politics towards the middle class, the main electorate of the 'Bürgerklub'.[55] Despite the broader election law the policy arena before the World War I was very polarized too.[56]

During the war there was a silent truce between the political parties, but the social situation did not improve for broad parts of the population at the end of the war, in contrary it even got worse. There was neither enough food nor enough resources for heating during the winter. These circumstances of a 'dying city'[57] ['sterbende Stadt'] led to strikes in Vienna in January 1918 and held until November until the total dissolution of the empire. From this moment on, Vienna had more than two million inhabitants and the administration of the whole empire to account for, but was only the capital of the Republic of (German-)Austria[58] a small state in Central Europe without any economic connection to the former parts of the monarchy. At the same time the other new states in Central Europe had food or rather resources as coal or wood or metal for the industry at their disposals. From the autumn of 1918, Vienna needed one whole year to reconstitute itself as a city, when it got a social-democratic city government as a result of the first free elections in May 1919.[59]

---

50 Cf. Mommsen-Reindl, Österreich, 461–463; Seliger – Ucakar, Wahlrecht, 119; Maderthaner, Zeit, 230; Reinhard Pohanka, Eine kurze Geschichte der Stadt Wien [A Short History of the City of Vienna], Wien/Köln/Weimar 1998, 181f.

51 Cf. Seliger – Ucakar, Wien, 850f; Peter Csendes, Geschichte Wiens [History of Vienna], Wien 1990, 129.

52 Cf. Seliger – Ucakar, Wien, 830f.

53 Cf. Seliger – Ucakar, Wien, 872f.

54 Cf. Seliger – Ucakar, Wien, 901–907; Maderthaner, Zeit, 223–225.

55 Cf. Pohanka, Geschichte, 186f.

56 Cf. Pohanka, Geschichte, 192.

57 A metaphor, not least used by the current city administration itself: Wien.at: Wien im Ersten Weltkrieg. Wohin der Krieg führt [Vienna in the First World War. Where the War Leads to], https://erster-weltkrieg.wien.gv.at/site/, 9 May 2014.

58 German endonym: 1918/1919: Deutschösterreichische Republik, from 21st October 1919 on Republik Österreich.

59 Cf. Dieter A. Binder – Ernst Bruckmüller, Essay über Österreich. Grundfragen von Identität und Geschichte 1918–2000 [Essay about Austria. Fundamental Questions about Identity and History], München 2005, 65; Pohanka, Geschichte, 196; Maderthaner, Zeit, 329–335, 340f; Csendes, Geschichte, 140.

The federal reforms in 1920 when Vienna became an own federal part of Austria are crucial for the following development[60]: from 1919 on the SDAP[61] won every election in Vienna until 1932. In this time their election output increased from 60.6% in 1919 to 66% in 1932.[62] This big support of the social reform policy through workers and low earners led to similar tensions between the conservative government of the state and the city council as they existed in Hungary at the same time. The SDAP 'war in permanenter Opposition, die nur allzuleicht als Opposition aus Prinzip, als Fundamentalopposition mißverstanden werden konnte' ['was in permanent opposition, which could be too easily misunderstood as opposition as a matter of principle, as fundamental opposition'][63] especially on the level of the federal state. These tensions led to the events of February 1934, when the SDAP became illegal after a decade (1919–1929) of more or less compromised political solutions.[64] This particular step marks the end of the development of pillarization. From this moment on the society of a strong bipolar antagonism and the political culture of conflict became more intense.[65]

Nonetheless the development according to the election law and within the workers-movement led to a situation in which '[d]ie politische Kultur der 1. Republik viele Merkmale auf[wies], die einer "demokratisch-industriellen" Gesellschaft zugeschrieben werden' ['the political culture of the first republic showed many characteristics of a "democratic-industrial" society'][66], and yet the most important groups, which had particular connections to this 'Tradition gesellschaftlichen Gestaltens' ['Tradition of social organizing'][67] were not able to identify themselves with the polity of the republic, instead they made the design of the political system to a question of party policy[68] as it is observable in the patterns of the street naming.

---

60 Cf. Selinz – Ucakar, Wien, 999–1007; Binder – Bruckmüller, Essay, 14; Maderthaner, Zeit, 347–349; Walter Goldinger – Dieter A. Binder, Geschichte der Republik Österreich 1918–1938 [History of the Republic of Austria 1918–1938], Wien/München 1992, 95–100.

61 1918/1919: Sozialdemokratische Partei Deutschösterreich [Social-democratic Party of German-Austria], cf. Mommsen-Reindl, Österreich, 461.

62 Cf. Selinz – Ucakar, Wien, 1139; Maderthaner, Zeit, 391.

63 Rainer Nick – Anton Pelinka, Bürgerkrieg – Sozialpartnerschaft. Das politische System Österreichs. 1. und 2. Republik. Ein Vergleich [Civil War – Social Partnership. The Political System of Austria. 1St and 2nd Republic. A Comparison], Wien/München 1983, 25.

64 Cf. Nick – Pelinka, Bürgerkrieg, 25.

65 Cf. Mommsen-Reindl, Österreich, 443, 464; Selinz – Ucakar, Wien, 1014–1021, Binder – Bruckmüller, Essay, 9; Manfred Oberlechner, Strukturelle Versäulungen in Österreich und den Niederlanden. Gemeinsamkeiten, Unterschiede, Auswirkungen [Structural Pillarisation in Austria and the Netherlands. Similarities, Differences, Consequences], in: Österreichische Zeitschrift für Politikwissenschaft 34/2, Wien 2005, 191–206, here 192, 195; Arend Lijphart, Typologies of Democracy Systems, in: Comparative Political Studies 1/3, Thousand Oaks 1968, 3–44, here 18.

66 Nick – Pelinka, Bürgerkrieg, 110.

67 Nick – Pelinka, Bürgerkrieg, 109.

68 Cf. Nick – Pelinka, Bürgerkrieg, 109f.

Although the nationalism had other directions than in Hungary, the national tendency in Austria was pointing to become again a part of the German Reich.[69] Beside that the question of viability was raised often during the interwar period, it was connected with the discussion about an 'Anschluss' in the early years of the first republic. Reasons behind questioning the viability changed after the raise of National Socialism in the German Reich. The political elite of Austria was afraid of the viability because of the competition with the German Reich for an economic independence and the idea about an 'Anschluss' became more unpopular.[70] Other popular ideas of revisionism were the restoration of the Habsburg monarchy in the rows of the CSP and even until the early 1990s the South Tyrol[71]-issue.[72] Especially the importance of the monarchy for the conservative parts of the societies in Budapest and Vienna can be observed in the sources of the street name analysis.

Name-changes

Sources for the analysis are the official street name lists of the two cities, where the administration was collecting street and place names according the date of decision of the responsible office. Therewith, one can track back the changes of the names during the inter-war period. For Vienna it can be observed through the list of the 'Konskriptionsamt' ['Administration for Collecting Statistical Data'], which ends in 1930.[73] Other important sources are the official publications and documents of the administration, such as gazettes, proceedings and the maps of the city.[74]

Budapest has similar sources. First of all, the city archive has a very good street name lexicon with details about different names, including all the name changes back to the first naming of the street; the lexicon includes also detailed references especially to general acts of the administration.[75] In other words, the lexicon contents correspond with the official record of street names written down in 1945/1946 by the public administration. Compared to the Budapest street name

69 Cf. Goldinger – Binder, Geschichte, 27, 100.

70 Cf. Goldinger – Binder, Geschichte, 129–133.

71 German and Ladin endonym: Südtirol, Italian endonyms: Alto Adige, Sudtirolo.

72 Cf. Peter Loewenberg, Austria 1918. Coming to Terms with the National Trauma of Defeat and Fragmentation, in: Karl Müller – Hans Wagner (Eds.), Österreich 1918 und die Folgen. Geschichte, Literatur, Theater und Film [Austria 1918 and the Aftermath. History, Literature, Theater and Film], Literatur und Leben 76, Wien/Köln/Weimar 2009, 11–24, here 20–22; Nick – Pelinka, Bürgerkrieg, 15.

73 Cf. Straßenverzeichnis 25 [Street-name Directory], Vienna, Wiener Stadt- und Landesarchiv (WStLA), Konskriptionsamt, 1.1.8.B53.

74 Cf., *e.g.*, Stadtplan vor 1920 [city map before 1920], Vienna, WStLA, Pläne und Karten [Plans and Maps], 3.2.1.1.P5.

75 Cf. György Mészáros, Budapest teljes utcanévlexikona [Budapest all-encompassing Street-name Lexicon], Budapest 1998.

lexicon, the collection of street names of Vienna is more topical[76], but its assembling is a little different. It is not possible to trace back the names of a street until the first naming of a street or place within the entry of the current street-name. Nevertheless, it is a useful help to get a first impression of street name changes for a more general study of a street-name as Dietz Bering and others have pointed out.[77] Along official lists, one can find some help in archived newspapers for example in form of publications about the public discussions of the street name changes. The following overview about street name changes in Budapest and Vienna is based mostly on the lists mentioned above and the statistical data is collected within those lists.

When it comes to a street name study with a big dataset, as is the case for Vienna and Budapest, one might have to categorize the street names to see the developments of street naming processes and -backgrounds. Therefore different levels of categories are required. The used levels of categorization are inspired by the categorization system of Dietz Bering and others.[78] However it is alternated for this paper as followed: First of all there is a general first level of categories such as district, year of naming, erasing a name, or the name cluster. Also the naming process belongs to first level with its values 'new introduced names', 'completely changed names', or partly changed names, which will be further called 'modified names'.

The political motivation for a name change causes each time different general connotations and references. These connotations constitute the second level of categories. In the sources and discourses in newspapers one can observe different categories. Geographical orientation ('local', 'within the official boundaries', 'outside the official boundaries'), local political meaning and general political orientation based on political parties, *i.e.* policy orientation, are such categories. Furthermore there are critical categories as there is the category for the reference towards a national identity, the category for the polity orientation or the above-mentioned policy-orientation. Less critical to define are the religious, military, as well as social references of the name and its historical context. Those are the two most important category-levels for this paper, while a more detailed analysis will be part of the more extensive Ph.D. research.[79]

76 Cf. Peter Autengruber, Lexikon der Wiener Straßennamen. Bedeutung, Herkunft, frühere Bezeichnungen [Lexicon of Street-Names of Vienna. Meanings, Origins, Earlier Designations], Wien 2012.

77 Cf. Dietz Bering – Klaus Großsteinbeck – Marion Werner, Wegbeschreibungen. Entwurf eines Kategoriensystems zur Erforschung synchroner und diachroner Straßennamenkorpora [How to Get Somewhere. Draft of a System of Categories for Studying Synchronic and Diachronic Street-Name Corpora], in: Zeitschrift für Germanistische Linguistik 27, Berlin 1999, 135–166, here 140, esp. footnote 29.

78 Cf. Bering – Großsteinbeck – Werner, Wegbeschreibungen, 147.

79 Cf. Bering – Großsteinbeck – Werner, Wegbeschreibungen, 150–155.

Name Changes in Budapest

The following examination of the name changes in Budapest and Vienna is based on the categories described above. One has to consider some meaningful facts around the context of the name changes in the cityscape of Budapest. At first, the main important political conflicts were caused by the democratic revolution in March 1918, the following socialist revolution in the spring of 1919, the subsequent right-wing revolution in the autumn of 1919 and its consolidation after 1920. Second, within that the political situation in Budapest was very radicalized between liberals and MSZDP on the one side and the conservatives on the other side, but after 1920 the groups were more or less united in questions of revisionism. The context of the political conflicts and changing political leadership elite made it possible to change street names.

Already when Károlyi was in charge in 1918, one was able to see a change in the dominating ideology, although the government changed only a few street names. At this point, it is very important to emphasize that the political power in Hungary was extremely centralized around the government of the young state. For the street names, this means that general changes in the government of the state influenced the names of the streets of Budapest more than in Vienna. As far as it was visible in the name directories, the city governments managed to rename only fourteen names in 1918 and 1919 in Budapest. The main reason of this small number is the short period of office of the democratic coalition as well as of the communist movement. These are the main reasons why the analysis of this time is more explicit and does not allow much generalization. The new democratic government in Budapest and the parties of the coalition as well as the city government tried to emphasize the independence from the Habsburg Empire in street names. There are two examples from 1918, which all took place in the city center. Therefore, on a very central square only a few kilometers away from the eastern railway station, the square with the name 'Blaha Lujza tér' ['Blaha Lujza Square'] was introduced. That is interesting insofar as this is one of the first street names referring to a woman, Blaha Lujza, who was, first of all, not part of the aristocracy and second she was still alive in 1918 and very popular in the wider parts of the population and known as 'the national nightingale'. No other name had to be erased by the government for this introduction.[80] Very obvious was the recognition of the new role of the population at the 'Nép körút', which means 'Ring Road of Nation' or 'Ring Road of People'. But in that case, the city government had to erase the former name, 'IV. Károly király út' ['King Karl IV Street'], this name was introduced only two years before the renaming and was dedicated to the Habsburg King Karl IV of Hungary.[81] He was the formal king of Hungary from 1916 until 1922, the year of his death. This example shows that the tendency

80 Cf. Mészáros, Budapest, 112.

81 Cf. Mészáros, Budapest, 267.

is symbolic, but it is clearly for the benefit of the independence, democratization and the people of Hungary, as was pointed out above.

In the same way, the former King Franz Joseph was erased and instead of his name Kossuth Lajos and Petőfi Sándor were introduced to the map of Budapest.[82] This renaming meant a very strong break to the policy of remembrance by the officials. Before this renaming, only a few names were dedicated to the national heroes of the fight of independence of the 1848 revolution as they are mostly remembered until nowadays, because they fought against the Habsburgs. Those heroes were very popular in the population and since the independence of Hungary it was easier to introduce for instance the name of Kossuth Lajos in 1918 and to erase such an important Habsburg king as Franz Joseph was. Kossuth was the most radical and engaged fighter against the Habsburg Monarchy as well as Petőfi Sándor, who was a young poet and seems to have held his status of the 'national poet' of Hungary until today.[83]

Emilia Palonen showed how important Kossuth Lajos and Petőfi Sándor were and still are. Referring to a survey made in 1999 it is pointed out, that 'certain names, such as Kossuth, Petőfi or Széchenyi seem to be well established and are used liberally and never removed from the streets. According to the survey [...] these are the three most popular characters of Hungarian literature and history among Hungarians.'[84] In the interwar years Kossuth was as important as he already was before the World War I. Remembered by different groups of the society as a hero of freedom, he still is a symbol for freedom, independent from a particular political party.[85] Nevertheless Kossuth remains a political symbol, 'Kossuth war für jeden, der den Anspruch hatte, auf große Volksmassen politisch zu wirken, das nationale Gütesiegel, mit dem er die nationale Glaubwürdigkeit seiner politischen Ware beweisen konnte.' [86] ['Kossuth was for everybody, who claimed to have a political influence on the masses, the national kite mark for proving the national credibility of the political product.']. In the same pattern the central street name of the Habsburg 'Föherceg Albrecht út' ['Grand Duke Albrecht street'] was

82 Cf. Mészáros, Budapest, 103.

83 Cf. Emilia Palonen, Canonisation and Recanonisation in Hungarian Street-Names, in: István Dobos – Mihály Szegedy-Maszák (Eds.), Kánon és kanonáció [Canon and Canonization], Budapest 2003, 152f.; András Gerő, Der Kossuth-Kult [The Kossuth-Cult], in: Holger Fischer (Ed.), Lajos Kossuth (1802–1894). Wirken – Rezeption – Kult [Lajos Kossuth (1802–1894). Work – Reception – Cult], Hamburg 2007, 167–194, here 180–193; György Dalos, Ungarn in der Nußschale. Geschichte meines Landes [Hungary in a Nutshell. History of My Country], München 2004, 101–104.

84 Palonen, Canonisation, 152. Palonen confers to Ágnes Kapitány – Gábor Kapitány, Magyarság szimbolumok [Symbols of Hungarians], Budapest 1999.

85 Cf. Katalin Gönczi, Lajos Kossuth oder die Personifikation der Freiheit. Eine Fallstudie zur Entstehung von nationalen Mythen in Ungarn [Kossuth or the Personification of Liberty. A Case Study on the Development of National Myths in Hungary], in: Holger Fischer (Ed.), Lajos Kossuth (1802–1894). Wirken – Rezeption – Kult [Lajos Kossuth (1802–1894). Work – Reception – Cult], Hamburg 2007, 137–154, here 148.

86 Gerő, Kossuth-Kult, 181.

renamed to 'Nagy Sándor út' ['Great Sándor Street'], who was also a fighter for Hungarian independence in 1848.[87] The 'Rudolf trónörökös tér' ['Crown Prince Rudolf Square'], which was introduced only in 1903, was renamed to 'Leinigen tér' ['Leiningen Square'], dedicated to Earl Leiningen-Westerburg Károly, who was a general of the Hungarian army in 1848 and 1849.[88] The same can be observed at the renaming of the 'Erzsébet királné útja' ['Queen Erzsébet Street'], which was also dedicated to a Habsburg and was renamed after 'Zrínyi Ilona', who again was a woman, who fought against the Habsburg and for the Hungarian independence in the 17th century.[89] Finally, the 'Országház tér' ['Square of Parliament'] became the 'Köztársaság tér' ['Square of Republic']. All those name-changes show the political view of the democratic movement especially around Károly Mihály to get

> 'total independence without the Habsburg's right to rule as kings' as well as the 'desire for the emancipation from German tutelage [...]. The entire party, Károly included, was imbued with Magyar chauvinism, [...] hoping that democratization and social progress would eliminate ethnic hostility toward a new type of Hungarian state.'[90]

The general directions in renaming do also not change with the beginning of the Socialist Soviet Republic in April 1919. Again only a few names were changed. All the names of 1918 stayed while a special committee for renaming was founded.[91] These names, which changed in the first half of 1919, show stronger opposition against the nobility and could be interpreted in a socialistic way of understanding history as well as symbols for national independence. This was possible because of the use of national symbols as there are Kossuth Lajos and others. Considering this

> 'Kun could argue, to base the fight for Hungary's national survival and greatness on a revolutionary alliance with Bolshevik Russia. [...] Inexorably, this dual appeal to patriotism and revolution impressed minor Socialist functionaries and the rank and file as well as a significant fraction of the leadership, not to mention the ideologically illiterate but fervently patriotic troops and masses.'[92]

Bearing this in mind, for example the street 'Főherceg Sándor utca' ['Archduke Sándor Street'] as well as the 'Főherceg Sándor tér' ['Archduke Sándor Square']

---

87 Cf. Mészáros, Budapest, 119.

88 Cf. Mészáros, Budapest, 250.

89 Cf. Mészáros, Budapest, 167.

90 Vermes, Politics, 110f.

91 Cf. Eva Bodnar, 'I Have Often Walked Down This Street Before ... But What Was it Called?' Changes to Street Names in Budapest from the End of Turkish Rule to the Present, in: Past Imperfects 15, Alberta 2009, 115–153, here 137.

92 Rothschild, Europe, 144.

modified into 'Sándor utca' and tér.[93] The titles of the nobility were lost in the process of name-modification. Another example is the introduction of the street name of Szentmarjay Ferenc, who was a Jacobin in Budapest in the 1790s and was remembered as a fighter for Hungary and the peasants and workers.[94] Especially with this name, one could see the symbolic attempt of the communist government to introduce such names. On the other hand, the street-name dedicated to the last German Emperor Wilhelm, which was introduced in 1914, was simply descriptively renamed into 'Váci utca' ['Vaci Street']. This time, the old name was returned, the street was already named Váci before 1914. The name has just a descriptive function as it shows the direction towards the town Vác in the north of Budapest.[95] After the end of the socialist domination and the conservative revolution around Horthy Miklós, who was in charge as regent until October 1944, the heroes of the 1848 revolution stayed in the public space and the Habsburg nobility returned to the street signs: 'Nép körút' ['Ring Road of People/Ring Road of Nation'] was renamed back into 'Károly körút' ['Ring Road of Károly'].[96] During the time of the conservative domination much more names were changed, this is why statistical-descriptive data would be more useful for the analysis. This quantitative analysis is based on a work in progress dataset and only a few test-categories of the two levels, which were described above. The following analysis is focused on names, which were introduced during the inter-war-period, and stayed unchanged since the year of introduction. When it comes to numbers, there are at the moment 362 new name introductions and 30 name changes from the time between 1919 and 1930[97], which are in use since the inter-war period and which were never changed again, neither by the radical Hungarian government during the Second World War, nor by the socialist governments until 1989, nor by the governments after 1990. One might call this a common, not-discussed part of local identity or a common sense. Because of that it is interesting to observe the current territory of Budapest for the street name analysis with the aim of getting a better understanding of the difficulties and implications of the daily use of those street names.

It is interesting to see that in Budapest the names, which have mostly lasted until nowadays, were not changed continuously. That means, there are two significant peaks, when names were introduced or changed: 1920 and 1930. In 1920, 102 new names were introduced in the name scape of Budapest and two were changed. In 1930, exactly 12 out of 125 names were changed, whereas all the other 113 were new names. Nearly one half of the names of 1920 and 1930 were

93 Cf. Mészáros, Budapest, 119, 206.

94 Cf. Mészáros, Budapest, 470, 73.

95 Cf. Mészáros, Budapest, 538, 86.

96 Cf. Mészáros, Budapest, 267.

97 The period of time and the number of names are based on the state of work.

introduced in current urban fringe districts, which were separated settlements around Budapest in the interwar-period.

One quarter of all names, which were introduced in the city are connected to places outside the State of Hungary, which is interesting so far as that migrants from the 'abgetrennte Gebiete'[98] ['detached parts'] probably lived in the areas around 'Klein-Budapest' ['Small-Budapest'][99] of 1873. Therewith, the introduced names are connected with the people, who came to different settlements and after a while, those communities became large enough for naming streets in the area of the settlement, as there is the 1920 introduced 'Brassói utca' ['Brássoi Street'][100], which is named after the city Braşov and was part of the Hungarian Kingdom and is part of Romania since the treaty of Trianon. The 'Kolozsvári utca' ['Kolozsvári Street'][101] is another example that shows the same pattern, in Romanian known as Cluj or in German as Klausenburg. This name 'Kolozsvári utca' ['Kolozsvári street'] is a good example insofar, as it was introduced three times, which is quite unusual in a name-scape and makes the street name to an unclear local reference. Both acts were in favor of the new names, which were dedicated to cities outside Hungary.

Another significant pattern is dedication to 'heroes'. 64% of out of all street names were dedicated to some kind of hero. Very important examples from this group are again Kossuth Lajos or Petőfi Sándor. Attention should also be paid to names including Damjanich János, a famous officer of the 1848/49 Revolution, born in the multilingual area of the Banat[102] and executed as one of the 13 martyrs of Arad in 1849. Next to 'Damjanich János utca' ['Damjanich János Street'] is a street dedicated to another important 'hero', which is 'Dessewffy Arisztid utca' ['Dessewffy Arisztid Street']. Dessewffy was one of the generals of the army of the 1848/49 Revolution. Both names were introduced in 1922. Further names with historical deepness belong to people behind the 'Jagelló út' ['Jagiellonian Street'][103] or the 'Hunyad lejtő' ['Hunyad Ascent'][104], both dedicated to dynasties of former Hungarian kings.

Not less meaningful are the 'heroes' taken as an 'anonymous' collective, mostly remembered and honored with four 'Hősök tere' ['Heroes' Square'], one

98 Tamás Faragó, Die Budapester Bevölkerungsentwicklung und die Zuwanderung. 1840 bis 1941 [The Development of the Inhabitants of Budapest and Migration. 1840 until 1941], in: Gerhard Melinz – Susan Zimmermann (Eds.), Wien – Prag – Budapest. Blütezeit der Habsburgmetropolen: Urbanisierung, Kommunalpolitik, gesellschaftliche Konflikte (1867–1918) [Vienna – Prague – Budapest. Blooming of the Habsburg Metropols: Urbanization, Local Politics, Conflicts of Society (1867–1918), Wien 1996, 58–72.

99 Faragó, Bevölkerungsentwicklung, 71.

100 Cf. Mészáros, Budapest, 119.

101 Cf. Mészáros, Budapest, 293.

102 Banat is the Romanian, German and Serbian name, Bánság is the Hungarian name.

103 Cf. Mészáros, Budapest, 248.

104 Cf. Mészáros, Budapest, 239f.

'Hős utca' ['Heroes' Street'] and one 'Hősök fasora' ['Heroes' Alley'].[105] All were introduced in 1920 in former independent settlements and later became part of Budapest, although the names were not changed. Within those names only two were introduced by erasing another one. Those former names belonged in one case to a local politician and the other one was 'Ferenc Jószef tér' ['Ferenc József Square'], which was erased in 1930.

All in all one can say that there are some patterns of name changing, which correlate with the symbolic name changes of the years 1918 and 1919. First of all the important break of the polity from a kingdom to a democracy was emphasized throughout street names in 1918 and 1919. Second the national identity of Hungary got a key position beyond 1918 and 1919. Third, especially when it comes to the remembrance of the Habsburg dynasty there are differences. Here one can see the approach of the restoration of the Hungarian Kingdom, which was not an issue at all of the government policies in 1918 and 1919. Finally the street names dedicated to settlements outside of Hungary show the migration of Hungarians, who moved from the new-founded countries into the capital of the post-Trianon Hungary.

Name Changes in Wien

Especially the Anti-Habsburg theme during the first months of post-Trianon Budapest, described above, can be observed in Vienna too. Main reasons for the name changes in Vienna were the elections in May 1919, when the political domination through the SDAP began. The new social-democratic city government founded a committee[106], which had to cancel double naming or names, which were not appropriate for the young political system as well as names which 'heute als unpassende Aeusserung [sic] der Liebdienerei einer vergangenen Zeit [scheinen]' ['seem to be today expressions of cajolery for a past time'].[107] The committee also had to work based on the general decision of the office council, which said that 'Umbenennungen nur in Fällen zwingender Notwendigkeit vorzunehmen sind' ['Names can only be changed if it is for compelling necessity'][108]. The

105 Cf. Mészáros, Budapest, 236f.

106 Cf. Einladung zur Sitzung des Komitees zur Umbenennung von Strassen, Gassen und Plätze vom 20. Oktober 1919 [Invitation to the Meeting of the Committee for Renaming Streets, Alleys and Squares from the 20 October 1919], WstLA, M.Abt. 116, A38: Straßenbenennungen [Street Naming], 1908–1925.

107 Umbenennung von Strassen [Street Name Changing], Mag. Abt. 18/2137/21, WStLA, M.Abt. 116, A38: Straßenbenennungen [Street Naming], 1908–1925. Cf. Oliver Rathkolb – Peter Autengruber – Birgit Nemec – Florian Wenninger, Forschungsprojektendbericht. Straßennamen Wiens seit 1860 als "Politische Erinnerungsorte" [Finale Science Project Report. Street-Names of Vienna since 1860 as 'Political Places of Memory'], Wien 2013, 33.

108 Umbenennung der Weintraubengasse im II. Bezirk [Renaming of the Weintraubengasse in the IInd District'], Mag. Abt. 18/4021/24, WstLA, M.Abt. 116, A38: Straßenbenennungen [Street Naming], 1908–1925, Vermeidung von Strassenumebennungen [Avoiding of Street

federal reforms after 1919 led to the situation that Vienna became an independent part in the federal system of Austria. Due to the federal sovereignty of Vienna the Social Democrats could stay in political charge until the middle of 1930s and managed to consolidate their view of history within the street names. According to the clear name giving policy, the city government changed 48 street names by the decision of the city council from 6 November 1919 and during the 1920s changed or introduced 274 names, which were not changed since and which are still in use. Most of the new ones can be found in the urban fringe districts of Vienna of the interwar-period, similarly to Budapest, because nearly 50% of those 274 names were introduced in the 12th, 13th and 21st district.

43 names of this first decision of 1919 were finally introduced. 37 of those street names referred to the Habsburgs or the Monarchy.[109] For example, along the 'Ringstraße' ['Ring Road'] of Vienna: parts of it were named after the Emperor Karl (last emperor of Austria), Emperor Zita (wife of Karl) and Emperor Wilhelm (last German Emperor Wilhelm II) and so on. Other examples are 'Franzensring' ['Franzens-Ring Road'], dedicated to the first emperor of Austria Franz I or as well as next to the ring road, the 'Maximiliansplatz' ['Maximilian Square'], dedicated to Archduke Maximilian, who initiated the construction of the church at that square, and also the 'Albrechtsplatz' ['Albrecht Square'] is such an particular case. The new names along the 'Ringstraße' can be categorized in local geographic names, names in favor of a democratic polity, or names of an explicit social-democratic policy. The parts of the 'Ringstraße', which were named after Emperor Karl, Emperor Zita and Emperor Wilhelm became local geographic names: 'Parkring' ['Park-Ring Road'], according to the park next to it, 'Opernring' ['Opera-Ring Road'] next to the opera and 'Kärtnerring' ['Kärtner Ring Road'], because of an older name of this part of the city. Those name changes might be interpreted as an anti-monarchistic polity approach.

Further there are three significant changes which show clear political preferences of the political system of the social-democrats: the 'Franzensring' became 'Ring des 12. November' ['Ring Road of the 12th November'], to commemorate the Annunciation of the Republic. Beside that the 'Maximilians Platz' became 'Freiheitsplatz' ['Freedom Square'] and the 'Albrechtsplatz' was named into 'Revolutionsplatz' ['Revolution Square'].

The *Arbeiterzeitung* ['Worker's Newspaper'] pointed out during the discussion about street name changes in the early November 1919 that 'die Einführung einiger Straßennamen, die an bedeutende Vorgänge des Revolutionsjahres erinnern' ['the introduction of some street names, which are commemorating the

---

Name Changes], Mag. Abt. 16/11255/1911,WStLA, M.Abt. 116, A38: Straßenbenennungen [Street Naming], 1908–1925.

109 The decision was changed later in different cases, cf. Umbenennung von Strassen [Street Name Changing], Mag. Abt. 18/2137/21, WStLA. M.Abt. 116, A38: Straßenbenennungen [Street Naming], 1908–1925.

events of the year of revolution'] are an 'erzieherische Notwendigkeit'[110] ['educative necessity'].[111] The names of the power-filled sites were changed by the local government all over the city.

There are a few interesting tendencies when it comes to a comparison with Budapest. In Vienna there are twice as many names as in Budapest with a connection to a local place, 17%, and there are not even 2% of the cases, which are dedicated to a place outside Austria. Name dedicated to local places were often named in the sense to save old field names as well as according to the fact that names should be a help for orientation and that is why the responsible offices had to take topographical or physical landmarks as well as the local history in consideration.[112] Those two percent of names, not in favor of revisionism, follow the tradition of thankful commemoration to specific help for example from the government of Argentina[113], which helped Vienna with a certain amount of money in months after the war. Beside that this is a great example for the public participation in a process of name change. There was a discussion about naming of a street in the city center in 'Argentinierstraße' ['Argentinier Street'] instead of the already existing 'Argentiniergasse' ['Argentinier Street'] in the 15th district.[114] However as the small firms of the industry and trade pointed out, the upcoming costs for the address-change were very high, so there was even public opposing participation against a name change. According to a letter to the local agency of the district the firms on the street had to change all signs of each company as well as every advertisement. Finally, against the will of the local companies the street name was still changed in 1921.[115] An example for revisionism might be given by the 'Südtiroler Platz' ['Südtiroler Square'], named in 1927, as for this the name 'Favoritenplatz' ['Favoriten-Square'], which was named after a district of Wien[116], was erased.

---

110 *Arbeiterzeitung*, Wien 1919 November 12th.

111 Cf. Amtsblatt der Stadt Wien, Wien 1919 November 22th, 2279–2781; Rathkolb – Autengruber – Nemec – Wenninger, Forschungsprojektendbericht, 33.

112 Cf. Schreiben von den Städtischen Sammlungen an die Magistratsabteilung 18 vom 25. November 1920 [Letter from the Städtischen Sammlungen to the Magistratabteilung 18], St. S. 573/20, WStLA, M.Abt. 116, A38: Straßenbenennungen [Street Naming], 1908–1925.

113 Spanish endonym: República Argentina.

114 Cf. IV. Umbenennung der Alleegasse in Argentinierstrasse und XV. Argentiniergasse in Herlachergasse [Name Change of the Alleegasse to Argentinierstrasse and XVth. Argentiniergasse in to Herlachergasse], Mag. Abt. 18/9/21, WStLA, M.Abt. 116, A38: Straßenbenennungen [Street Naming], 1908–1925. Another example is the Montevideogasse, cf. Benennungen von Verkehrsflächen im XIII. Bezirk. Gasse hinter der Lainzer Straße [Naming Areas Constructed for Traffic in the XIIIth District], Mag. Abt. 54/868/30, WStLA, Topographische Sammlung, 3.14.A3: Verkehrsflächen: Neubenennungen, Umbenennungen, Streichungen, 1917–1988 [Areas Constructed for Traffic: Naming, Renaming, Erasing, 1917–1988].

115 Cf. IV. Umbenennung der Alleegasse in Argentinierstrasse [Name Change of the Alleegasse to Argentinierstrasse], Mag. Abt. 18/9/21, 4, WStLA, M.Abt. 116, A38: Straßenbenennungen [Street Naming], 1908–1925.

116 Cf. Straßenverzeichnis 25 [Street Name Directory], 517, WStLA, Konskriptionsamt, 1.1.8.B53, Platzumbenennung IV. Bezirk [Square Renaming IVth District], Mag. Abt. 54/4142/27, WStLA, Topographische Sammlung, 3.14.A3: Verkehrsflächen: Neubenennungen, Umbenennun-

Most names had a local reference as one of the new names of the 'Ringstraße', *e.g.*, 'Parkring' ['Park-Ring Road'] or 'Opernring' ['Opera-Ring Road']. There is still one special case: the 'Burgenlandgasse' ['Burgenland Street'], where one street was newly named 'zum Gedenken an die Einverleibung des neuen Bundeslandes Burgenland in die Republik Österreich'[117] ['in memory of the annexation of the new federal state Burgenland to the Republic of Austria'].

Most of the other names without geographical references, which were introduced during the analysis period are dedicated to contemporary artists and academics in Vienna. There are more than two thirds of all street names dedicated to persons. Important persons of the cultural life became the key name group with nearly 50% of all street names, which were not dedicated to a place or to academics, which constitute the second most important group with around 28%. Among those persons, who were culturally important, one can group names into specific categories, as there are street names with a local reference or external geographic reference. First of all, according to the general directions negotiating identities of the young Republic of Austria, it is obvious, that there were few names introduced, which had a reference to the German Reich like the 'Goethegasse' ['Goethe Street'], 'Gottfried-Keller Gasse' ['Gottfried-Keller Street'] or the 'Grimmelshausengasse' ['Grimmelshausen street']. For all those street names changed by the decision of the city council in 1919, Habsburg references had to be erased.[118] Across that there is category of names with local reference, which shows the important role of the Burgtheater and its actors in Wien for parts of the population: 'Baumeistergasse' ['Baumeister Street'], 'Lewinskygasse' ['Lewinsky Street'], or 'Gabillongasse' ['Gabillon street'], this group even got an own name cluster.[119] All those names belong to the actors of the theater, showing respect to their long-lasting career. Finally, many local important persons were used for street-renaming, *e.g.*, 'Ebersberggasse' ['Ebersberg Street'] named after Ottokar Franz Ebersberg[120],

---

gen, Streichungen, 1917–1988 [Areas Constructed for Traffic: Naming, Renaming, Erasing, 1917–1988]; Autengruber, Lexikon, 279.

117 Straßenbenennung im Siedlungsgebiet No 3 Laa am Berge, X. Bezirk [Street Naming in the Settlement Area Nr. 3 Laa am Berge, Xth District], Mag. Abt. 18/963/24, WStLA, M.Abt. 116, A38: Straßenbenennungen [Street Naming], 1908–1925.

118 Cf. Amtsblatt der Stadt Wien, Wien 1919 November 22th, 2279–2781; Alois Sillaber, Straßennamen. Wegweiser zur Identität [Street Names. Directions to Identity], in: Stefan Riesenfellner (Ed.), Steinernes Bewusstsein I: Die öffentliche Repräsentation staatlicher und nationaler Identität Österreichs in seinen Denkmälern [Consciousness Made of Stone I: The Public Representation State and National Identity of Austria in his Monuments], Wien/Köln/Weimar 1998, 575–618, here 579.

119 Cf. Benennungen von Verkehrsflächen in der Gartenstadt 'Am Tivoli' im XII. Bezirk [Naming of Areas Constructed for Traffic in the Garden City 'Am Tivoli' in the XIIth District], Mag. Abt. 54/1630/28, WStLA, Topographische Sammlung, 3.14.A3: Verkehrsflächen: Neubenennungen, Umbenennungen, Streichungen, 1917–1988 [Areas Constructed for Traffic: Naming, Renaming, Erasing, 1917–1988]; Autengruber, Lexikon, 43, 66, 98, 181.

120 Cf. Benennungen einer Verkehrsflächen im Siedlungsgebiet No 14, Siedlung Hermeswiese, XIII. Bezirk [Naming of Areas Constructed for Traffic in the Settlement Area No 14, Settlement Hermeswiese, XIIIth District], Mag. Abt. 18/2024/26, WStLA, Topographische Samm-

the founder of the satire magazine *Kikeriki* and the *Illustrierte Wiener Extrablatt* ['Illustrated Viennese Extrablatt'], a daily newspaper, and there are also persons like Eduard Lötzl[121], an author from Vienna, who wrote especially about *Heimat* topics. The last two patterns can be observed more from the middle to the end of the inter-war period, while the first one reached its height in 1919 – according to the already mentioned city council decision of the November 1919.

When it comes to academics, Vienna during the interwar-period seemed to be very Central European, as there are commemorations to Ernst Mach, Ignaz Philipp Semmelweis and more international Konrad Duden[122] or Louis Braille. Professors of the University of Vienna of the 19th and early 20th century are also academically significant and are considered in street names. In addition to those academics, local scientists such as archaeologist Dr. Friedrich Kenner – his main field of interest was the roman history of Wien – become a part of the name scape since 1925.[123]

Examples for different political ideologies as well as the will of political actors to implement names connected to a special government system can be seen at the 'Habsburgplatz' ['Habsburg Square'] in the 16th district, which got the name 'Schumeier Platz' ['Schumeier Square'], dedicated to a local social-democrat and the 'Kaiserplatz' ['Emporer Square'] in the 20th district, which after the change got the name 'Engels Platz' ['Engels square'] after Friedrich Engels. One can find a few more important authors of the social-democratic idea like for the Austrian Party: Viktor Adler, Leopold Winarsky, Alois Langenau or Anton Schlinger or important Germans such as Ferdinand Lasalle and August Bebel.[124] Within this memory policy in favor to commemorating progressive persons in general and especially persons connected with the SDAP, the place 'zwischen dem Rathause, dem Universitätsgebäude, der Ringstraße und dem Parlamentsgebäude'[125] ['between city hall, the building of the university, the 'Ring Road' and the Parlia-

---

lung, 3.14.A3: Verkehrsflächen: Neubenennungen, Umbenennungen, Streichungen, 1917–1988 [Areas Constructed for Traffic: Naming, Renaming, Erasing, 1917–1988]; Autengruber, Lexikon, 73.

121 Autengruber, Lexikon, 75.

122 Cf. Benennung einer Gasse am Küniglberg im XIII. Bezirk [Naming an Alley at the Küniglberg in XIIIth District], Mag. Abt. 54/2787/29WStLA, Topographische Sammlung, 3.14. A3: Verkehrsflächen: Neubenennungen, Umbenennungen, Streichungen, 1917–1988 [Areas Constructed for Traffic: Naming, Renaming, Erasing, 1917–1988].

123 Cf. Straßenbenennung im X. Bezirk [Street Naming in the Xth District], Mag. Abt. 18/3236/25, WStLA, Topographische Sammlung, 3.14.A3: Verkehrsflächen: Neubenennungen, Umbenennungen, Streichungen, 1917–1988 [Areas Constructed for Traffic: Naming, Renaming, Erasing, 1917–1988].

124 Sillaber, Wegweiser, 579.

125 Umbenennung des Dr. Karl Luegerplatzes und eines Teiles der Wollzeile im I. Bezirk [Renaming of the Dr. Karl Luegerplatzes and of a Part of the Wollzeile in the Ist District], Mag. Abt. 18/3295/26, WStLA, Topographische Sammlung, 3.14.A3: Verkehrsflächen: Neubenennungen, Umbenennungen, Streichungen, 1917–1988 [Areas Constructed for Traffic: Naming, Renaming, Erasing, 1917–1988].

ment'], named after Karl Lueger in 1907, got the name Rathausplatz because of the new construction of the city hall, while the Dr. Karl Luegerplatz was replaced to another square in the city center, where it is until today.[126] At the same time, this part of the 'Ringstraße' was named after 'Ring des 12. November' ['Ring Road of the 12th November']. The political approach of naming streets and commemorating specific persons, who played a leading role in different uprisings, can be observed in the name introductions in 1930. The 'Weitmosergasse' ['Weitmoser Street'] is a representative case, 'Erasmus Weitmoser[,] Gewerke in Gastein und Führer der Salzburger Knappen im Aufstand des Jahres 1525'['Erasmus Weitmoser, craftsmen in Gastein and leader of the miners of Salzburg during the revolt in the year 1525']'[127] or the 'Sickingengasse' ['Sickingen Street'], named after 'Franz von Sickingen (1481–1523) Führer im fränkischen Ritteraufstand der Jahre 1522 und 1523' ['Franz von Sickingen (1481–1523) leader during the Franconian revolt of knights in the years 1522 and 1523']'[128] are examples for this pattern. Another typical case is the whole area around the 'Achtundvierziger Platz' ['48er Square'], where one can find names of seventeen craftsmen, who died during the 1848 revolution, introduced in 1929.

Conclusion

All in all this paper tried to give a short overview about the street naming during the interwar period in Budapest and Vienna. The aim was to show different developments and change-patterns within the renaming process, which also show the political conflicts of the societies of the interwar period: or example either more external and more focused on (historical) important politicians or with a stronger focus on a differentiated society within artists and academics and especially with less monarchical dedication.

With particular reference to the theoretical idea that place names are a media of power introduced by political institutions on the one hand and that they are a part of the mass media system of the official collective memory on the other

126 Cf. Umbenennung des Dr. Karl Luegerplatzes und eines Teiles der Wollzeile im I. Bezirk [Renaming of the Dr. Karl Luegerplatzes and of a Part oft the Wollzeile in the Ist District], Mag. Abt. 18/3295/26, WStLA, Topographische Sammlung, 3.14.A3: Verkehrsflächen: Neubenennungen, Umbenennungen, Streichungen, 1917–1988 [Areas Constructed for Traffic: Naming, Renaming, Erasing, 1917–1988]; Autengruber, Lexikon, 233; Sillaber, Straßennamen, 577.

127 Benennungen von Verkehrsflächen in der Gebietsansiedlung am Wienerberg im X. Bezirk [Naming of Areas Constructed for Traffic in the Settlement at the Wienerberg in the Xth District], Mag. Abt. 54/857/28, WStLA, Topographische Sammlung, 3.14.A3: Verkehrsflächen: Neubenennungen, Umbenennungen, Streichungen, 1917–1988 [Areas Constructed for Traffic: Naming, Renaming, Erasing, 1917–1988].

128 WStLA, Topographische Sammlung, 3.14.A3: Verkehrsflächen: Neubenennungen, Umbenennungen, Streichungen, 1917–1988 [Areas Constructed for Traffic: Naming, Renaming, Erasing, 1917–1988]: Benennungen von Verkehrsflächen in der Gebietsansiedlung am Wienerberg im X. Bezirk [Naming of Areas Constructed for Traffic in the Settlement at the Wienerberg in the Xth District], Mag. Abt. 54/857/28.

hand and because of the relatively easy way to change them they are vulnerable for changes.

The cases of Budapest and Vienna demonstrate that the social and multinational differentiation of the population can cause a more differentiated street name cityscape. The political break of the end of World War I made it possible to change place names according to the varying dominating political ideologies and government systems. In Budapest the name change were as radical as in Vienna. Nevertheless there are some differences between both cases. During the first phase in 1918/1919, the new street names of Budapest concentrate on an opening to the democratization. Street names, dedicated against the nobility were often changed in favor of street names, which tried to consider broader starting-points of identification bear broader parts of the population than the nobility in mind. Only in one case the street name underlines the socialist ideology. After the conservative revolution, historical national heroes became an important part of the cityscape as well as names dedicated to places outside Hungary. That means, street names, which were reflecting a broad society and not only particular groups of the population got less frequent. Names of cities outside the Hungarian country were even repeatedly existing and names of persons, who could be characterized as a kind of 'hero' of 'the' Hungarian nation got more frequent. Nevertheless one has to admit, that those names were also common identity-building role models. Whereas in Vienna, the democratization was the first main-topic too, the erasing of Habsburg names was much stronger, because the first new elected city government erased Habsburg-mentioning names. Instead of these, names dedicated to artists, social-democratic politicians and scientists were introduced, which might be a sign for the caution opening up to democracy based on the differentiation of society since the end of the 19th century, even though this change in the name scape can be seen as a radical break. Categorizationwise one can observe, that place names from outside the borders of the new Austrian country are quite rare. Another difference between both cities is the dealing with double naming. Vienna tried to avoid strictly all double namings or names, which were too similar. Budapest instead had a few double namings, which are in use until today. Both instances show, that the way of the seizure of power and the time in charge are very important factors for the question how much and how a government can change names. In other words: how a government can (re)settle the own ideology and respectively for how long the institutionalization of the names lasts.

All in all, it is also very important to remember that the government of Vienna is based on a broader population, which had the right to vote. The governments since the late 19th century gradually opened the society to democracy unsuccessfully when it comes to questions of a positive identification with the new governmental system during the interwar-period. In that manner one has to read a lot of street name changes in Vienna as particular statements for a social-democratic republic and not for the Republic of Austria. As for Hungary, the lack of democratic culture in 1918 seems to have made it possible that a less institutionalized but a more radical introduction of democracy, which was strongly affiliated with socialistic ideas, failed in the same way by introducing a more pluralistic memory as the young Soviet Republic failed to introduce its view. The governments between 1920 and 1934 could promote a more conservative view of the society affiliated to the idea of Hungarian nation and represented by the aristocracy instead. Both in Vienna and in Budapest the interwar period was a time of conflicting memories, while every dominant group tried to emphasize the own view of history combined with the intention to make it the view of the society.

Ofer Waldman

'I wanted to show – we are here!' Memory Activism in the Former Sudetenland

Hebrew University of Jerusalem

Preface

The innovative moment of the rise of the field of memory studies is by now, in itself, a mnemonic phenomenon. The re-discovery of the dialectical relationship between history and memory as past oriented realms at the backdrop of the numerous historiographical 'turns' and the rising human rights discourse of the 1990s will stand at the center of the following words, extended by its investment in contemporary social action, referred to as 'memory activism'. These following words seek to accomplish a critical view of a distinct case study of memory activism, while examining the social and historical backdrops against which it takes place. [1] In order to do so, *i.e.* to interweave the critical text with the description of the contemporary action, I chose a textual strategy taken from Ronit Lentin[2], interjecting narrating textual sections into the scholarly text, re-contextualizing the different segments of my research. These 'interjections' will be made distinct through slightly narrower margins and 'italics' formatting.

Opening

Upon arriving at the north bohemian village of Lobendava (Lobendau) in the last august week of 2012, a twenty members strong Czech-Austrian-German group,[3] participating in this year's 'Spurensuche'-project – searching for traces in the Sudetenland – arrived at a church standing on the main village road. In front of the entrance one could see war memorials for the Austro-Hungarian casualties of the First World War, concentrated around a massive granite obelisk with the simple inscription – 'Die Hei-

1 This research was made possible through the generous support of the Konrad Adenauer Foundation.

2 Ronit Lentin, Co-Memory and Melancholia. Israelis Memorializing the Palestinian Nakba, Manchester 2010.

3 The author of this paper was also a member of the 'Spurensuche'-group of 2012. I am deeply grateful to Dr. Christiane Brenner from the Collegium Carolinum in Munich for introducing me to this project.

mat gibt Dank' – ['The fatherland shows gratitude']. The group entered the building, which stands in a miserable condition; the paint which peels off from the walls, reveals hidden biblical German phrases, one written just below Maria holding her dying son, stating – 'Es ist vollbracht.' ['It is done.']

Based on on-site observations during the 'Spurensuche'-week in the summer of 2012, interviews with its participants as well as textual sources regarding the participating organizations, the following paper wishes to outline dissimilar Austrian-German and Czech discourses concerning the Czech border regions, emanating from the same historical event – the expulsion of the Ethnic Germans from Czechoslovakia after the Second World War. The articulation of these respective different discourses and collective memory frames regarding these regions, documented during the 'Spurensuche'-week, will be addressed at the backdrop of memory activism related research.

Historical Background

German speaking population inhabited the Bohemian and Moravian landscapes since the 11th century, concentrating in the course of time mainly along the borders to German speaking regions (Silesia, Saxony, Bavaria, Upper- and Lower Austria), as well as in some 'language islands' as Brno (Brünn)and Olomouc (Olmütz)[4], making up for as much as a third of the region's population.[5] At the face of the rising Czech-German interplay of language-based nationalism that swept across the region starting from the late 19th century, the Bohemian and Moravian Germans were increasingly considered to pose a single national unit, referred to as 'Sudeten Germans'. This term, deriving from the Sudeten Mountains in Bohemia, remains – although often used – rather problematic, being intertwined with the nationalistic phase in which it was coined, as well as overlooking the affiliation of these Germans to the Habsburg crown rather than to Germany.[6] Its further use in the following study as well as in the German, Austrian, and Czech discourses must therefore be observed with a due critical notion.[7]

4 Joseph B. Schechtman, European Population Transfers, New York 1946, 27–29.

5 Detlef Brandes, Der Weg zur Vertreibung 1938–1945 [The Path towards the Expulsion 1938–1945], München 2005, 284f.

6 'The Sudeten Germans are affiliated with Hessen or Bavaria as little as they are affiliated with the German speaking parts of Switzerland [...]', Hans Grimm to Hans Ehard, 1947 February 24th, cited in: K. Erik Franzen, Der vierte Stamm Bayerns. Die Schirmherrschaft über die Sudetendeutschen 1954–1974 [The Fourth Tribe of Bavaria. The Patronage over the Sudeten Germans], München 2010, 82.

7 Andrea Hohmeyer, Aufklärung über 'Böhmische Dörfer'. Zu den Schwierigkeiten einer adäquaten Nomenklatur in Darstellungen über Böhmen und Mähren [Clarification over 'Bohemian Villages'. Regarding the Difficulties of an Adequate Nomenclature in Descriptions over Bohemia and Moravia], in: Andrea Hohmeyer – Ernst Erich Metzner (Eds.), Spurensuche in Sprach- und Geschichtslandschaften [Searching for Traces in Landscapes of Language and

After the First World War, the Sudeten Germans underwent a paradigmatic change, turning from members of the dominant national group of the Habsburg Empire into a large minority within the newly formed Czechoslovakia, which embodied the clash between the ideal of a modern nation-state and the multiethnical reality of East Central Europe.[8] The embittering aftermath of the world economic crises at the end of the 1920s was felt especially in the heavily industrialized German regions[9], as well as the winds of radical German nationalism, which blew across the border deepened the antagonist and irredentist stance of an overwhelming majority of the Sudeten Germans towards the Czechoslovakian state, reflected in the rapid rise of the German nationalist 'Sudetendeutsche Partei' (SdP [Sudeten Germany party]).[10] In an attempt to restrain the possibility of war, western leaders – without a Czechoslovakian representative – signed with Nazi-Germany the agreement of Munich, which forced the annexation of the Sudetenland to the German 'Reich'; soon afterwards, in March 1939, the Wehrmacht occupied the rest of Czechoslovakia. The Sudeten Germans, from which a vast majority greeted their invading co-nationals, were positively discriminated by the occupation regime in former Czechoslovakia, taking an active role in its institutions.[11]

The fleeing Czechoslovakian leadership set up its exile residence in London. Headed by Dr. Edvard Beneš, it propagated a removal of the German population from Bohemia and Moravia in the case of an allied victory. Preliminarily aimed at the group of Nazi-Collaborators, these plans soon encompassed a full scale

History], Münster 2003, 277–290. (I am deeply thankful for this reference to Prof. Ingeborg Fialová).

8 'One says regarding the first Czechoslovak Republic that it indeed inherited the weaknesses of the old Austrian-Hungarian monarchy, but none of its strengths.' [Translation of the Author, O.W.], see Rudolf Hilf, Das sudetendeutsche Problem in der Zwischenkriegszeit und die Position der Linken. [The Sudeten German Problem in the Interwar Period and the Position of the Left], in: Leopold Grünwald – John Bunzl (Eds.), Sudetendeutsche – Opfer und Täter. Verletzungen des Selbstbestimmungsrechts und ihre Folgen 1918–1982 [Sudeten Germans – Victims and Perpetrators. Injuries to the Right of Self-Determination and their Consequences], Wien 1983, 25–40, here 25.

9 See Franzen, Stamm, 18–21. Over 70% of Czechoslovakian industry was placed in 'German hands'. See Joseph B. Schechtman, Postwar Population Transfers in Europe 1945–1955, Philadelphia 1963, 101. See also Zdeněk Kárník, České země v éře první republiky (1918–1938) [The Bohemian Lands in the Era of the First Republic], díl I. (1918–1929), Praha 2000, 203–207, in: Dieter Gosewinkel – Matěj Spurný, Staatsbürgerschaft und Eigentumsentzug in der Tschechoslowakei nach 1918 und 1945 [Citizenship and Expropriation in Czechoslovakia after 1918 and 1945], Forthcoming, 3.

10 The Sudetendeutsche Partei [SdP], representing the separatist inspirations of the Sudeten Germans, whose leader Konrad Henlein agitated in coordination with the National Socialist Party of Germany, won 70% of the German votes in the Czechoslovakian elections of 1935, and as much as 91% votes in the local elections of 1938. See Hilf, Problem, 34–36. See also Schechtman, Postwar, 53. Compare also Brandes, Weg, 13.

11 Schechtman, Postwar, 53. Compare also Brandes, Weg, 134.

ethnic cleansing[12] of all German speaking individuals.[13] Evoking a Sudeten German collective guilt and betrayal towards the Czechoslovakian state[14], the Czech population started expelling ethnic Germans on the heels of the retreating Wehrmacht. Succeeding this phase of so called 'wild' expulsions [wilde Vertreibungen], in which the Germans suffered between 19,000 – 30,000 civilian casualties[15], the newly installed government in Prague, with the approval of the victories allies given at the Potsdam conference[16], executed an organized removal of nearly all German speaking population from Bohemia, Moravia and Slovakia, effecting more than three million persons. Merely 300,000 ethnic Germans were allowed to stay or were forcefully kept back as essential workers in key industries.[17]

The former German regions, referred to as 'border regions' – the term 'Sudetenland' was prohibited by law[18] – suffered a rapid degeneration following the dramatic population reduction. The massive repatriation and other social engineering efforts of the Czechoslovakian authorities[19] failed to fully re-inhabit these land stretches. Roughly five years after the expulsion, some regions inhabited merely a third of their original population size, resulting in an abandonment of numerous villages and urban districts, as well as key regional industries.[20] Some rem-

---

12 Yfaat Weiss, Ethnic Cleansing, Memory and Property – Europa, Israel/Palestine, 1944–1948, in: Raphael Gross and Yfaat Weiss (Eds.), Jüdische Geschichte als Allgemeine Geschichte [Jewish History as General History], Göttingen 2006.

13 Brandes, Weg. Also see Claudia Kraft, Der Platz der Vertreibung der Deutschen im historischen Gedächtnis Polens und der Tschechoslowakei/Tschechiens [The Place of Expulsions of the Germans in the Historical Memory of Poland and Czechoslovakia/the Czech Republic], in: Christoph Cornelißen (Ed.), Diktatur – Krieg – Vertreibung. Erinnerungskulturen in Tschechien, der Slowakei und Deutschland seit 1945 [Dictatorship – War – Expulsion. Memory Cultures in the Czech Republic, Slovakia and Germany since 1945], Publication of the German-Czech and the German-Slovak historians' commission 2005, Essen 2005, 329–354, here 330.

14 Philipp Ther, Die dunkle Seite der Nationalstaaten. »Ethnische Säuberungen« im modernen Europa [The Dark Side of the Nation State. 'Ethnic cleansing' in Modern Europe], Göttingen 2011, 151. Compare also Gosewinkel – Spurný, Staatsbürgerschaft.

15 This is the recent evaluation of the German-Czech-Slovak historian commission, in: Norman M. Naimark, Fires of Hatred. Ethnic Cleansing in Twentieth-Century Europe, London 2001, 120.

16 Brandes, Weg, 458. Compare also Schechtman, Postwar, 75–80.

17 Leopold Grünwald, Der sudetendeutsche Widerstand gegen Hitler (1938–1945) [The Sudeten German Resistance against Hitler], in: Leopold Grünwald (Ed.), Sudetendeutsche – Opfer und Täter. Verletzungen des Selbstbestimmungsrechts und ihre Folgen 1918–1982 [Sudeten Germans – Victims and Perpetrators. Injuries to the Right of Self-Determination and their Consequences], Wien 1983. Compare also Schechtman, Postwar, 93.

18 *Ibid.*, 67.

19 *Ibid.*, 104–106. Most of the repatriated ethnic Czechs came from the Volga Region, Poland and France, as well as a large number of forced workers returning from Germany. Compare Petr Mikšíček, Die Besiedlung der Grenzregionen [The Settlement of the Border Regions], in: Zmizelé Sudety. Das Verschwundene Sudetenland [The Vanished Sudetenland], Praha 2006, 96.

20 Compared to the 1930 census, the population density in the former German regions decreased by 33.9% by the year 1952. *Ibid.*, 97.

nants of German settlement were removed by the authorities[21]; others 'vanished' in the Bohemian forests. The triumph of nature over the ruins, widely described in German 'Ruin Literature'[22] as a marker of abolishment of traces of human civilization, reached its definite expression in these regions, creating 'Postkulturlandschaften'[23], their barrenness leading one observer to tag them as 'Czech Siberia'.[24] Even after more than half a century of communist rule, Soviet intervention, revolution, and economic growth, the traces of the traumatic depopulation are still omnipresent in the border regions.

The Tour

These landscapes are the scenery, in which the 'Searching for traces – with the bicycles through the Sudetenland' project takes place since 2005, planned and executed by the Czech organization 'Antikomplex', with the cooperation of the 'Junge Aktion der Ackermann Gemeinde' [Young Action of the Ackermann Gemeinde – the youth movement of the Munich based Catholic Sudeten German expellees organization], as well as by the 'Jugend-Kontakt-Organisation' (JUKON [the youth organization of the German minority in the Czech republic]). This project is funded by the Czech-German Future Foundation, the German Ministry of Internal Affairs[25], and a minimal participation fee from the participants.

Every year, a group of around twenty young participants explores one segment of the Czech-Austrian-German border regions. During the tours, resonating Central European recreational hiking traditions reaching back as far as the German youth movement 'Wandervogel', the group members literally search for traces of vanished German villages, farms and grave yards, and try to comprehend the changes that places, which used to be predominantly German and now are populated by others, have gone through. This objective is achieved with the assistance of graphic materials, comparing old photos dating from the time prior to the expulsion of the Sudeten Germans with the present condition, complemented by written and oral testimonies. The group also seeks for 'official' past representations, as in 'Heimatmuseen' [museums of local history] or other types of folklore preservation sites. The on-site explanations during the tour were provided by

21 As late as 1959 the Politburo of the ČSSR ordered the detonation of 35,000 abandoned German buildings. German buildings were also destroyed on festive occasions like 1st of May, 9th of May or the commemoration of the October revolution. *Ibid.*, 98.

22 Compare Winfried Georg Sebald, Luftkrieg und Literatur [Aerial Warfare and Literature], Frankfurt am Main 2001.

23 Mikšíček, Besiedlung, 90.

24 Ther, Nationalstaaten, 193f.

25 The jurisdiction of the German Federal Ministry of Internal Affairs evolving around cultural and educational projects concerning the German Expellees is anchored in the Federal Law of Expellees [Bundesvertriebenengesetz], in: Gesetz über die Angelegenheiten der Vertriebenen und Flüchtlinge [The Law Regarding the Matters of the Expellees and Refugees], http://www.gesetze-im-internet.de/bundesrecht/bvfg/gesamt.pdf, 18 May 2014.

Ondřej Matějka, the head of 'Antikomplex', who sheared the tour guidance with C., a co-worker of 'JUKON'. At the end of every tour day, the participants recapitulated and discussed their impressions and thoughts within the group.

Discussion

The act of re-examining the remnants of the past German-Czech rupture, coupled with a discussion regarding this very act and its meaning in a contemporary binational frame, leads me to labeling the 'Spurensuche'-project as a memory project and its participants as 'memory activists'.[26] This requires a short terminological inquiry. Why tag the 'Spurensuche' as a 'memory project' and not merely a historiographical endeavor? Wherein lays the difference between these two past-oriented realms?

Both history and memory are connected with a notion of the past. Yet unlike the remembered past, hence a past whose existence depends on a remembering human agency, the historical past (in the sense of historiographical past) is an abstraction, a *durée artificielle* lacking any subjective, personal reference, as Maurice Halbwachs, the pioneer of collective memory studies[27], states.[28] According to Halbwachs, historiography, being a critical, empirical discipline, aims at organizing its findings in a homogenized historical realm, removing any subjective layer from its findings.[29] This somewhat rigid concept of historiography was adjusted in recent decades, mainly through the recognition of the historian's subjective stance, manifested in the narrative strategies of his or her writings.[30] At the core of this narrative revolution of historiography stands the linkage between the subjective positioning of the historian in the present and the way she or he approaches the past. And yet this new notion of history did not resolve the principle perplexity between memory and history.

The fruits of historiographical research occupy a prominent role in the construction of memory, than it is historiography, which often supplies collective memory with its building blocks, its 'images' or 'icons', revealing new facts about

26 Yifat Gutman, Looking Backward to the Future. Memory Activism and Oppositional Knowledge-Production in Past-Oriented Political Discourse, Current Sociology, Forthcoming.

27 Maurice Halbwachs, La mémoire collective [Collective Memory], Paris 1950, 75, quoted in Jan Assmann, Das kulturelle Gedächtnis. Schrift, Erinnerung und politische Identität in frühen Hochkulturen [Cultural Memory and Early Civilization. Writing, Remembrance, and Political Imagination], München 1992, 43.

28 As this paper discusses German, Austrian and Czech collective memory forms, and following Halbwachs's notion that every memory is a manifestation of collective memory [see last remark], every reference to 'memory' following should be understood as 'collective memory'.

29 Assmann, Gedächtnis.

30 Hayden White, Metahistory. The Historical Imagination in Nineteenth Century Europe, Baltimore 1973.

constituent moments in the past of nations or other large social groups.[31] A prominent example of this linkage between memory and history is provided by Pierre Nora's *Lieux de Mémoire* [Realms of Memory].[32] Based on his claim, stating that the collective bonds of society are dissolving and with them the social ability of collective remembering, Nora drafts his realms of memory as the last strongholds of (remembered) symbols of collective identity. These sites of memory, which can be of the most diverse nature – Nora counts geographical spaces, famous books, and the French language itself as such sites – are constituted by historical phenomena absorbed with a 'material, functional, symbolic'[33] meaning. They are generators of collective identity embedded in a body of historical facts and patterns, remnants of a collective memory which, according to Nora, is drained of all its symbolic charge by today's historical research (writing at the end of the 20th century).

'A human self is a diachronic identity', states the philosopher Thomas Luckmann[34] acknowledging like Nora the relation of identity with the dialectical tension between past and present, best manifested in the agency of memory. Yet, whereas Nora sees the realms of collective memory lose their symbolic weight under the critical scalpel of historiography, other social scientists tend to subordinate historiography to collective memory. 'Only meaningful history gets to be remembered; only remembered history is meaningful', states Jan Assmann.[35] Memory is sketched here as history, perceived through the prism of meaning. Referring to this subject in his later writings, Assmann claims that memory is knowledge about the past with an identity index.[36] History, even while accepting the subjective influences of the present on the historian, is looking to the past from the present, and as such is committed to the primacy of the past. Memory, being a social construction[37], is the present looking at itself with images, icons, and symbols of the past, and as such is committed to the primacy of the present. The memorized past is therefore a social 'creation', or *Schöpfung*[38], its limits defined more by the dictum of contemporary social arrays than the empiric imperative of scientific historiography.

---

31 Aleida Assmann calls the pool of historical facts from which collective memory is drawing its images 'archive memory', the collective memory itself 'canonic memory'. See Aleida Assmann, Canon and Archive, in: Astrid Erll – Ansgar Nünning (Eds.), Media and Cultural Memory, Berlin 2008, 97–107.

32 Pierre Nora, Between Memory and History. Les Lieux de Mémoire [Realms of Memory], in: Representations 26, Special Issue: Memory and Counter-Memory, Berkeley/Los Angeles 1989 7–24.

33 *Ibid.*, 19.

34 Assmann, Canon, 109.

35 Assmann, Gedächtnis, 52.

36 Jan Assmann, Collective Memory and Cultural Identity, in: New German Critique 65, Durham, NC 1995, 125–133.

37 *Ibid.*

38 Assmann, Gedächtnis, 48.

In a recent case study underlining this methodological approach towards memory studies, Harald Welzer examined the *Tradierung*, the tradition of passing on German family memories regarding the Second World War.[39] Welzer's observations showed beyond any doubt that the majority of Germans is well aware of the official historical description of the war, which includes wide scale atrocities committed by members of the Wehrmacht and the SS, culminating in the mass murder of European Jewry. Yet, when confronted with war recollections implying complacency of members of the older generation in these atrocities, the mechanism of *Tradierung* inside the family revises the memory – in the form of a story which 'runs through the family' – over and over, until it is washed clean of any indicting elements; the necessity to preserve one's integrity, defined by contemporary social conventions, overcomes historical accuracy, turning war criminals to hidden resistors to Nazi rule. Welzer draws a picture of the collective memory as a house, its floor made of the loyalty of the family members preventing them from accepting horrific truths about their relatives, its walls representing the restrictions and requirements posed by dominant social conventions.[40] These conventions assume a higher hierarchic stance over historical facts in the process of memory construction, leading Welzer to claim that his study – or for that matter any 'collective memory study' – is not 'about the past, but about the present'.[41]

The tagging of the 'Spurensuche'-project as a memory project arises therefore from its contemporary nature, focusing its interest on the present manifestations of the expulsion of the Sudeten Germans from Czechoslovakia. Driven by the above specified understanding of memory as an identity constructing, contemporary social phenomenon, 'memory activists' seek to challenge the hegemonic memory frames through social action in order to influence the dominant social identity. Following the definition of Yifat Gutman, memory activism is a 'transnational strategy of peace activism in which fragments of a contested past gain visibility through on-site commemoration with the aim of creating a more tolerant and peaceful society in the future'.[42] Based on the understanding of the key role of memory as a binding agency between the past and the collective (mostly national) identity, memory activists disseminate 'oppositional knowledge', *i.e.* non-consensual interpretations of the past, wishing to 'shift the normative center of society'.[43]

39 Harald Welzer – Sabine Moller – Karoline Tschuggnall (Eds.), Opa war kein Nazi. Nationalsozialismus und Holocaust im Familiengedächtnis [Grandfather Was Not a Nazi. National Socialism and Holocaust in Family Memories], Frankfurt am Main 2002.

40 *Ibid.*, 200.

41 *Ibid.*, 12.

42 Gutman, Future, 4.

43 Patrick G. Coy – Lynne M. Woehrle – Gregory M. Maney, Typology of Oppositional Knowledge. Democracy and the U.S. Peace Movement, in: Sociological Research Online 13/4/3, Guildford 2008, http://www.socresonline.org.uk/13/4/3.html, 18 May 2014.

The Participating Organizations

The group climbed the bell tower of the Lobendava Church, from which one could get a fair view of the village below. The young Czech church care-taker, working for the Catholic Church in the Czech Republic, explained that the bells, like the rest of the church, are not used by the locals. 'Most of these locals are either Roma, pushed out of the central parts of the Czech Republic, or Vietnamese, who control the cross border trade with the Germans around here. Both groups have no affinity to the church. The few Czech locals either go to their own church – or to no church at all.'

Some of the participants waited in the church's garden for the rest of the group to finish the tour, when suddenly the bells began ringing. Starting off with some hesitation, soon the sound gained projection and volume and resonated all across the small village. A few moments later a group member from the city of České Budějovice (Budweis), appeared in the church's door with enthusiastic face, clearly being the one ringing the bells in the tower. When asked why she chose to do so she replayed – 'Ich wollte zeigen – wir sind da.' – ['I wanted to show – we are here.']

This short phrase encloses many of the layers and indicators, contradictions, and hidden meanings typical for this unique project; by deconstructing it and facilitating its different parts, this phrase may be used as an index for the second part of this paper, analyzing the 'Spurensuche'-project. 'I wanted to show – we are here': Who are 'we', what is the nature, the motivation and importance in 'showing' that these 'we' are 'here' – and what is the nature of the place, of the so called 'Sudetenland'?

'Antikomplex'

The 'Spurensuche'-project is open to anyone who wishes to participate in it; nevertheless, the lion part of the participants is affiliated with either the Czech 'Antikomplex' or the German 'Junge Aktion der Ackermann Gemeinde'.

'"Antikomplex" is a citizens' association, involved in the field of the Czech reflection of the German history in Bohemia, Moravia and Silesia.'[44] This quote, taken from the Internet overture of this 1998 founded organization, cites remarkably both the past oriented 'German history' as well as the contemporary 'Czech reflection'. Ondřej Matějka, one of the organization's founding members, characterizes 'Antikomplex' as a 'memory and education' organization, emphasizing its self-assigned active role in Czech society.[45] The 'memory' segment of this claim is best exemplified in one of the main projects of this organization, the exhibition

44 Antikomplex Opening Site, http://www.antikomplex.cz/de, 18 May 2014.

45 All quotes of Ondřej Matejka, unless stated otherwise, are taken from a series of interviews conducted with him during the 'Spurensuche'-tour in the summer of 2012.

'Das verschwundene Sudetenland' ['The vanished Sudetenland'].[46] This touring exhibition, accompanied by a book carrying the same title[47], comprises mainly graphical exhibits supplemented by textual references, documenting the developments in the Czech-Austrian-German border regions since the expulsions of the Sudeten Germans. By using similar technics as in the 'Spurensuche'-tour, the initiators of the exhibition present pictures of areas previously inhabited by Germans, both from the time prior to the expulsions and from recent years. The visualization of the massive changes these regions have went through poses a diachronic challenge to the dominant Czech discourse regarding the Sudetenland and its former German inhabitants.

'We had and we have a German Complex', stated once the Czech historian Vitězslav Gardavský.[48] Indeed, starting from the era of German dominated imperial frame of the Habsburg Monarchy, through the dialectic development of the language-based nationalism of German and Czech speaking populations in Bohemia, Moravia, and Silesia and the traumatic events of the 1930s and 1940s, the Czech modern national identity was constantly formed *vis-à-vis* German presence.[49] This complex is mirrored in the ambivalent attitude towards the Sudeten Germans and their expulsion. The bare terminology surrounding the common Czech-German history is disputed up until these days – resonating alternative historical narratives by providing a vast range of terms such as 'German speaking population', 'Sudeten Germans', or even 'Our Germans'[50], as well as several descriptions of the expulsions such as 'deportation', 'punishment', 'displacement', 'emigration', or 'population removal'.[51]

The official Czech historiography after 1945 attempted to overcome this ambivalence by reducing the multinational Bohemian history to a narrow description of a mere ethnic-national conflict, which could only be solved through the forced removal of Germans following their claimed collective betrayal of the Czechoslovakian state.[52] Yet, this teleological narrative[53], emphasizing only the national

---

46 The members of Antikomplex are well aware of the problematic dimensions of the term 'Sudetenland', using it consciously as an irritation, as previously described.

47 Zmizelé Sudety. Das Verschwundene Sudetenland, Praha 2006.

48 Gardavský, Vitězslav, Fenomén Německo. Studie ke konkrétní dialektice univerzalismu a partikularismu [The Phenomenon Germany. Study of the Concrete Dialectic of the Universal and the Particular], Praha 1967, 7. Quoted in Ferdinand Seibt, Deutsche, Tschechen, Sudetendeutsche. Analysen und Stellungnahmen zu Geschichte und Gegenwart aus fünf Jahrzenten [Germans, Czechs, Sudeten Germans. Analysis and Commentary Regarding the History and Presence from Five Decades], München 2002.

49 Kraft, Vertreibung, 342.

50 This surprising phrase can be found in several texts from the 1920s and 1930s. Ondřej Matejka from Antikomplex, consciously resonating this past discourse, makes frequent use of this term.

51 Thomáš Feřtek, Die Fotografien sind das schmerzliche Gedächtnis des Ortes [The Photos Are the Painful Memory of the Place], in: Zmizelé Sudety. Das Verschwundene Sudetenland, Praha 2006, 68.

52 Brandes, Weg, 459.

53 Kraft, Vertreibung, 336.

prism of the expulsions, oversees a further crucial aspect of the mass deportations. The newly formed Czechoslovakian state did not only lay on the ethnic-national demarcation line in the second half of the 1940s, but also represented the borderline between liberal democracies and socialist egalitarian states, thus embodying the two main hermeneutical axis of European history in the 20th century.[54] And yet, the social aspect of the deprivation of the Germans citizens' rights (expropriation, annulling of citizenship, and deportations) based on collective criteria and its ramifications on the Czechoslovakian society find little if any echo in the Czech public discourse of the time[55], although none of the involved Czech statesman tried to disclaim their validity.[56] Resulting from this propagated ignorance, the expulsions of Sudeten Germans was treated in the dominant Czechoslovakian discourse as a closed historical chapter, which required no further elaborations.

Early articulations of doubt regarding this dominant national narrative, which eventually culminated in the work of 'Antikomplex', circulated through the *samizdat* [underground publications] dating back to the late 1970s. First articulated 1978 by the Slovak historian Ján Mlynárik under the pseudonym 'Danubius'[57], dissident Czechoslovakian historians argued that the expulsions of the Sudeten Germans, based on collective criteria, undermined the democratic foundations of Czechoslovakia. The denial of the protection of law from collectively defined social groups did not make halt with the Germans; other groups were soon to follow. The massive expropriations of the Germans were perceived as harbingers of the communist collective doctrine's implementation after the takeover of the communist party in 1948.[58] Other ramifications of the expulsions, also expressed among others by the 1989 elected Czechoslovak president Vaclav Havel, were the loss of the bridging function the Germans had between Czechoslovakia and Western Europe, which lead to an 'Eastening' of the state[59], referring to the unpopular ties to the soviet influenced eastern bloc.

The increasing pursuit of these themes is one of the indicators of the re-birth of a post-communist Czech civic society[60]; it is also the framework in which the

54 Dan Diner, Das Jahrhundert verstehen [Understanding the Century], Frankfurt am Main 2001.

55 Kraft, Vertreibung, 330. Recent studies try to offer new concepts regarding the conjunction between the ethnical racism intrinsic to the modern national state and the means through which the state executes its authority – among other things though the establishment of a homogenized national narrative, excluding and including on the base of racist criteria. See Naimerk, Fires; Ther, Nationalstaaten.

56 Beneš was quoted saying that 'One has to combine the national revolution with the social one', in Brandes, Weg, 222.

57 Danubius (Ján Mlynárik), Tézy o vysídlení československych Nemcov [Theses regarding the deportation of the Czechoslovak Germans 1945–1947], in: Leopold Grünwald (Ed.), Wir haben uns selbst aus Europa vertrieben [We Expelled Ourselves from Europe], München 1985.

58 Kraft, Vertreibung, 339. See also Schechtman, Postwar, 89f.

59 *Ibid.*, 349.

60 Kraft, Vertreibung, 330.

work of 'Antikomplex' is to be located, an organization which wishes to initiate both a re-thinking process of the past role of the German-Czech coexistence for the Czech society, as well as a critical reflection of the established Czech discourse concerning the expulsion of the Sudeten Germans and its consequences, not so much for the Germans, but rather for the Czechs and Slovaks. In their pursuit for reshaping the dominant Czech discourse, the members of 'Antikomplex' make conscious use of the dialectical relations between past and present. The visualization of the current precarious state of the Sudetenland is instrumentalized in order to tackle questions regarding the German-Czech past, which are used in order to articulate questions regarding today's Czech society (the present looking at itself through the past). These questions are then embedded in pedagogical programs for the Czech education system, which are disseminated through nationwide teachers' seminars. The members of 'Antikomplex' thus embody both the historian's role according to Nora – no longer an 'absence obsessed with objectivity'[61], but interpreter of the present, applying moral judgment[62] while serving as a bridge between past and present, as well as the memory activist role according to Gutman, actively influencing the Czech discourse through social interaction. The authors of the 'Das verschwundene Sudetenland' write:

> 'How can all these disturbing findings concerning the border region be transformed, so that something new will arise, so that "Sudetenland" will not be only an irritation, but [...] will become a symbol of a fresh beginning in a place, which for us means lost and decay [...].'[63]

The target audience of 'Antikomplex' is therefore primarily the Czech society; although it is engaged in several cross-border projects, it remains first and foremost an actor in the internal Czech discourse.

Junge Aktion der Ackermann Gemeinde

Ondřej Matějka describes the core motivation of 'Antikomplex' with the following words: 'Freedom through re-processing the past. Like the Germans.' There are several ways to encode this somewhat ironic phrase; the dissonance between the alleged, similar re-processing of the past and its massive, non-spoken periodization gap is one of them. Whereas the meaning-charged term of German 'Vergangenheitsaufarbeitung' ['Re-processing the past'][64] seeks to describe a process that began soon after the war in the Western occupied zones, constituting the later

61 Nora, Memory, 18.

62 Kraft, Vertreibung, 342.

63 Vorwort: Über das Projekt 'Das Verschwundene Sudetenland' [Preface: Over the Project 'The Vanished Sudetenland'], in: Zmizelé Sudety. Das Verschwundene Sudetenland, Praha 2006, 62. [translated by the author, O.W.]

64 And not the criticized term 'Vergangenheitsbewältigung' – [overcoming the past].

Federal Republic of Germany, making use of a more or less liberal discourse protected by free speech laws, the Czech discourse, as shown here, gained the same preconditions around the year 1989, *i.e.* more than four decades later. The discursive frame for the 'Junge Aktion der Ackermann Gemeinde', with which the majority of the German speaking 'Spurensuche'-participants are affiliated with, originates from this aforementioned German 'Vergangenheitsaufarbeitung', whose main subject is guilt, its ramifications, denials, acceptance, delegations, and manifestations. Generally subdivided in generational phases, it is usually categorized using hermeneutical axes stretching between perpetration and victimhood, as well as between generalization and differentiation.[65]

The 'Ackermann Gemeinde', founded 1946 (the 'Junge Aktion', its youth movement, was founded 1950), aligned at its first years with the general notion of an integral, generalized victimhood of the German nation[66], placing the soldiers returning from the war or from captivity, the victims of the bombings of German cities, those expelled from East and Central Europe, and to some extent the victims of racial or political prosecutions, in a joint pool of victims, canceling any differentiation of the circumstances of their suffering. For the vast majority of Germans and Austrians after the war, the guilt for the mass suffering inflicted through Germany inhered on the 'demon(s) from Berlin', a small group of high ranking Nazis, identified and punished in the Nuremberg processes[67], coloring the Germans as a politically 'unmündig' [immature, non-liable] collective.

Nevertheless, the Catholic 'Ackermann Gemeinde', founded by former activists of German Catholic organizations in pre-war Czechoslovakia[68], soon developed its own version concerning the war guilt, which serves up to these days as its fundamental paradigm.[69] Like other religious institutions in post-war Germany, it wished to tell the war story along Christian *topoi*. The perceived German political 'Unmündigkeit' [non-liability], relativizing any responsibility for the horrors of the war, was transformed to a human subordination at the face of the divine stance, rejecting human capability of understanding divine justice, annulling the distinction between different levels of responsibility or between cause and consequence in the war context; the notion of guilt was thus transformed to a religious

65 Karl Jaspers, Die Schuldfrage [The Question of Guilt], Zürich 1946. The distinctly different Austrian mnemonic process found, as a result of the small number of Austrian participants, factually no resonance during the tour; its description would therefore exceed the boundaries of this paper, both thematically and physically.

66 Constantin Goschler, 'Versöhnung' und 'Viktimisierung'. Die Vertriebenen und der deutsche Opferdiskurs ['Reconciliation' and 'Victimization'. The Expellees and the German Victim's Discourse], in: Zeitschrift für Geschichtswissenschaft 10, Berlin 2005, 873–884.

67 Bernhard Giesen, The Trauma of Perpetrators. The Holocaust as the Traumatic Reference of German National Identity, in: Jeffrey C. Alexander (Ed.), Cultural Trauma and Collective Identity, Berkeley/Los Angeles 2004, 112–154.

68 Integration und Dialog – Sechs Jahrzehnte Friedensarbeit [Integration and Dialog – Six Decades of Working for Peace], Schriftenreihe der Ackermann-Gemeinde 38, München 2007.

69 Weg und Ziel [Path and Goal], Schriftenreihe der Ackermann-Gemeinde 24, München 2004.

concept of sin. Subsequently, the war was no longer perceived as a German crime against others, which was than avenged, among other forms, through the expulsions of the Sudeten Germans; it became rather a human crime against god, placing the burden of guilt on modernity and materialism, and on leaving the Christian righteous path. These evils are perceived as common to all conflicting parties of the war, and were atoned through the *via dolorosa* of the Sudeten Germans, repenting for Europe's sins.[70] The suppressed argument in the transformation of 'guilt' to an all human 'sin', *i.e.* the relativization of German war guilt, met a contemporary German need, and as such harvested criticism of some contemporary observers.[71]

Three imperatives arise from this perception. At first, the notion of a 'human sin' implies a human collective, free of any national or ethnic differentiations, resulting in the supranational, European language of the 'Ackermann Gemeinde'.[72] The Catholic paradigm also induces the imperative to forgive and to ask for forgiveness, as a part of the process of repentance.[73] This conciliatory imperative increasingly gained importance in the texts of this organization, alongside an outspoken negation of vengeance of any kind – either against the Germans or against the expelling Czechs.[74] The third imperative of the 'Ackermann Gemeinde', resulting from the first two, lays in its fundamental future orientation. The belief in a divine plan behind the war relativized human responsibility to its proceedings and made any attempt to understand its causal background redundant. Thus, the 'Ackermann Gemeinde' propagated a mutual German-Czech forgiveness and the foundation of a unified Europe, as well as the wish to 'draw a line under the past'.[75]

These three imperatives delineate the nature of the 'Ackermann Gemeinde' and its youth movement, the 'Junge Aktion', until these days. Embedded in the 'Aktion West-Ost' of the Association of the German Catholic Youth (BDKJ [Bund

70 Gilad Margalit outlines in his research of German war memorials the different forms with which the German suffering was projected on Christian symbols of suffer. See Gilad Margalit, The German Conscience of Guilt and its Repercussions after 1945, in: Yfaat Weiss – Gilad Margalit (Eds.), Memory and Amnesia. The Holocaust in Germany, Tel Aviv 2005.

71 'Yet the religious acknowledgment of the original sin may not become a veil for a false German collective guilt acknowledgment, exchanging dishonestly one with the other.' See Jaspers, Schuldfrage, 76.

72 Compare: Weg und Ziel.

73 The most prominent example appears in the Lord's Prayer: '[…] and forgive us our sins, as we also have forgiven our debtors', Matthew 6:9–13.

74 Pater Paulus Sladek OSA, 'Predigt vom 5 August1955' [preach from 5 August 1955], in: Zukunft trotz Vergangenheit [Future Despite the Past], Schriftenreihe der Ackermann Gemeinde, München 2005.

75 This charged term of a 'Schlussstrich' was widely used by the 'Ackermann Gemeinde'. One of its founders, Hans Schütz, claimed: 'Both nations (Germans and Czechs) must draw a line under the past. Both have made mistakes.' See Not signed, 'Für ein freies und christliches Europa.' [For a Free and Christian Europe], *Main Post*, Frankfurt am Main 1951 July 30th, 118, as well as Not signed, 'Both Sides Have to Finally Draw a Line Under the Past.', *Limburger Neue Presse*, Limburg 1951 May 2nd.

der Deutschen Katholischen Jugend]), the 'Junge Aktion' actively promotes encounters with Czech and Slovak youth, as well as the learning of east European languages, history and culture. Its four basic principles – 'Christian life', 'Human rights', 'Encounter with the middle and east European neighbors', and 'Europe of the people'[76] – disclose both the commitment of the 'Junge Aktion' to the European-Christian collective as well as its avoidance of a clear affiliation with Germany (the word 'German' rarely appears in the organizations' texts).

'We' – The Group

Let us return to the scene in front of the church in Lobendava (Lobendau) and to the phrase 'I wanted to show – we are here', as well as to the questions' index arising from it. What group did the young Czech participant in the 2012 'Spurensuche'-project refer to by saying 'we are here'? Does this 'we' encompass both 'Antikomplex' and the 'Junge Aktion', *i.e.* the Czech, German and Austrian participants of the 'Spurensuche'-project?

Many aspects of this project might suggest the existence of a coherent 'Spurensuche'-group. For one, aiming at avoiding any dominance of one nationality and alienation of the respective other, the bi-national, cooperative nature of the project was maintained at all levels – both at the preliminary, preparatory phase, as well as throughout the tour, which was guided by a German-Czech co-team. Furthermore, both 'Antikomplex' and the 'Junge Aktion' commonly comply with Gutman's definition of memory activists, acting as a social *avant-garde* trying to reshape the national discourse inside their respective societies regarding the German-Czech past, present and future. The latter similarity is underlined through the non-consensual nature of the organizations' actions; the notion of inviting Germans and exploring the Czech border regions with them, thus assuming an active German role in the Czech national memory is remote of being widely accepted in Czech society. On the other hand, the notion of cooperating with Czech organizations and relying on their expertise regarding the Sudetenland stands in clear contrast to the strictly nostalgic tours executed for instance by the 'Sudetendeutsche Landsmannschaft' (SL ['Sudeten German Landsmannschaft']) – the largest organization of Sudeten German expellees – which are organized by Germans and for Germans alone.

However, does the simultaneity of action imply a consistency of goals – can one presume that the 'Searching for traces' group is trying to create a common memory or narrative of the past? Does the fact that both organizations are characterized as memory activists, cooperating in the same memory project, mean that they act for the same memory frame – that they commonly re-member?[77]

76 Leitsätze der Jungen Aktion [Principles of the Young Action], See Weg und Ziel.

77 Jefferey Olick, Collective Memory. The Two Cultures, in: Sociological Theory 17/3, Washington 1999, 333–348, here 342.

Memory activism complies, based on the afore-mentioned definitions of memory activists, with two main context-frames – social and chronological. Can one, following the Welzerian metaphor of the 'collective memory house' as representing these context-frames, then speak of a joint memory house of the members of the 'Searching for traces project'?

The question regarding the social context of the 'Junge Aktion' is rather complex, since there is only partial correlation between its perceived European aspiration and its immediate German discursive surroundings. Inspired by the renewed legitimation given to German victimhood claims, marking a unique German notion of the prevailing human rights discourse of the 1990s[78], most German expellees' organizations seek to reanimate past discussions regarding the expulsions. The two most prominent examples of this phenomenon are the 'Preußische Treuhand' ['Prussian Trustee'] and the 'Bund der Vertriebenen' (BdV ['Alliance of the Expelled']), latter seeking for recognition of diverse cultural and national deprived rights of the expelled Germans from Central and Eastern Europe, the former seeking to readdress questions of property and restitution.[79] For these and similar organizations, the definition as a Sudeten German derives from the catastrophe of the expulsions, fixing all members of this group in a permanent antagonistic position towards the Czech nation. The 'Ackermann Gemeinde' and its 'Junge Aktion' wish to break this Gordian knot, both by rejecting any national based differentiation between perpetrators and victims and by propagating a Christian-European discourse, which assembles both Germans and Czechs in a homogenous pool. Their strived context is therefore an inclusive one, overlooking any German affiliation, as seen in the following statement of a senior 'Junge Aktion' activist: 'The admission of the Czech Republic into the European Union is a dream coming true for the "Junge Aktion".'[80]

The group traveled through several kilometers of forests and soft hills. Every now and then Ondřej Matějka pointed at the traces of a crossroad, stating that it led to German villages which no longer exist. 'All this areal was used as a soviet military practicing ground. The Russian tanks used the German ruins for target practice.' We arrived in a small town, its streets built as a patchwork of old, crumbling German houses and low standard housing, which are – as Matějka explained – products of communist architecture. 'The misfortune of the city [...] the fact it looks so miserable is not only because of the population exchanges after the Second World War,' explained Matějka, 'but also because here was a center of the soviet army stationed at this area after 1968.'

78 See Goschler, Versöhnung; also see Elazar Barkan, The Guilt of Nations. Restitution and Negotiating Historical Injustices, New York 2000.

79 Goschler, Versöhnung.

80 Junge Aktion, Munich 2003.

The core of 'Antikomplex's' non-consensual message consists of a critical stance towards the expulsions of Sudeten Germans, naturally without challenging the notion regarding the negative role played by the latters before and during the Second World War. For the organizations' activists, the expulsions mark a deep injury of the Czech moral integrity and serve as the harbinger of the traumatic decades of communist rule, drawing a direct line from the expulsions to the Prague spring and its traumatic end. The challenge 'Antikomplex' poses for the Czech society is excruciating, establishing a causal link between the deeds of Czechoslovakian society and its fate under Soviet forced communist oppression, a link which, according to 'Antikomplex', is repressed and tabooed. The materialization of this alleged taboo is the desolate condition of most of the border regions, the result of decades of negligence, which serve as home to the poorest, most rejected parts of Czech society – immigrants, Roma and Sinti, as well as drug dealers and a thriving sex industry:

> 'The tragedy of Czech society is that its border zones, its periphery [...] became its nightmare, zones of decay, of amnesia and of repressed feelings of guilt.'[81]

The periodization frame with which 'Antikomplex' corresponds discloses its relevant social context. By referring to 1968 – the year of the Prague spring – it hooks up with the dominant, collective Czech periodization, creating a linkage between ever present discursive themes and its own challenging messages. 'Antikomplex' draws two strings from the well-known symbol '1968' – one to the past, to 1945–1946, establishing a causal linkage to the expulsions, and one to 1989 and further, pointing at the current situation of the Sudetenland as the result and the signifier of the first two chronological anchors.

The difference in the social contexts of 'Antikomplex' and the 'Junge Aktion' – the former acting within the boundaries of Czech society, the latter striving a supranational, European frame – is thus enhanced through the different periodization frames both organizations relate to. As such, the universal discursive frame regarding the Second World War, in which the 'Spurensuche'-project takes place, applies for both organizations; its boundaries are set both by the global human rights discourse, as well as through the comprehension of the current period in time regarding the war as the threshold between memory and history.[82] This last notion, based on the disappearing of the last eyewitnesses of the war, intensifies the urgency around war memory disputes.

Within this common frame, the members of the 'Junge Aktion' consider the participants of the 'Spurensuche'-project as a homogenous reconciliatory group,

---

81 Ivo T Budil, Das Sudetenland als gesellschaftliche Herausforderung [The Sudetenland As a Social Challenge], in: Zmizelé Sudety. Das Verschwundene Sudetenland, Praha 2006, 74.

82 Norbert Frei, 1945 und Wir. Das Dritte Reich im Bewusstsein der Deutschen, München 2005. Jan Assmann named this phenomenon as the 'floating gap', separating the communicative, experienced memory, from the cultural memory. See Assmann, Gedächtnis, 48f.

serving as a model for a future oriented Czech-Austrian-German coexistence, an orientation which is inherent to the term 'reconciliation', presuming a pragmatic, hierarchic superiority of such future co-existence over disputing upon a 'true' version of the past.[83] *Vis-á-vis* this approach stand the members of 'Antikomplex'. While condemning the expulsions of the Sudeten Germans, they turn their gaze to this past rupture and acknowledge its consequences, while trying to disseminate their perception within Czech society. Although both organizations act synchronically, they do so in two distinct different social and periodization-related contexts[84]; the 'Spurensuche'-project has, in fact, no present tense – it has a Czech past and a (German) European future. Considering these distinct different social and chronological contexts, the 'we' in the phrase of the young Czech lady in front of the church does not necessarily include the Austrian and German participants; there are rather two perceptions of 'we' in this project. The walls of the Welzerian common memory house thus crumble and fall.

'To Show' – The Tour

The afore-mentioned notion regarding the expulsions as undermining the democratic foundations of Czechoslovakia, leveling the way to the 1948 communist seizing of power and the suspension of democratic principles and of liberal human rights, serves as the background for 'Antikomplex's' condemnation of the expulsions of Sudeten Germans. While establishing the causality between the expulsions and communist rule, 'Antikomplex' wishes to mark the forced removal of Sudeten Germans as a traumatic event, as a breach of the Czechoslovak moral integrity, casting a long shadow up until today. Corresponding with a growing tendency in social sciences applying the terminology of personal, psychological trauma on collective, social groups[85], these Czech memory activists refer to the expulsions as traumatic both to society and to the landscape. In the publications of 'Antikomplex' the Sudetenland is explicitly referred to as an invitation to mourn:

> 'The landscape of the Sudetenland, empty from human presence, with its loneliness and traces of that which disappeared invites up to our days to do so [to mourn].'[86]

This leads us to the question regarding the possible role the Czech-Austrian-German 'searching for traces' project takes in this frame of mourning, in an at-

83 Gutman, Future.

84 This notion leads Claudia Kraft to the conclusion, that a Czech-German 'Memory community' ['Gedächtnisgemeinschaft'] cannot exist. See: Kraft, Vertreibung, 347.

85 Jeffrey C. Alexander (Ed.), Cultural Trauma and Collective Identity, Berkeley/Los Angeles 2004.

86 Carsten Lenk, Verschwundenes Sudetenland – Vergessene Trauer [Vanished Sudetenland – Forgotten Mourning], in: Zmizelé Sudety. Das Verschwundene Sudetenland, Praha 2006, 76–78.

tempted healing of the proclaimed Czech Trauma. The joint act of touring the Sudetenland might suggest an interweaving of the German and Czech discourses, possibly aiming at a new, synthetic act of 'co-memoration'. The reciprocal attendance of Czechs and Germans in the respective other discourse – the deliberate act of making the respectively other attend one's own discourse – is one of the intrinsic features of the 'Spurensuche'-project, distinguishing it from the accustomed, exclusive national monolog typical for Czech and German approaches to the Sudetenland and its history.[87] Returning to the key phrase of this paper, 'I wanted to show – we are here', the question arises – what is the nature of the act of 'showing', of the tour itself?

Resembling cases of memory projects, which encounter past population removals through contemporary bi-national action, convey some relevant insights regarding the nature of the 'Spurensuche'-tour. The aforementioned work of Yifat Gutman approaches one such example, examining the activities of Israeli-Palestinian groups attending the memory of the expulsions of the latters from Israel during the 1948 war. Conducting her research within the same field, Ronit Lentin offers further analytic tools regarding what she calls a 'commemoration of a contested past'.[88] These tools should, however, be applied with awareness to the paradigmatic difference between the post-conflict German-Czech frame, strengthened by the vivid vision of a Czech-German future posed by the European Union, and the ongoing Middle Eastern conflict-plagued environment.

Lentin sketches the outlines of a commemoration theory in her work (written in her texts as 'co-memoration'), trying to uncover the different strategies and motivations standing at the base of bi-national commemoration of violent population removals, pointing towards the intrinsic imbalance between partners of such memory projects, one representing the former perpetrator, the respective other the former victim. Although initiators of such projects always conceive themselves as equality motivated peace activists[89], this dichotomist division remains an insurmountable signifier in every stage of the alleged common commemoration.

> *After visiting another former German town which today offers a rather decayed visage, Ondřej Matějka stated: 'So tragic, so ironic, well, the Czechs actually won, but what did we get from this, well, Pyrrhic victory, the pretty homogeneity which costs us so much.'*

Using Lentins words, the catastrophe of victims of expulsions – in our case, the Sudeten Germans – comprised of violent forced removal from vast land stretches, is transformed into a trauma of the expulsions' perpetrators – the Czechs. With-

87 Kraft, Vertreibung, 344.

88 Lentin, Co-Memory.

89 Lentin, Co-Memory, 137. Also see: Yifat Gutman, Consensual Forms, Contested Memories. Memory Activism and the Reuse of National Commemorative Practices in Israel, 2001–2010. Forthcoming, 4.

out questioning the historical burden which is laden upon the Sudeten Germans, who actively, overwhelmingly supported the national socialist aggression policy, the expulsion of over 3 million ethnic Germans from Czechoslovakia in perceived by all the members of the 'Spurensuche'-project as a traumatic rupture. And yet, in the organizations' publications, 'Antikomplex' does not emphasize this traumatic aspect, but rather the Czech melancholy (using Lentins words), deriving both from the betrayal of liberal democratic principles after the war and its grave consequences. This melancholy is evoked through a notion of absence, of the 'vanished Sudetenland'. Clearly, a place cannot disappear – in this phrase the term 'Sudetenland' is transformed from a geographical term to a signifier of a social-chronological phenomenon.[90] The spatial memory[91] of the Sudetenland is perceived and presented as a memory of an absence – 'roads which suddenly end, apple trees in the midst of forest, a pile of stones which makes little sense'[92] – turning it not to a *Lieu de Mémoire*, but much more to a *Lieu d' Oubli*, a realm of oblivion, from which all memory is drained.

> *After dinner, the group set at the hostel, discussing the impressions of the passing day. M., a Czech participant, reflected upon some of the settlements we saw on the way: 'I forgot [during the tour] sometimes that we are in the Czech Republic, it looks here so different than where I live [...] the Germans [participants] are much more connected to the land here [...] where I come from it is very rich, no ruins, few unemployed people, not like here, here there are many problems, unemployment, drugs, prostitution. Now I know what faces our republic has.'*

Yet, the drained memory of the *Kulturlandschaft*[93] of the Sudetenland did not disappear, according to 'Antikomplex'; rather, it still dwells in the culture of those who were forced to leave it – the Sudeten Germans and their descendants. These Germans serve in conjunction with the Sudetenland as living *Lieu de Mémoire*, so to speak, islands of a vivid memory of German life in the Czech border regions, holding the key to these locked landscapes.[94] It is through this prism that the Czech perception of the joined commemoration act should be deciphered. Lentin writes explicitly, that the descendants of the expellers need the descendants of the

90 I owe this insight to Kateřina Kovačková from the University of Munich.

91 Lentin, Co-Memory, 21.

92 Ondřej Matejka refers to the 'Invisible German places is the middle of our Czech villages and cities'. See Preface, Zmizelé Sudety. Das Verschwundene Sudetenland, Praha 2006, 63.

93 Cultivated landscape, cultural landscape – this term contains all layers comprising a stretch of land, combining the geographical, the cultural and the social features of a place.

94 'If we want to discover the richness hidden in the landscape of the border regions, we have to start communicating with its old inhabitants.' Ondřej Matejka, Das Sudetenland – was wir verloren haben und was wir gewinnen können [The Sudetenland – What We Have Lost and We Can Gain], in: Zmizelé Sudety. Das Verschwundene Sudetenland, Praha 2006, 92.

expellees, since the latters 'possess the memory they [the descendants of the expellers] are trying to promote'.[95]

By inviting the members of the 'Junge Aktion', many of them descendants of Sudeten Germans themselves, to jointly tour the Sudetenland and commemorate its past, 'Antikomplex' attempts to perform a symbolic act of reintroducing the German memory to the landscape, of retrieving German presence to the border regions. This act, much like the comparison of old photos with the current state of the landscape, poses a diachronic challenge, an act of amendment, offering a symbolic, yet hypothetical alternative historical development to the one which actually occurred. This aspect is enhanced though the sole usage of the German language as a means of communication, although some of the German speaking participants possess Czech language skills. This gesture of retrieving the German language to the landscape has another aspect, however; the spoken language of the border regions these days is Czech, and so, acting as translators or even interpreters, the members of 'Antikomplex' – in an intended friendly gesture – encapsulated these participants, placing the Czech translators as intimidators between the symbolically revived German past and the existing Czech present.

For the German participants, the acceptance of the assigned role or narrow definition solely as representatives of the expulsion's victims in the frame of the act of 'co-memoration' is, to say the least, problematic. Their commitment to the Catholic paradigm of the 'Ackermann Gemeinde', regarding the guilt of all nations resulting from the war as a unified, *i.e.* undifferentiated human sin, does not imply a 'historic blindness'. The members of the 'Junge Aktion' are aware of the events of the Second World War, as well as to the chronological time border separating German perpetration from Sudeten German victimhood – that is, in a rough generalization, the year 1945. This notion offers yet another motivation for the members of the 'Junge Aktion' to defy the dichotomy offered by Lentin, intrinsic to bi-national commemoration projects, distinguishing between former perpetrators and former victims. Therefore, the tour has two non-corresponsive meanings: For the 'Junge Aktion' it is perceived as a part of a unifying agenda, which includes the inspiration to make 'Europe tangible'.[96] The Czech members, on the other hand, appropriate and instrumentalize[97] through the joint commemoration the German presence, language, and memory, which serve as a legitimizing stance in the process of establishing a link to the decayed border regions. The symbolic retrieval of the Germans, aimed at healing the visible rupture in the Sudetenland, is perceived as a step towards overcoming the Czech melancholia, originating in the German expulsion trauma.

95 Lentin, Co-Memory, 134.

96 'With our work we set the fundament [for a unified Europa] and make Europa for anyone tangible.' Weg und Ziel, 12.

97 Lentin, Co-Memory, 144–146.

'Here' – The Place – And Conclusion

In an interview given to a Prague radio station, Ondřej Matějka stated to following:

> 'Our goal is to discover and experience the traces of the German past in the Sudetenland. This means: vanished settlements, remnants of houses, apple trees in the middle of forests, old, nearly vanished paths in the midst of fields. All of this can be found in the Sudetenland; its discovery attracts us. It is as if one had an "Atlantis", which one can reach and explore not so far away from Prague.'[98]

'Atlantis' – a mythical place, a place without contours and yet with defined boundaries, open for every interpretation inflicted upon it – serves here as an invitation to explore and to cast new meanings into the landscape. For Matějka, the Sudetenland is a question that needs to be answered:

> 'Many questions remain. Few ways which reach a destination [...] few settlements, where people live. And even more questions. These questions are today's Sudetenland.'[99]

The description of the Sudetenland as a question, as an open space, defies hermetic hermeneutical confinements and transforms the Czech border regions from a 'Place of Occurrence'[100] to a 'Place of Possibility'[101], allowing these to contain different, contesting, and nontraditional narratives. The gesture challenging and destabilizing these confinements is the Czech-Austrian-German commemorational act of the 'Spurensuche'; its literal symbolic expression is the ringing of the forgotten German church bells in a landscape, which has sunken into oblivion. After attending the questions regarding the group ('we') and the tour ('to show'), this paper will conclude with the question regarding the place – 'I wanted to show, we are HERE.'

The different processes described in this paper all aim at re-opening the hermetic symbolic space called 'Sudetenland' in order to re-form it. Taking advantage of its peripheral status, delaying or even suspending both Czech and German dominant discourses, 'Antikomplex' and the 'Junge Aktion' act to re-write a

---

98 Ondřej Matějka, Interview in Radio Prague 1 April 2008, see http://www.radio.cz/de/rubrik/begegnungen/spurensuche–mit–dem–fahrrad–durchs–sudetengebiet, 10 May 2013.

99 Petr Pithart, Was im Sudetenland verschwunden ist und was von ihm blieb [What Disappeared from the Sudetenland and What Was Left], in: Zmizelé Sudety. Das Verschwundene Sudetenland, Praha 2006, 13.

100 Lentin, Co-Memory.

101 Jeffrey C. Goldfarb, The Politics of Small Things. The Power of the Powerless in Dark Times, Chicago 2006.

spatial memory of the Sudetenland and instrumentalize it according to their own discursive needs.

When referring to the Sudetenland, the characteristic paradigm of the 'Junge Aktion' is transformed to a terminology, compatible with the notion of a national de-differentiation. Referring either to macro level terms such as 'Central Europe' or micro level terms like 'Bohemia' and 'Moravia' (and 'Saxony' or 'Bavaria'), the members of the 'Junge Aktion' refrain from using the terms 'Germany' or 'Czech Republic'. By trying to diffuse the national affiliation of the region, taking advantage both of its rather unique history and of the legitimacy of the joint tour, they wish to pose an example for a de-nationalized European space.

> *The tour began in the village Dolní Poustevna (Niedereinsiedel), which lies on the Czech-German border. Those who arrived directly from Germany took the route through Neustadt in Saxony and the village of Sebnitz, crossing the stream Vilémovský Potok (Sebnitz) and entering the Czech Republic. The immediate sight after crossing the border was rather striking. Rows of shops selling cheap alcoholic beverages and cigarettes, split asphalt, and broken pavements welcomed the newcomers. One of the participants, arriving on a BMW motorcycle, wanted to park it in front of the hotel. Ondřej Matějka from 'Antikomplex' advised him to park it rather in a closed garage. Looking at me [coming from Israel] he smiled and said – 'Welcome to the Gaza strip of the Czech Republic.'*

The landscape of the Czech border regions bears visible remnants of rupture, resulting from the past 70 years of Czech history. The expulsions of the Sudeten Germans, the break-down of social textures as a result of the rapid depopulation, the traces of soviet presence, the massive negligence, and the formation of problematic social structures are omnipresent along the border. This fractured 'Postkulturlandschaft'[102] and the historical processes that enabled it serve as a mirror according to 'Antikomplex', allowing for a 'gloomy self-awareness' of the Czech society.[103] The Sudetenland therefore serves as an analogy to the entire Czech Republic; the reasons for its current state are perceived by 'Antikomplex' as paradigmatic for a whole raw of contemporary Czech social and political grievances.[104] The abstention of the Czech society confronting the ill-development in the border regions is interpreted therefore by 'Antikomplex' as analogous to an evasion in confronting these vary same grievances.

With its diverse actions – one of them being the co-organization of the 'Spurensuche'-tour – 'Antikomplex' wishes to defy the silencing taboo surrounding both past and present of the Sudetenland, utilizing its state to launch a wide ranging Czech social discourse. The confrontation with compromising histori-

---

102 Mikšíček, Besiedlung, 90.

103 Matějka, Sudetenland, 93.

104 Budil, Sudetenland, 73.

cal crossroads, assuming responsibility for past grievances, marks a crucial building block in the formation of the post-communist liberal-democratic civil society for 'Antikomplex'. The Sudetenland, an 'identity endowing phenomenon'[105] transforms from a signifier of trauma and melancholy to a signifier of amendment.

In the joint act of 'co-memoration', both partners are dependent of the legitimizing participation of the respective other. 'Antikomplex' requires the symbolic retrieval of the Sudeten Germans in order to bring the Czech process of mourning to an end, reconnecting to the landscape and turning it to a place of amendment; the 'Junge Aktion' is dependent of the Czech invitation and of the joint act of touring in order to substantiate its reconciliatory vision. Nevertheless, the analytical methodology, which derives from signposting the 'Spurensuche'-project as a memory project, and its participants as memory activists, negates perceiving it as a genuine collective venture. A common memory project assumes a common social context, consisting of common periodization and discursive frames; having said that, the contradictory momentum in the 'Spurensuche'-project becomes all the more omnipresent. In nearly every segment of this project, one encounters two distinct narratives and perceptions, as the two interpretations to the sentence 'I wanted to show – we are here' suggest. For the Czech participants, this tour is both an act of overcoming a national melancholia as well as an act of amendment through the establishment of a genuine link to the landscape of the border regions. It is therefore an exclusive, past-oriented project, confined to the boundaries of the Czech national discourse. On the other hand, for the German participants, the 'Spurensuche'-week offers a chance to demonstrate the power of reconciliation based on Christian forgiveness. Rejecting any readdressing of past issues, the members of the 'Junge Aktion' turn their gaze to a united, Christian-European future. Therefore, they comply with an inclusive, future oriented perspective of the project – 'showing' a Christian 'we' in a European 'here'.

105 Tomáš Kafka, Das Sudetenland ist noch nicht verloren [The Sudetenland Is Not Yet Lost], in: Zmizelé Sudety. Das Verschwundene Sudetenland, Praha 2006, 79.

II. (Individual) Mind and Memory

Maria Bianca Fanta

Unknown Life Stories of Communist Editors – Journalists of the Party Newspaper *Österreichische Volksstimme*

Andrássy University Budapest

> 'We will fight a ruthless and consistent fight in the editorial office for the utmost accuracy in our coverage and the most diligence in handling articles we receive. We have to work consistently on raising the political sense of responsibility, the political knowledge and the journalistic skills of our cadre, to find new journalistic cadre and to develop them.'[1]

Erwin Zucker-Schilling, editor-in-chief of the communist main organ *Österreichische Volksstimme* [Austrian Voice of the People] from 1945 to 1957, outlines the tasks of the communist party press in a speech in 1955. His wording emphasizes the way communist party journalism had to function at that time: diligent, predetermined, focused solely on the work in the editorial office, politically educating, collectively working, as well as strictly disciplined.

The *Österreichische Volksstimme* was founded with the initiation of the party papers in Austria in August 1945 and was one of the Austrian Communist Party's (Kommunistische Partei Österreichs, KPÖ) most essential instruments in self-assertion. However, the editors Zucker-Schilling referred to as 'journalistic cadre' are mostly unknown to the public today since the majority of historical communication research in Austria has focused almost exclusively on 'famous' personalities.[2]

---

1 Erwin Zucker-Schilling, Aufgaben und Verbreitung der Parteipresse, Referat am 8. Plenum der KPÖ, Wien am 15. und 16. November 1955 [Tasks and Distribution of the Party Press, Presentation at the KPÖ's 8th Plenary Assembly, Vienna on 15 and 16 November 1955], Alfred Klahr Gesellschaft Wien (AKG), Zentrales Parteiarchiv (ZPA) der KPÖ.

2 Famous names of the KPÖ press were for example Eva Priester or Fritz Jensen. See Claudia Trost – Eva Priester, Ein biografischer Abriss [A Biographical Survey], in: Hans Hautmann (Ed.), Die Alfred Klahr Gesellschaft und ihr Archiv. Beiträge zur österreichischen Geschichte des 20. Jahrhunderts, Alfred Klahr Gesellschaft Quellen & Studien, Wien 2000, 347–370; Eva Barilich – Fritz Jensen, Arzt an vielen Fronten, Biografische Texte zur Geschichte der österreichischen Arbeiterbewegung 5 [Doctor on Many Fronts, Biographical Texts on the History of the Austrian Labor Movement], Wien 1991.

The following contribution is based on a dissertation project which is interested in the life stories of all *Volksstimme* journalists, not only the prominent ones.[3] The objective of the Ph.D. project is to illustrate the lives of the journalists to learn more about their professional and political career. This intention is based on the question: Who were the journalists of the *Österreichische Volksstimme*?

A newspaper is the product of a collaboration between different people. It originates from the sum of numerous articles written by distinct editors. This excerpt from the dissertation project aims to demonstrate that the one exemplary and distinct journalist biography of the KPÖ press does not exist – rather, this paper proposes the diversity of these journalist stories full of detours, escapes, and dead ends. People of different origin, age and experiences, but similar political notions and ideals. This notion not only emerged through archival research, but also in the course of several interviews. The author was able to talk to a journalist, who seized the initiation of the party paper as a stepping stone to establish himself in journalism, but who would soon feel the full force of the paper's limits, and therefore turn away from the KPÖ to pursue his career; the author also talked to a KPÖ journalist who accepted these limits and remained a faithful party journalist to the *Österreichische Volksstimme* until its termination in 1991.

As of now, a comprehensive study of the communist press in Austria or of the *Österreichische Volksstimme* does not exist; several publications discuss this topic[4], occasionally a biography of one or the other 'famous' communist journalist can be found.[5] So far, however, the KPÖ press in the Second Republic has played only a minor role.[6]

3 The Ph.D. project 'Journalists of the Communist Party Newspaper "*Österreichische Volksstimme*"' (working title) was started at the Andrássy University Budapest in 2011. It focuses on the life stories of those journalists who worked at the newspaper in the period 1945 to 1956.

4 See Theodor Venus, Die kommunistische Presse Österreichs seit 1945 [The Communist Press in Austria Since 1945], in: Vorarlberger Landesmuseum (Ed.), Max Haller, (Ausstellung Vorarlberger Landesmuseum 23.7.–20.9.1992), Bregenz 1992, 71–78; Michael Graber, Die 'Volksstimme' [The 'Volksstimme'], in: Franz Ivan (Ed.), 200 Jahre Tageszeitung in Österreich 1783–1983. Festschrift und Ausstellungskatalog, Wien 1983, 309–318; Otto Langer, Der Wiederaufbau der kommunistischen Presse [The Rebuilding of the Communist Press], in: Heinz Pürer (Ed.), Die österreichische Tagespresse. Vergangenheit, Gegenwart, Zukunft. Eine Dokumentation von Vorträgen des Symposions '200 Jahre Tageszeitung in Österreich', Journalistik 5, Salzburg 1983, 97–102.

5 *Inter alia* Erica Fischer, Das Wichtigste ist, sich selber treu zu bleiben. Die Geschichte der Zwillingsschwestern Rosl und Liesl [The Main Thing Is to Stay True To Oneself. The Story of the Twin Sisters Rosl and Liesl], Wien 2005; Jenö Kostmann, Zeitzeuge [Contemporary Witness], in: Friedrich Stadler (Ed.), Vertriebene Vernunft. Emigration und Exil österreichischer Wissenschaft 1930–1940. Emigration – Exil – Kontinuität. Schriften zur zeitgeschichtlichen Kultur- und Wissenschaftsforschung 1, 2 vols., Münster 2004, 836–842; Peter Guttmann – Ernst Epler, Lebensstationen eines kommunistischen Journalisten [Life Stages of a Communist Journalist], Wien 2006; Hartmut Krones – Marcel Rubin, Österreichische Komponisten des XX. Jahrhunderts 22 [Austrian Composers of the XXth Century], Wien 1975; also see footnote 3.

6 This circumstance is emphasized by the fact that scientific papers on Austria's party press and journalists' biographies still rely heavily on information from the 1970s and 1980s, due to a lack of alternatives. For instance: Rudolf Tschögl, Tagespresse, Parteien und alliierte Besatzung.

But who were these 'journalist cadre' of the communist press, whose workday was 'a constant struggle against the controlled, manipulated, dictated malicious lie, a constant struggle for the discovery of the truth behind the lie'?[7] Who declared their 'most powerful weapon' 'class consciousness, Marxist knowledge, a close relationship to the party and the workforce, never flagging vigilance, collective collaboration and constant self-control'?[8]

The life stories of three journalists of the *Österreichische Volksstimme* will illustrate the diversity of biographies as well as the repercussions of the persecution of journalists by the 'Ständestaat' [Austrofascism] and National Socialism, the continuities and discontinuities in the Austrian press system, and the control by the communist party. Finally, this outline will be complemented by additional life stories of communist editors.

Detours, Escapes, Dead Ends. The Lives of Communist Editors

Journalist A is a dedicated communist and becomes an editor for the Carinthian KPÖ party paper *Volkswille* [The Will of the People] in 1946. He has soon managed to establish a good reputation as committed editor. In 1953, however, he has to leave the *Volkswille*: as a former Scottish soldier – during the NS regime, Journalist A had survived as a Jewish emigrant to Scotland and enlisted with the Scottish army – he is no longer welcome in times of 'heightened vigilance', because during the Cold War both Great Britain and Soviet Union clarified the position. Later, he will comment his expulsion with the following words: 'It was a bad time. But that didn't happen to me only. Others lost their positions too.' Nevertheless, Journalist A applies again for the KPÖ press two years later, this time at the *Österreichische Volksstimme* in Vienna. His involvement with the Scottish army does not seem to be a problem anymore and he is immediately hired. This time he is allowed to stay until the termination of the communist paper in 1991.

In the days of the Austrian-Hungarian monarchy, Journalist B was born in present-day Slovakia. Her mother is a passionate partisan of the Social Democrats and writes articles for newspapers with titles such as 'The Academic and Cui-

Grundzüge der Presseentwicklung in der unmittelbaren Nachkriegszeit 1945–1947 [Daily Press, Parties and Allied Occupation. Essential Press Developments in the Immediate Post-War Era 1945–1947], Ph.D. thesis Wien 1979; Fritz Hausjell, Journalisten gegen Demokratie oder Faschismus. Eine kollektiv-biographische Analyse der beruflichen und politischen Herkunft der österreichischen Tageszeitungsjournalisten am Beginn der Zweiten Republik (1945–1947) [Journalists Against Democracy and Fascism. A Collective-Biographical Analysis of the Daily Newspaper Journalists' Professional and Political Origin at the Beginning of The Second Rebulic (1945–1947)], Europäische Hochschulschriften 40/Kommunikationswissenschaft und Publizistik 15, Frankfurt am Main 1989.

7 In der Zeitungsfabrik. An der Erzeugungsstätte der 'Volksstimme' [In the Newspaper's Factory. At the Place of Production of the 'Volksstimme'], *Österreichische Volksstimme*, Vienna 1951 August 5th, 5.

8 *Ibid.*

sine' or 'Holidays from Marriage'. Since her school days, Journalist B is a communist and survives the NS regime in China, where she works in hospitals and field hospitals. Following her return to Austria, she publishes initial texts in the *Österreichisches Tagebuch* [Austrian Diary] in 1947. She establishes herself in journalism and works as culture critic for the *Österreichische Volksstimme*, also for the *Abend* [Evening] and the *Stimme der Frau* [Voice of Woman]. She publishes two books true to party principles; later publications, however, display distinct personal opinions. Subsequently, the journalist is no longer allowed to review films of political content for the newspaper, she is excluded from the party and eventually ostracized. In 1959, Journalist B embarks on a mountain hike from which she never returns. Police assume she committed suicide. Later it is revealed that Journalist B had been fired a few days before her disappearance.

Journalist C, born in 1925, is a journalist for the *Volksstimme* since day one. As a 20-year-old, he contributes to the setup of the paper prior to its first publication and learns the journalist craft in the local department of the *Volksstimme*.

Journalist C had survived the war in Vienna. As a 'Geltungsjude' he had to perform forced labor; he was sent to a SS camp twice. During the war he joined a communist resistance group and entered the communist party in 1945.

In 1947, however, he is only to receive half his salary for his articles; he protests and leaves both paper and party. When he later marries a woman who is still employed at the *Volksstimme*, she is fired immediately.

After he had turned his back on the KPÖ in 1947, his career proceeds. His intentions to work for the newspaper *Neues Österreich* [New Austria] are initially rendered impossible by his job at the *Volksstimme*. Instead, he works for the French occupation paper *Welt am Abend* [World in the Evening]; it is only after this 'cleansing', as he calls it, that he can begin his work as editor with *Neues Österreich*.

Journalist C moves on to the *Kurier* and becomes reporter in chief under Hans Dichand. Subsequently, he works for different magazines and becomes chief press officer at the 'Wiener Handelskammer' [Viennese Chamber of Commerce]. In the 1970s, he returns to *Kurier* as chief of the local department.

The Journalistic Scenery in Austria after 1945

These three journalist stories exemplify the contemporary historical discontinuities and general symptoms of the history of the Austrian press. Simultaneously, there are also points of contact: aspects and factors that are similar in all biographies.

After 1945 it was not possible to rebuild Austrian journalism, which had existed before 1938 – although it must be emphasized that the destruction of journalist criticism happened well before 1938 with the ban of party papers in 1933.[9]

9 How many Austrian journalists emigrated in the 1930s is unknown. Since 50 to 70 percent of Viennese journalism was created by Jewish editors in the First Republic, it can be assumed that

Too many journalists did not return from exile after 1945 and many others had not survived the war at all. Due to their experiences with the instrumentalization of the media in the Second World War, the Allies endeavored alterations. Simultaneously, 'denazification' progressed only partially and deficiently[10]; at the beginning of the Second Republic, 37 percent of all daily newspaper journalists had gained journalistic work experience under the NS regime.[11]

Almost none of the exiled journalists returned after 1945: merely 5.5 percent of experienced journalists returned to Austria in the first three postwar years of 1945 to 1947.[12]

In 1945, the *Österreichische Volksstimme* also had problems in finding qualified employees for their editorial office. The *Rote Fahne* [Red Flag], the main organ of the KPÖ in the First Republic, only had a very small editorial team; additionally, they had to bemoan the loss of several editorial staff members who died in the heat of persecution after 1938. Erwin Zucker-Schilling on the beginnings of the partisan paper:

> 'A crucial task in the beginning was understandably the compilation of an editorial team and the determination of the political-journalistic face of the paper. Almost no one was left from the communist daily press' former members of staff at that time. Many of our best comrades fell victim to the Nazi regime.'[13]

The Recruiting of Experienced Journalists

Despite the small number of returning journalists, some daily newspapers like the *Arbeiter-Zeitung* [Newspaper of the Workers], the main organ of the SPÖ, and the *Österreichische Volksstimme* were able to recruit more than half of their edito-

many journalists emigrated. See Fritz Hausjell, Österreichische Journalisten und Publizisten im Exil [Austrian Journalists and Publicists in Exile], in: Friedrich Stadler (Ed.), Vertriebene Vernunft I. Emigration und Exil österreichischer Wissenschaft 1930–1940, Emigration – Exil – Kontinuität 1, Münster 2004, 204–342, here 304.

10 Fritz Hausjell, Entnazifizierung der Presse in Österreich [Denazification of the Austrian Press], in: Sebastian Meissl – Klaus-Dieter Mulley – Oliver Rathkolb (Eds.), Verdrängte Schuld, verfehlte Sühne. Entnazifizierung in Österreich 1945–1955, Symposium des Instituts für Wissenschaft und Kunst März 1985, Wien 1986, 171–201.
For the National Union of Journalists' denazification measures see: Fritz Hausjell, Die mangelnde Bewältigung des Vergangenen. Zur Entnazifizierung und zum Umgang von Journalistinnen und Journalisten mit der nationalsozialistischen Vergangenheit nach 1945 [The Insufficient Coping with the Past. On the Denazification and Journalists' Approach to the National Socialist Past after 1945], in: Hans Heinz Fabris – Fritz Hausjell (Eds.), Die vierte Macht. Zu Geschichte und Kultur des Journalismus in Österreich seit 1945, Wien 1991, 29–49.

11 Hausjell, Journalisten, 325.

12 *Ibid.*, 337.

13 Erwin Zucker-Schilling, So begann es [This Is How It Started], *Österreichische Volksstimme*, Vienna 1965 August 1st, 1.

rial team from returned expatriates from 1945 to 1947.[14] The repatriation rate was the highest among communist journalists: at the KPÖ press, the returned emigrates dominated clearly with more than 27 percent. The editorial team of the *Volksstimme* was staffed with numerous professional newcomers returned from exile – as indicated by journalist A's biography – as well as expatriate journalists with work experience.

Siegfried Klausner (1881–1951), for instance, whose name was 'inextricably linked to Vienna's glory days of journalism'.[15] As an educated lawyer, he had started his journalistic career at the daily newspaper *Die Zeit* [The Time] in 1910; in 1918 he moved on to *Abend* where he became editor-in-chief in 1925. Klausner survived the NS regime in Yugoslavia where he was an active partisan. After his return to Vienna in 1945, he became head of the local department of the *Österreichische Volksstimme*, where he trained many young journalists. 'He was a fantastic journalist because people from boulevard are good journalists. Those are researchers and whistleblowers. Those are the ones with nerves', a journalist who had once been a newcomer at the local department of the *Österreichische Volksstimme* will say in an interview for this Ph.D. project about Klausner.

Although the majority of KPÖ journalists emigrated or turned to illegality due to the prohibition in 1933, and some fell victim to National Socialism later, it is fair to say that the Austrian Communist Party managed to gain comparatively many experienced journalists for the *Österreichische Volksstimme* in the first reconstruction years of the Second Republic. Among those accomplished publicists, who started at the *Österreichische Volksstimme* in 1945, was Jenö Kostmann, who had already gained experience as editor of the *Rote Fahne*, the communist main organ of the First Republic, for example. Kostmann, born 1906 in Vienna, emigrated to Prague already in 1935. His career at the *Rote Fahne* began in 1930, on 19 February 1934 he was arrested and was deported to the detention camp in Wöllersdorf where he stayed until July 1935.[16] In 1935, the party sent him to Prague, where the *Rote Fahne* had been produced, 'to resume his work alongside editor-in-chief Erwin Zucker-Schilling'.[17] From November 1938 to November 1945, Kostmann lived in London, where he worked as editor-in-chief of the weekly paper *Zeitspiegel* [Mirror of Time], which was published by Austrian emigrants.[18] In November 1945, he was allowed to return to Vienna as the 'counterpart' to the editor-in-chief

---

14 Fritz Hausjell, Österreichische Journalisten und Publizisten im Exil (1933/34 bis 1945). Eine Fallstudie [Austrian Journalists and Publicists in Exile (1933/34 to 1945). A Case Study], in: Friedrich Stadler (Ed.), Vertriebene Vernunft I. Emigration und Exil österreichischer Wissenschaft 1930–1940, Emigration – Exil – Kontinuität 1, Münster 2004, 204–342, here 306.

15 Unser Dr. Siegfried Klausner gestorben [Our Dr. Siegfried Klausner Died], *Der Abend*, Vienna 1951 July 4th, 2.

16 Personal File Jenö Kostmann, Österreichische Journalistengewerkschaft [National Union of Journalists], Vienna.

17 Kostmann, Zeitzeuge, 837.

18 Personal File Jenö Kostmann, Questionnaire Vienna 1946 March 15th, Journalistengewerkschaft Vienna.

of the *Arbeiter-Zeitung*, Oscar Pollack.[19] At the *Volksstimme*, Kostmann combined his journalistic experience with 'profound knowledge and unconditional devotion to the party'[20], portrays the paper its deputy editor-in-chief.

However, many experienced journalists did leave the *Volksstimme* editorial office rather early again since they were needed for the establishment of individual states' issues. Richard Schüller, born in 1901, is a good example: in the 1920s, Schüller was a representative of the 'Communist Youth-International' in the executive committee of the 'Komintern' before working at the *Rote Fahne* like Kostmann. In 1934, Schüller emigrated to Prague, 1935 to Moscow. In 1941 he voluntarily enlisted in the Red Army; from 1942 onwards he was working as an editor for the radio station 'Radio Moskau für Österreich' [Radio Moscow for Austria]. Following his return to Vienna, Schüller was editor of the *Österreichische Volksstimme* from 1945 to 1947 before he was appointed editor-in-chief of the 'Neue Zeit' [New Time] in Linz.[21]

Simultaneously, new, young people had to be trained; many who returned from emigration in 1945 had the chance to gain first journalistic experience abroad – with the organization 'Young Austria' in England for instance – and were keen on contributing to the newly founded Austrian papers.

Other young professional newcomers came from Austrian resistance groups, as the example of Journalist C illustrates. While he was a member of a communist resistance group during the war, he became a full member of the communist party after Austria's liberation and transferred from a Viennese state organization to the *Volksstimme* editorial office to work as a local reporter.

In contrast to Journalist C, who joined the KPÖ in 1945, the resistance fighter Antonie Lehr became a KPÖ member in 1927. In the 1930s, she worked for the news organization of the 'Communist International' in Vienna before continuing her work illegally in France. Disguised as Frenchwoman, Lehr returned to Vienna in 1943, when she was arrested a year later and deported to Auschwitz and then to the KZ Ravensbrück, where she was supposed to be shot. Owing to the solidarity of other women – who hid Lehr and helped her acquire a new identity – she was evacuated to Sweden by the Red Cross in April 1945.[22] In 1946, Lehr returned to Austria; from 1954 at the latest, the business graduate worked as full-time editor for the *Volksstimme*.

---

19 Hausjell, Journalisten, 638.

20 Jenö Kostmann zum Sechzigsten [Jenö Kostmann to the Sixtieth], *Österreichische Volksstimme*, Vienna 1966 December 12th, 4.

21 Portfolio S, Documents on Richard Schüller, AKG Vienna; File 19675, Dokumentationsarchiv des Österreichischen Widerstandes (DÖW), Vienna; Hilde Koplenig, Emigration in die Sowjetunion [Emigration into the Sowjet Union], in: Friedrich Stadler (Ed.), Vertriebene Vernunft. Emigration und Exil österreichischer Wissenschaft 1930–1940. Emigration – Exil – Kontinuität. Schriften zur zeitgeschichtlichen Kultur- und Wissenschaftsforschung II, Münster 2004, 976–979, here 978.

22 File 50104/609 DÖW Vienna; as well as Personal Document on Antonie Lehr, Journalistengewerkschaft, Questionnaire Vienna 1954 January 11th.

The Lenghty Search for Journalist Biographies

An editorial archive of the *Österreichische Volksstimme,* which preserves all these life stories, does not exist. This presents a profound problem in the investigation of Austrian media history, since editorial archives are mostly absent and general newspaper articles are rarely provided with a byline. Additionally, contemporary registers and indexes only contain names of 'important' editors. Therefore, studies on individual Austrian newspaper editorial offices are quite difficult to conduct and consequently very rare or available in limited dimensions only.[23] Nevertheless, the author of this ongoing dissertation project was able to record about one hundred names of former *Volksstimme* journalists, who worked for the communist main organ between 1945 and 1956. In order to counteract the information deficiency, all issues of the party paper between 1945 and 1956 were examined and all names or abbreviations from identified articles annotated. In sum, 3,800 issues have been edited and processed. All possible names were then researched in different archives in order to establish a comprehensive journalist database. These pieces of data are complemented by two detailed interviews with former journalists, who worked for the *Volksstimme* in the 1940s and 1950s.

The investigation period comprises the interval 1945 to 1956 – since an investigation of the entire history of the *Österreichische Volksstimme*, that is from its founding in 1945 to the paper's termination in 1991, would, according to the author, surpass the dissertation's dimensions to focus on the journalists biographies.

The Investigation Period 1945 to 1956

The year 1945 sees a realignment of the Austrian press market. To label this process as 'zero hour', however, would be too far-fetched considering the backdrop of Austrian 'denazification' policy.[24] The first party papers are published again on 5

---

23 Exceptions are among others: Miriam Machtinger, Die Folgen der Pressepolitik im "Ständestaat" und im "Dritten Reich" auf den sozialdemokratischen Journalismus am Beispiel der "Arbeiter-Zeitung" – eine kollektivbiographische Analyse zu Verfolgung, Widerstand, Exil, Holocaust und Anpassung der Journalisten der "Arbeiter-Zeitung" [The Consequences of Media Policy in the "Ständestaat" and the "Third Reich" on the Social-Democratic Journalism by Example of the "Arbeiter Zeitung" – A Collective Biographical Analysis on Persecution, Resistance, Exile, Holocaust and Adaption of the Journalists at the "Arbeiter Zeitung"], diploma thesis Wien 1994; Gerda Steinberger, Vernichtung, Vertreibung, Anpassung und Aufstieg von Journalisten im "Ständestaat" und im "Dritten Reich". Eine Analyse am Beispiel der "Neuen Freien Presse" (1933–1939) [Extinction, Expulsion, Adaption and Rise of Journalists in the "Corporative State" and the "Third Reich"], diploma thesis Wien 1990.

24 Many editors of National Socialist papers continued their work in the editorial offices after 1945. See Hausjell, Entnazifizierung, 171–201; Uwe Andreas Mauch, Der nationalsozialistische Journalist Dr. Manfred Jasser. Eine biographische Studie zu Nazifizierung und Entnazifizierung des österreichischen Pressejournalismus im "Ständestaat", im "Dritten Reich" und in der Zweiten Republik [The National Socialist Journalist Dr. Manfred Jasser. A Biographical Study on Nazification and Denazification of the Austrian Press Journalism in the "Corporative State" and "Third Reich" in the Second Republic], diploma thesis Wien 1990; Oliver Rathkolb,

August 1945: the SPÖ releases the *Arbeiter-Zeitung* after an eleven-year break, the ÖVP revives the *Kleine Volksblatt* [People's Newspaper] and the KPÖ publishes the *Österreichische Volksstimme* for the first time.[25] The foundation of the party papers in 1945 marks the beginning of the longstanding partisan press monopoly in East and South Austria; the party press plays a long and essential role in Austria. The investigation period 1945 to 1956 may also be regarded as a period of tension: a 'Cold Peace'[26] dominated the international scene at that time. Austria was on the geographical fault line of this 'global ideological conflict'[27], which was evident in the belligerent journalism of the (party) paper's media coverage. Disruptions in general characterize this period simultaneously, both at home and abroad: the communist accession to power in Hungary and Czechoslovakia, the Berlin Blockade, the breach between Stalin and Tito, the atomic arms race, the signing of the NATO Pact, the final division of Germany, the Korean War, Stalin's death, etc. The crisis year of 1956 was of special importance with regard to staff turnovers and conflicts within the main organ – changes, which are also apparent as 'fault lines' in the journalists' biographies.

The Newspaper as an Instrument of Agitation

The 'editorial collective' of the *Österreichische Volksstimme*, as the editorial team liked to call themselves, had a strong ideological attachment to the official party policy, with one of their main duties representing the principles resolved by the central committee. The so-called editorial policy assumes an important role in the case of the *Österreichische Volksstimme*, since, as a media-internal factor, this policy limits the journalists' creative freedom[28], because the editorial policy of

---

US-Medienpolitik und die "neue" österreichische Journalistenelite [US Media Policy and the "New" Austrian Journalist Elite], in: Hans Heinz Fabris – Fritz Hausjell (Ed.), Die vierte Macht. Zu Geschichte und Kultur des Journalismus in Österreich seit 1945, Wien 1991, 51–79, here 51.

25 On an overview of Austria's Party Press see Tschögl, Tagespresse, 166–205; Fritz Plasser – Peter A. Ulram, Öffentliche Aufmerksamkeit in der Mediendemokratie [Public Attention in Media Democracy], in: Fritz Plasser (Ed.), Politische Kommunikation in Österreich. Ein praxisnahes Handbuch, Schriftenreihe des Zentrums für angewandte Politikforschung 29, Wien 2004, 37–99, here 43. Timetable on the History of the Austrian Daily Press since 1945 at Peter Muzik, Die Zeitungsmacher. Österreichs Presse. Macht, Meinungen und Milliarden [The Newspaper Makers. Austrian Press. Power, Opinion and Billions], Wien 1984, 120–121.

26 Eric Hobsbawm, Das Zeitalter der Extreme. Weltgeschichte des 20. Jahrhunderts [The Era of the Extremes. World History of the 20th Century], München [10]2010, 288.

27 Berthold Molden, "Die Ost-West-Drehscheibe". Österreichs Medien im Kalten Krieg ["The East-West-Hub". Austria's Media in the Cold War], in: Manfried Rauchensteiner (Ed.), Zwischen den Blöcken. NATO, Warschauer Pakt und Österreich, Schriftenreihe des Forschungsinstitutes für politisch-historische Studien der Dr.-Wilfried-Haslauer-Bibliothek 36, Wien 2010, 687–774, here 689.

28 See Norbert P. Feldinger, Parteien und Parteipresse. Die Tageszeitungen der politischen Parteien in Österreich nach 1945 [Parties and Partisan Press. Daily Newspapers of Austrian Political Parties after 1945], Salzburg 1995, 175.

the main organ is synonymous with the party's policy. Since the *Österreichische Volksstimme* was clearly a political paper, the proper editing of information was of secondary importance: sparse reading incentives but a maximum of information defined the paper's profile. This layout should not only address educated officials, indeed, the *Volksstimme* was meant to appeal to a broader audience.[29]

> 'The "Volksstimme" was a partisan paper, but more popular than our paper in the First Republic; we wanted it to be a paper of the conscious, fighting working class but at the same time a paper that appeals to other demographic groups as well, it was supposed to be the voice of the people. That is how the new name of our party's main organ came into existence.'[30]

However, compared to SPÖ and ÖVP, the KPÖ was determined to use the party paper as a means of agitation in the Second Republic. Main reasons for this approach were the belligerent ideological orientation of the party as well as the marginalization and isolation of the KPÖ by the governing parties.[31]

This belligerent ideological orientation is also apparent in the diction of the KPÖ administration's resolutions with regard to the work of the *Volksstimme* editorial team, which indicates how communist journalism functions: solely focused on the work within the editorial office, politically educating, collectively working and fighting, as well as strictly disciplined. The party considered its main organ a 'mass paper', which was supposed to address all issues 'that interest the masses of working people'.[32] With regard to foreign affairs, the *Österreichische Volksstimme* was supposed to 'unravel western "democracy" through a persistent and constant revelation of facts', especially since good accentuated information on foreign affairs was an 'intricate part of the party's fight'.[33] The party also ensured that the 'achievements of the Soviet Union and people's democracies' would receive special emphasis within the coverage of the *Österreichische Volksstimme*.

The Sunday Magazine as Exile for Critical Minds

The Sunday supplement of the *Volksstimme* was far less 'predetermined' and 'politically educating'. In Rosa Breuer-Grossmanns biography, the weekend supplement is identified as 'exile of the party's critical minds'.[34] Breuer-Grossmann's life story is incomparable – and yet it is doubtlessly aligning itself along the collection of

29 See Feldinger, Parteien, 32f.

30 Erwin Zucker-Schilling, So begann es [This Is How It Started], *Österreichische Volksstimme*, Vienna 1965 August 1st, 1.

31 See Feldinger, Parteien, 178.

32 Beschluss des Sekretariats über die Arbeit der Redaktion der 'Volksstimme' [Secretary's Resolution on the Editorial Work of the 'Volksstimme'], Vienna 1954 January 5th, AKG Vienna.

33 *Ibid.*

34 Fischer, Treu bleiben, 199.

communist editors' biographies. Similar to Journalist B, Rosa Breuer-Grossmann (born in Vienna in 1920) had been a convinced communist since her school days. From 1938 she was an active member of the resistance movement. In 1943, she was caught and arrested and, just like her father, tortured for days by the *Gestapo*. On the way to another interrogation, Rosa Breuer-Grossmann lunged herself out of the window of the 4th floor – and survived.[35]

In 1945 she began working for *Jugend voran* [Youth to the Fore], the weekly paper of the KP affiliate 'Freie Österreichische Jugend' (FÖJ [Free Austrian Youth]): 'Her reports manifest how close she is to the lives of the small men, much closer than the intellectual editor-in-chief Breuer.'[36] At that time, Georg Breuer was not only editor-in-chief of *Jugend voran* but also Rosa Breuer-Grossmann's husband.

They had met each other in 1945 as Breuer had returned home from England, where he had survived the NS regime as a Jewish emigrant. On behalf of the FÖJ officials, Rosa Grossmann had organized an accommodation in Vienna for him. Georg Breuer worked as editor-in-chief for the paper *Jugend voran* until 1949. From 1950 to 1955, Breuer was editor of the *Brücke* [Bridge], the paper of the 'Austrian Soviet Society'.[37] From 1955, Breuer was a permanent employee of the *Österreichischen Volksstimme* working on a fixed rate, 'later only employed externally due to his critical attitude after 1956'.[38]

Rosa Breuer-Grossmann was also making a career as journalist: from 1946 to 1947, she worked as editor for the *Welt am Montag* [World on Monday], from December 1948 as editor for the magazine *Stimme der Frau*.[39] On 1 January 1950, Rosa Breuer-Grossmann superseded Hilde Mareiner as editor-in-chief of the *Stimme der Frau*, in 1960 she changed to the Sunday supplement of the *Volksstimme*:

> 'When she criticized the Soviet nuclear bomb tests during the Berlin crisis in the Stimme der Frau in 1960, her article was used as an opportunity to shift her to the editorial office of the Volksstimme's supplement.'[40]

In 1969, she left the KPÖ. Her husband Georg Breuer was already 'removed' from the *Volksstimme* in 1959 due to his 'euro-communist attitude'. He worked as freelance journalist subsequently and co-founded the Austrian 'Ostermarschkomitee' ['Easter March Committee'] against nuclear hazards.[41]

---

35 File 00651, DÖW Vienna.

36 Fischer, Treu bleiben, 152.

37 Personal File Georg Breuer, Journalistengewerkschaft Vienna.

38 Sonja Frank (Ed.), Young Austria. ÖsterreicherInnen im britischen Exil 1938–1947. Für ein freies, demokratisches und unabhängiges Österreich [Young Austria. Austrians in British Exile 1938–1947. For a Free, Democratic and Independent Austria], Wien 2012, 77.

39 Personal Document Rosa Breuer, Questionnaire, Journalistengewerkschaft Vienna.

40 Fischer, Treu bleiben, 199.

41 See Georg Breuer, Rückblende. Ein Leben für eine Welt mit menschlichem Antlitz [Retrospect. A Live for a World with a Human Face], Wien 2003.

The *Volksstimme*'s' Sunday supplement offered ample room for articles by freelance journalists and authors as well as experts in the fields of culture, natural science and technology. The rest of the editorial office was divided into resorts: chief editorial, internal affairs, foreign affairs, economy and parliament, national union, local, culture, supplement, and sports (initially, the paper also had a Lower Austria resort). Many creative artists worked in the culture resort. Some of them also worked as painters, composers or dramaturges, which, according to the records, was not welcomed by the party. The editorial team was to focus solely on their work within the editorial office; individual exceptions had to be approved extraordinarily.[42]

Marcel Rubin, who worked as editor for the *Österreichische Volksstimme* from 1948 to 1969, was not only a music critic but also a composer. Born in Vienna in 1905, he commenced to study law but decided to move to Paris to study composition when he was 20 years old. In the summer of 1931, Rubin received his law degree in Vienna but returned to Paris in mid March of 1938. Being a 'hostile foreigner', he was put into a French concentration camp in 1939 and released in 1940. In 1942, Rubin travelled to Mexico City where he worked as conductor, composition teacher and secretary of the Austrian Antifascist Committee.[43] In 1947 Marcel Rubin returned to Vienna where he was offered to work as music critic for the *Volksstimme.* This position was especially appealing to Rubin as he credited music criticism with educational and culture-political features. Additionally, he could organize his time freely – thus leaving him enough time to work as a composer.

> 'Furthermore, the contract with the Volksstimme was quite beneficial to his personal intentions as a composer: he had no editorial hours and received a fixed salary for periodic culture critiques and articles as he officially worked as part-time editor. He could also choose freely which concerts he wanted to review as well as the general topics of his articles.'[44]

In 1969, Marcel Rubin left the KPÖ and resigned from his work as critic.[45]

---

42 Beschluss des Sekretariats über die Arbeit der Redaktion der 'Österreichischen Volksstimme' [Secretary's Resolution on the Editorial Work of the Austrian Volksstimme], Vienna 1954 January 5th, AKG Vienna.

43 File 1932, DÖW Vienna.

44 Krones – Rubin, Komponisten, 30.

45 Rubin was not only a musician and composer: from 1948 to 1965, he was also honorary secretary of the 'Austrian Componist Association'; founding member of the Austrian Association of Contemporary Music; from 1964, Rubin was chairman of the Author, Composer and Music Publishers Association (AKM), from 1975 president of the AKM; from 1974, Rubin was president of the Composer and Author Council of CISAC – Conféderation Internationale des Sociétes d'Auteurs et Compositeurs. Following his return to Vienna in 1947, Rubin's composer career advanced and earned him international acclaim. Numerous prizes: 1964 Conferral of Professor title, Grand Prix of the City of Vienna, Gran Austrian State Prize, Order of Merit for Science and Art.

Résumé and Prospect

Only a few journalists originally expelled by the NS regime returned from exile, since Austria and its newly founded papers showed no efforts as to their return. However, the life stories of Klausner, Schüller, Kostmann, and their colleagues at the *Österreichische Volksstimme* refute this image to a certain extent. These editors returned to write, to support the creation of a democratic press, and to establish their own existence. Nothing could stop them from pursuing their cause, despite the sorrow and deprivations they had experienced in the past. The stories of the editors at the *Österreichische Volksstimme*, whether they have been identified or remained anonymous, emphasize one basic aspect: the biographies are very different. Some were already working as journalists and editors in the 1930s, others learned the journalistic trade after 1945. Some had been active members of the Austrian Communist Party since the 1920s, others joined only after the end of the NS regime. They were workers, students or soldiers, resistance fighters, prisoners or expellees. Some were able to flee and spend the NS era in exile in countries all over the world, fighting, working, and suffering. Nevertheless, they all have one thing in common: the disunity of their life stories. This disunity constitutes the intrinsic pattern of their biographies.

An analysis of the life stories of the editors of the *Österreichische Volksstimme* shall answer questions with regard to persecution, resistance, exile, party cleansing, fidelity to party principles and control, which will be a prominent aspect in the aforementioned dissertation project. Questions regarding the paper's self-image and the journalist's role model will also be investigated. The biographies, which have only been outlined in this excerpt, are intended to provide an insight into the life of a KPÖ journalist after 1945. How multifarious it can be, but also how similar aspects may arise out of various life stories due to political and media-political situations. About a dozen additional biographies shall complement this picture and demonstrate further aspects in order to free the unknown editors of the post-war era – at least partially – from their anonymity. After all, the previously outlined life stories reveal one certain truth: that they are worth being told.

Dominik Hofmann-Wellenhof

Identity Crises in Austrian Jewish Refugee Autobiographies: Frederic Morton's Search for Belonging to a New Homeland

University of New Orleans

The Modern Form of Exile – Estranged by the Challenges of Today's Rat Race

In all autobiographies of Austrian Jewish refugees before, during, or after World War II, the topic of undergoing a certain personal change, of destroyed or altered identity, and the notion of alienation, homesickness, and uprootedness plays an important role.[1] Of course, this is not very surprising considering the fact that many of these autobiographers not only lost their family members to the Nazis, but also quite literally their Austrian identity. All of a sudden, their mother tongue was the language of the enemy, for example. Some of the exiled Jews decided to totally abandon and drop the German language; they would not even speak it with their family members anymore (some spoke French until their English was good enough to carry on a conversation, for example). Others would do quite the opposite and cling on to their mother tongue as the only possession (often quite literally) they had left and, more importantly, the only part of their Austrian identity that was still 'theirs', now that their home country was taken away by the Nazis and former neighbors, and even friends had turned into enemies.

The attitude towards their old and new language often correlated with the general attitude towards their old and new *Heimat*. The sociological term 'alrightnick' refers to an immigrant, who does not question the new culture in the least, and accepts and worships America and the 'American way of life' more than any American would. A 'beiunsnick' on the other side keeps living in the past, marvels about the time in Austria ('bei uns' [at home]) and generally did not wish to assimilate and adapt to the 'American way of life'.[2]

1 Cf. Ruth Klüger, Still Alive. A Holocaust Girlhood Remembered, New York 2001; Egon Schwarz, Refuge. Chronicle of a Flight from Hitler, New Jersey 2002; Walter Abish, Double Vision. A Self-Portrait, New York 2004.

2 Siegfried Beer, Exile between Assimilation & Re-Identification. The Austrian Political Emigration to the USA, 1938–45, in: Walter Hölbling – Reinhold Wagnleitner (Eds.), The European Emigrant Experience in the USA, Tübingen 1992, 39–50.

Most of the time, Jews who fled from Nazi oppression cannot be put in one of those categories so easily of course. Most of them adapt to a certain extent and have a very ambivalent relationship to their home country Austria. A good example for the ambiguity of exiled Austrian Jews towards their old and new home country is Frederic Morton. I had the pleasure of interviewing Mr. Morton in connection with the research I did for my Ph.D. project in German studies. In this regard, my main aim was to look into the shifts of identity in certain Jewish refugees and how they appear in their autobiographies.

Frederic Morton was born in Vienna in October 1924. His parents were both Jewish but by no means orthodox, but rather 'typical Viennese', as Morton describes them. Together with Morton's brother, the family of four fled to London in 1939 and then emigrated to New York. Back then, Morton's last name was still Mandelbaum. Morton says that in 1940 his father decided, with a heavy heart, to change their family name to Morton to be able to join the then anti-Semitic Labor Union in the United States. Frederic Morton first worked as a baker but starting in 1949 he studied English literature. Later on, he taught at a college in Salt Lake City for some years but gave it up in order to become a full time author and columnist (*The New York Times*, *Playboy*). In 1951, he visited Austria again for the first time after the Second World War, and in 1962 he returned, this time to Salzburg, to marry his fiancée, Marcia, whom he had met in college. Morton is most famous for his biography of the Rothschilds.[3]

In his autobiography 'Runaway Waltz'[4] Morton describes his father as the typical 'alrightnick' who blames himself for his poverty and lack of success in the first years in New York, rather than considering the extremely difficult circumstances and terrain New York proved to be. Frederic, on the other hand, did not want to cope with the 'American way of life' and criticizes its anti-social tendencies. This is also why he supported the McGovern campaign for president in 1972 (which McGovern lost to Nixon). In 'Runaway Waltz' Morton presents a very ambivalent picture both of New York and of Vienna. While he criticizes New York – and by extension the United States – for its notion of ruthless individualism, he also admits that the city made an impression on him. Not surprisingly, he first noticed this fact away from 'home' (New York that is), in Salt Lake City, where he had difficulty adjusting to the 'blandness' of his students.[5]

Morton's relationship to Vienna is an ambiguous one as well. In 'Runaway Waltz' Morton describes his feelings when he sees a swastika on a hotel wall in Vienna: 'On the instant I become the emigrant Jew recklessly returned to Hitler land. I stop, petrified.'[6] Even though decades have passed, all of a sudden he experiences the same fear and the impulse to run away. In general, though, the reader

3 Frederic Morton, The Rothschilds. A Family Portrait, New York 1961.

4 Frederic Morton, Runaway Waltz. A Memoir from Vienna to New York, New York 2005.

5 Cf. Morton, Waltz, 72.

6 Morton, Waltz, 194.

gets the feeling that Morton is reconciled with Vienna. Not only has he been invited to different conferences on anti-Semitism, the Austro-American relationship, etc. by well-known politicians, and accepted the Austrian citizenship (which the former mayor of Vienna, Helmut Zilk, personally offered to him). Morton feels connected to the city and if it were not for his love of the English language, Morton might even have moved back to Austria.

Yet, Frederic Morton is unable to fully come to terms with either of the two countries, a fact that is pointed out clearly in certain episodes described in 'Runaway Waltz'. Morton remembers his younger self's feelings during his first train ride that took him out of his hometown and then refers to its implication on his present life: 'I never really got off the [train] that rolled me out of Vienna in 1939. New York did not end my emigration. [...] Let Americans keep rushing after fulfillments ever receding. I know that I'm beyond arrival.'[7] Here it becomes obvious that even after decades, Frederic Morton still has not arrived in America, and will never fully get there either.

The reason for Morton's life in limbo is not so much his forced rupture with Austria as a beloved homeland (which subconsciously makes a full acceptation of a new home-country impossible), but rather his notion of exiled existence in the modern society of the first world. In his essay 'Exile – The Modern Heritage'[8], Morton stresses inner ruptures and discontinuities often experienced by *émigrés*. He asks for the reason of his own identity crisis and describes his feelings 'about being adrift, unmoored, homeless'.[9]

The psychological consequences of exile are ambiguous according to the author; exile has the potential to be both rupture and bridge. Facing the loss of one's old identity, *Heimat*, family and friends, exile builds bridges between the individual destinies of refugees, but also an alliance with the growing number of citizens that have become strangers to their own world.

In order to facilitate the interpretation of this slightly cryptic bond, a complicity of displaced individuals, Morton goes back in his own past and his beginnings in the 'Big Apple'. He adds an unknown detail to his experiences as a baker's apprentice described in 'Runaway Waltz': After a long day's work, Frederic makes his way home from the bakery to his parent's apartment on the wondrous and glamorous Broadway. In his ragged clothes, the teenager feels like an intruder.[10] A Maraschino-cherry serves the young refugee as an admission ticket to the fabulous New Yorker glitter in these situations – the delicious taste of the cherry allows the apprentice to dream of future fame and his very own bakery. The cherry,

7 Morton, Waltz, 98.

8 Frederic Morton, Exile – The Modern Heritage, in: Sandra Wiesinger-Stock – Erika Weinzierl – Konstantin Kaiser (Eds.), Vom Weggehen. Zum Exil von Kunst und Wissenschaft, Wien 2006, 34–41.

9 *Ibid.*, 34.

10 This feeling of illicit trespassing in a different culture is also mentioned in Morton's autobiography several times

which Frederic took from the bakery for the sole purpose of creating a sensation of fitting in, serves as a symbol for structure and hope in a life out of place.

Young Frederic then reads Joseph Roth's 'Radetzkymarsch'.[11] The novel tells the rise and fall of Lieutenant Joseph Trotta, who saves the emperor's life and thus achieves fame and fortune. Yet, Lt. Trotta feels hollow and unhappy, a paradox that confuses young Frederic. He cannot comprehend the negative development and the slow but steady decline of the Trotta-family. The Trottas could eat as many Maraschino-cherries as they wanted, yet the fruits would leave no sweet taste in their mouths. Their new lives revolved around protocols and details and had no cozy corners – 'it was a surprising form of exile'.[12]

Morton evolves from a baker's apprentice to an author and encounters the shady side of exile. His own writing about his exile is a topic he cannot escape from. Therefore it is no coincidence that Morton's first bestseller is a biography about one of the most successful emigrant families in modern times, 'The Rothschilds'.[13] By writing the book, Morton is able to tell the story of the triumphant recreation of a new home, a second *Heimat*. Furthermore the biography serves as a classic example for narration as therapy – the story as a hearth in the wilderness of experience, as an antidote to exile.[14] In his essay 'Exile – The Modern Heritage', Morton compares the telling of stories with the cutting of a trail through a jungle. Landmarks are set up through the implementation of a beginning, a middle, and an end. Tricky problems are solved in the end with the guidance of moral standards: 'At the end of a good story the reader has a roof over his head.'[15] Hence, one's own existence is domesticated through narratives.

The irony in Morton's critique about a 'good' narrative is unmistakable. It becomes particularly obvious when he seemingly reproaches the sabotage of the therapeutic story by different authors and continues to claim '[that] the therapeutic story has continued to make our mainstream writers rich.'[16] Morton considers World War II the last good saga in black and white. Here we had the obvious evil in the shape of the Nazis and brave protagonists represented by the Allied Forces who would triumph in the end. Yet Morton does not see salvation in this triumph, just like there is no redemption for him in his personal success.[17]

---

11 Joseph Roth, Radezkymarsch, Berlin 1932.

12 Morton, Exile, 36.

13 Cf. Morton, Rothschilds.

14 Cf. Morton, Exile, 36.

15 *Ibid.*, 37.

16 Ibid.

17 Similar to Frederic Morton, Ruth Klüger also rejects the common anticipation that the story of survival in Auschwitz is tantamount to a success story. In her autobiography 'weiter leben' she emphasizes that the aim of her book is not to tell the tale of an adventure that ended well: 'Der Bericht, der eigentlich nur unternommen wurde, um Zeugnis abzulegen von der großen Ausweglosigkeit, ist dem Autor unter der Hand zu einer 'escape story' gediehen. Und das wird nun zum Problem meines Rückblicks.' [The report which was originally undertaken for the sole purpose of bearing witness to a great hopelessness has developed into an escape story. And

The above-mentioned personal success is launched by the adaptation of Morton's Rothschild-biography into a Broadway musical. All of a sudden, the author finds himself in the very center of the previously distant fabulous and exquisite New York. In the midst of the glitter, he has longed for for many years, the prosperous writer feasts on all different kinds of metaphorical Maraschino-cherries. Yet Morton cannot disguise his feelings of deracination and homelessness. Now the author comes to understand the dilemma of the 'Radetzkymarsch's protagonist.

Tackling the question of the location of a 'home', Morton describes the crisis of deliberate homelessness of the modern man. In his view, the crisis started with the quest for absolute individual fulfillment, which is only possible through the abandonment of communal ties, and thus in a way through the leaving of one's home and *Heimat*. The difficulty of the obsessive centrifugal upward mobility in the developed world is a central topic in 'Runaway Waltz'. Morton, himself a victim to this obsession, takes umbrage to the 'mobility of fragmentation'[18] in his essay 'Exile – The Modern Heritage'.

He does this by the usage of a metaphor. In our society, there is a rainbow leading away from the native hearth to a treasure of gold. The hearth has what we need most – warm, familiar faces that is. According to the rainbow, that does not suffice though, and, therefore, we become gold diggers; lost frantic human fragments.[19] Morton describes these lost souls as candidates for psychiatrists (whose services he himself made use of[20]), rehab centers, mental homes, and correctional facilities. These fragmented individuals were easy prey for Hitler's promises of wholeness and retrieval of a lost homeland – 'One People, one Empire, one Leader'.[21]

In December 2012, I had the honor of meeting Frederic Morton within the scope of an interview for my doctoral thesis in his apartment in New York. Dur-

that is the problem of my review.'] Ruth Klüger, weiter leben. Eine Jugend, Göttingen 1992, 139.

18 Morton, Exile, 38.

19 Cf. ibid., 211: 'As a writer I am basically an individualist, which already is already an inner conflict. I try to fight it but at the same time I live from it [...] it is very complicated. Anyway: This American way of superficially feeling well content in this world superficially – I have never accepted that in myself and it is a matter of fact that this country, where which everyone wants to go to, has the highest percentage of nervous breakdowns, depressions, the worst crime rate, the highest percentage of prison inmates, and so on. So every pathological symptom that a society could possibly have is the worst here. And the whole world wants to come here! This is a highly interesting matter, a very tragic one too [...] but a thing that fascinates me. [...] 'The Western Culture, which is a culture coined by stress and pressure, keeps chronically consoling itself by assuring itself that there will be a paradise one day.' See: James Joyce, A Portrait of the Artist as a Young Man, New York 1964; Thomas Mann, Zauberberg, Berlin 1924.
Morton, Exile, 39.

20 Cf. Morton, Exile, 37.

21 Cf. *ibid.*, 39.

ing our conversation, Morton once again expressed his concern about modern society's struggle for fulfillment and his own involvement in the conflict:

> 'Als Schriftsteller bin ich überhaupt ein Individualist, so ist das schon ein innerer Konflikt. Ich versuche es zu bekämpfen, aber gleichzeitig lebe ich auch davon [...] es ist sehr kompliziert. Jedenfalls: Diese ganze amerikanische Art, sich oberflächlich in dieser Welt wohlzufühlen – das habe ich nie in mir selbst akzeptiert und die Tatsache ist natürlich, dass dieses Land, wo alle Leute herkommen wollen, den größten Prozentsatz von Nervenzusammenbrüchen, Depressionen, größte Kriminalität, größten Prozentsatz von Gefängnisinsassen hat und so weiter. Also jedes pathologische Symptom, das eine Gesellschaft haben kann, ist hier am ärgsten. Und die ganze Welt will hierher! Das ist eine hochinteressante Sache, eine sehr tragische Sache [...] aber eine Sache, die mich fasziniert.'[22]

The unprecedented American individualism ties in with Morton's understanding of the 'American dream' as a typical Jewish and Christian messianism: 'Die westliche Kultur, die ja eine unerhörte Stresskultur ist, tröstet sich chronisch immer weiter, dass es einmal das Paradies geben wird.'[23] Homeless people in the streets of New York keep struggling day by day, assuring themselves that they will be rock stars and millionaires one day, singing: 'New York, New York, I'll be a number one. If I can make it there I can make it anywhere.' Chastening themselves, they suffer from being their own messiah. This ascetic optimism leads them farther and farther away from their hearth and causes fragmentation, alienation, and identity crises.

While politics abuse the loss of identity, serious literature addresses the issue. According to Morton, important authors first learn away from home what the heart itself is, for the heart is no longer home. In search for an explanation of this statement, Morton cites James Joyce's 'A Portrait of the Artist as a Young Man'[24]: The young man, heading for Ireland, who bids farewell to his mother annotates in his diary: 'My mother said she prayed [...] that in my own life I may learn away

---

22 Interview with Frederic Morton in Dominik Hofmann-Wellenhof, Identity Crises in Austrian Jewish Refugees' Autobiographies. Frederic Morton's and Ruth Klüger's Search for Bridges in a New Homeland, Ph.D. thesis Graz 2013, 211: 'As a writer I am basically an individualist, which already is already an inner conflict. I try to fight it but at the same time I live from it [...] it is very complicated. Anyway: This American way of superficially feeling well content in this world superficially – I have never accepted that in myself and it is a matter of fact that this country, where which everyone wants to go to, has the highest percentage of nervous breakdowns, depressions, the worst crime rate, the highest percentage of prison inmates, and so on. So every pathological symptom that a society could possibly have is the worst here. And the whole world wants to come here! This is a highly interesting matter, a very tragic one too [...] but a thing that fascinates me.' [Translation by the author]

23 *Ibid.*: 'The Western Culture, which is a culture coined by stress and pressure, keeps chronically consoling itself by assuring itself that there will be a paradise one day.' [Translation by the author]

24 Joyce, Portrait.

from home what the heart is and what it feels.'[25] Thomas Mann's 'Zauberberg' serves as another literary example for the thematization of disorientation and dislocation respectively.[26]

Life in distance – far away from the homely hearth and even from the familiarity of narrative conventions – is also the topic of authors in the 1930s and 1940s, who had to escape from fascism. Good authors emancipated themselves from differentiating in black and white, good and bad.[27] Pursuant to Morton, these authors described and still describe the burning up of the hearth, a dilution which the core of humankind suffers from unrelenting progress. Exile, which is everyone's heritage and destiny in modern age, was put in focus by these authors. Therefore, a quote by the poet Gerald Manley Hopkins fittingly underlies Morton's plea for a reconnection with his hearth: 'Mine, o thou lord of life, send my roots rain.'[28]

Frederic Morton's essay reveals that exile, in a certain way, is every modern man's destiny. Thus the quintessence of his initially rather cryptic description of a bridge is that a person in exile shares his or her inner rupture with everyone and that forced (in the case of people in exile) or deliberate deracination from the hearth is our ultimate fate. Hence, paradoxically, we are all connected through our inner ruptures caused by our exile. Alienation and inner fragmentation are a natural part of our lives, according to Morton. By breaking with our hearth, we step on the bridge that leads us to other people in exile.

Morton's skepticism of the modern *Zeitgeist*, which uproots humankind through its challenges and sends us into psychological exile, is also shared by certain scholars like David Morley and Kevin Robins.

> 'There can be no recovery of an authentic cultural homeland. In a world that is increasingly characterized by exile, migration and Diaspora, with all the consequences of unsettling and hybridization, there can be no place for such absolutism of the pure and authentic. In this world, there is no longer any place like *Heimat*.'[29]

Here as well, the constantly changing and shifting modern world is blamed for the notion of homelessness and estrangement. In Morton's autobiography 'Runaway Waltz', the author's grandfather serves as an example for the toll that modern exile takes on those, who put work over life. The writer's grandfather is characterized as 'a man who worked instead of lived. Work engulfed his existence,

25 Morton, Exile, 39.

26 Mann, Zauberberg.

27 Cf. Morton, Exile, 39.

28 *Ibid.*, 40.

29 David Morley – Kevin Robins, No Place like *Heimat*. Images of Home(land) in European Culture, in: Erica Carter – James Donald – Judith Squires (Eds.), Space & Place. Theories of Identity and Location, London 1993, 3–31, here 27.

devoured all love, warmth, joy, leisure, ease'.[30] In 'Crosstown Sabbath', Frederic Morton goes into more detail about his grandfather's work-obsessed life. He not only chimes in with the wife of the factory owner, Morton's grandmother, who is described as a harsh critic of her husband's lifestyle, but 'magnified, deepened, universalized [the accusation's] impeachment of the Western entrepreneurial ethos as poisoner of life'.[31]

Separating himself from his grandfather's and father's western work ethic and the growth of technology and compulsive consumerism, Morton at least achieves intellectual belonging. As briefly mentioned above it is especially the English language, which serves as fertile soil for the *émigré's* rootedness in America.

The English Language as an Anchor in the New Homeland

Even though Frederic Morton still speaks his mother tongue German eloquently and fluently, he has managed to gain extraordinary proficiency in English. Thanks to his eagerness to learn the language (*e.g.*, by studying the English dictionary on a daily basis), Morton has managed to make a living by writing. Today, the author's language of choice is English. When asked about publishing in German, the writer admits his struggles in that field:

> 'Ich habe das einmal gemacht und das war sehr hart. Es war für das 'Spektrum' in der Presse, damals war, glaube ich, 2000 Jahre Österreich' und es geht sehr schwer, denn ich bin ein besessener Stilist und ich habe einfach das Fingerspitzengefühl verloren. Wenn Sachen von mir übersetzt werden, werden mir Probekapitel geschickt und oft rufe ich dann meine Übersetzerin an, das ist eine Englischprofessorin an der Universität in Innsbruck [Susanne Costa] und wenn ich Meinungsverschiedenheiten mit ihr habe, dann stellt sich oft heraus, dass sie recht hat und nicht ich. Es fehlt mir das Fingerspitzengefühl. Auch das ganze Konzipieren kann

30 Morton, Waltz, 197.

31 Morton, Waltz, 198. The following passage sums up both the content of Crosstown Sabbath as well as Frederic Morton's attitude towards entrepreneurship and the compulsive pursuit of success in the 21st Century: 'He [Frederic Morton] enlisted Occidental history, religious as well as secular, to question the Judeo-Christian dynamic which had goaded unnumbered Grosspapas so formidably into the quicksands of success; used myth, psychoanalysis, sociology to document how the West's faith in individualist, do-it-yourself salvation sacrifices the warmth of 'us' to the insatiable ex-actions of 'me'; how the fundamentalism of the chosen ego promises milk-and-honey deliverance contingent on arduous infinite travail; how it embroils us in a fratricidal Armageddon, a free-for-all of ferocious strivers intemperately contending for a payoff equally intemperate, such as a regal fortune or an imperial victory or planetary fame; how our supremacy-wracked, celebrity-ridden, joy-parched, never-enough culture initially created the Sabbath as a one-day respite from the grasping, aggrandizing, manipulating it demanded, and how the Sabbath inevitably withered as the Western enterprise waxed, technologized, accelerated in pursuit of a redemptive jackpot ever receding; how this process paved our lilies and leisure, morphed hugs into pixels; how the apparatus of achievement in chronic overdrive will break its own flywheel with excess momentum and come down on the achiever like that exploding press did on Grosspapa, buried on the other side of the Zentralfriedhof wall [...] '.

> ich nur auf Englisch, auf Deutsch fällt mir nichts ein, wenn ich mich hinsetze, das ist ganz seltsam.'[32]

In 'Runaway Waltz', Morton mentions his initial contact with English in the first chapter of his autobiography. He describes a visit to the movie theater of by Morton's twelve year old alter ego Fritz Mandelbaum. A great admirer of Fred Astaire (whose original first name is Fritz as well), the boy is eager to identify with his idol. Fritz draws parallels between the two of them; the boy is a bad student, Astaire's movie character an untalented dancing student. There are also other similarities between the two of them, yet but a major problem as well: In the synchronized movie, Astaire speaks 'Reichsdeutsch' like Hitler '[which] twists unnaturally out of His mouth, blurring and rasping'.[33] This auditive auditory detail destroys Fritz' illusion of connectedness. Only when Astaire suddenly succeeds with his dance moves and thus enchants his female dance instructor, he changes from German to English (songs were not synchronized in the movie). A wonderful transformation occurs: 'He [Fred Astaire] rises from the floor, suddenly commanding a language as new as His voice. This new voice is marvelously unblurred, untwisted [...] frees Him from the gravity pulling down sodden mortals. Fritz Austerlitz soars into Fred Astaire.'[34]

It may seem far-fetched to interpret this passage as a pure metaphor for Morton's future change of language. In this context, we must not forget that autobiographers screen their memory pool and select exclusive memories from it though. Within the detailed description of Astaire's transformation, Morton accentuates his linguistic alteration and ascribes it special importance. Different theories about on autobiographies agree on the fact that such an accentuation is constitutive for the self-perception of the autobiographer presented in his or her memoir: 'In Auswahl, Akzentuierung und Wertung geht der Verfasser nach dem Prinzip der Bedeutung vor; je wichtiger ihm etwas für die Entwicklung seiner Persönlichkeit erscheint, desto stärker wird es betont.'[35]

---

32 Interview with Frederic Morton. Hofmann-Wellenhof, Identity Crises, 216: 'I did that once and it was very tough. I did it for the 'Spektrum' in the newspaper 'Presse' for a series called '2000 Years Austria', I think. It is very hard because I am obsessed with style and I simply lost my sure instinct when writing in German. When my essays are translated drafts are sent to me. Often I then call my translator, a University professor [Susanne Costa] for English in Innsbruck [...] and if I disagree with her then it often turns out that she is right and I am not. I am missing the tact. Also the conceptual design works only in English. In German I have no ideas when I sit down and want to write. That is really strange.'

33 Morton, Waltz, 6.

34 *Ibid.*

35 Ingrid Aichinger, Probleme der Autobiographie als Sprachkunstwerk, in: Günter Niggl (Ed.), Die Autobiographie. Zu Form und Geschichte einer literarischen Gattung, Darmstadt 1989, 170–199, here 184: 'The author selects, accentuates, and evaluates according to the principle of meaning, the more important something seems for the development of his character the more it is emphasized.'

The analogy of Morton's change of language resulting in his ascension from a baker's apprentice to an acclaimed best-selling author cannot be denied. Morton's success surely does not solely rest on the acquisition of the English language. Yet, it played a major role enabling him to 'sorcer his blunder into a masterful joke'.[36] Writing in English not only enabled exiled authors better chances to be published during World War II; generally, fluency in English was and is an important if not decisive criteria for a successful assimilation. Fred Astaire's transformation from a clumsy German speaker to a dancing English singer therefore is also representative for Morton's life in a way.

In 'Runaway Waltz', Morton broaches the issue of language again in chapter III, '1942 – Manhattan Nocturne'. Fritz, who now calls himself Frederic, has to translate the German news for his supervisor Bert in the cellar of his bakery. Following his blunt order, Bert tells Frederic: 'You understand them. [...] You're German!'[37] This passage serves as proof for the often cited confusion between exiled Germans and Austrians.[38] Most of the time, Austrian recent arrivals were registered as 'Germans' in America before and during World War II (even though some who insisted were granted the denomination 'Austrian').[39] Frederic Morton underlines his Austrian roots in his autobiography, but keeps them to himself in front of Bert due to his supervisor's bad mood.

Morton talks about his assimilation in high-school in the same chapter. After a rough start, the 'kraut' manages to adapt; largely thanks to the acquisition of an English dictionary. Frederic is obsessed with learning as many new words as possible, he invests all his energy in perfecting the new language: 'The closer I get to the native tone, the better my chances to arrive in America'.[40] Former U.S.

---

36 Morton, Waltz, 6.

37 *Ibid.*, 25.

38 Even Austrian emigrants sometimes did sometimes not clearly differentiate between Austrians and Germans and identified with the Germans. The exiled *Austrian* scholar Walter H. Sokel serves as proof with the following statement: 'Und ich fand, daß es meine Aufgabe, meine Mission sei, die *deutsche* Literatur und das andere bekanntzumachen bei den avantgardistischen Amerikanern und den amerikanischen Linksintellektuellen.' [And I thought that it was my mission to advertise the *German* literature to the vanguard Americans and the leftist intellectuals. (Emphasis by the author)]. Original Quotation in: Beatrix Müller-Kampel, Lebenswege und Lektüren. Österreichische NS-Vertriebene in den USA und Kanada [Ways of Life and Readings. Austrian Nazi Refugees in the US and Canada], Tübingen 2000, 55.
Yet the majority of Austrian emigres identified specifically with Austria and also distanced themselves explicitly from Germany: The Austrian exiled scholar Harry Zohn documented this with his statement: 'Man wollte doch seine Muttersprache und Kultur pflegen und sagen können: *Jetzt wird Österreich wieder unabhängig und mit Deutschland nicht mehr in einen Topf geworfen.*' [On the foundation of the 'Austro-American Association' in New York. Emphasis added] Original Quotation in: ibid., 230. [One wanted to nourish his culture and mother tongue. We wanted to be able to say: *Now Austria will be independent again and won't be lumped together with Germany any more.*]

39 Cf. Peter Eppel, Exiled Austrians in the USA 1938–1945. Immigration, Exile, Remigration, No Invitation to Return, in: Walter Hölbling – Reinhold Wagnleitner (Eds.), The European Emigrant Experience in the USA, Tübingen 1992, 25–38.

40 Morton, Waltz, 28.

Ambassador to Austria Henry Grunwald thinks that a foreign accent is something normal in the US and does not isolate the speaker from the American society.[41] Also, there are still enclaves in the US, where foreign languages exist relatively undisturbed by English (*e.g.*, French in parts of Louisiana). Still, language acquisition is undoubtedly an essential part of any immigrant's assimilation. In Frederic Morton's essay 'Fritz! Es ist ein Traum!' [Fritz! It is a Dream!], the author gets to the point about the problems that foreign students were facing at American schools: 'Außerhalb der Hörweite der Lehrer war er [the foreign accent] immer noch Anlass für groben Spott.'[42] ['Out of the teachers' hearing range he [the foreign accent] still was cause for brute mockery.']. Morton mentions an initial feeling of insecurity also in 'Runaway Waltz'. He laments about his position as a 'writer in English overcoming so much German in the brain'.[43] From this, one can conclude that the narrator thinks of the German language rather as a bothersome obstacle.

Just like some immigrants feel truly naturalized once they start dreaming in English[44], Frederic feels the most intense connection to America cursing at a fraudulent barman: 'I had a flicker of belonging; as if I had connected for a moment to some mainstream running across the country [...] – and the connection was my shout, *Fuck you!*' Me, crying out the two most American of all words. Without any accent whatsoever.'[45] In this frustrating situation (being fooled out of his cake for his movie idol Fred Astaire), Frederic paradoxically feels attached to the new culture for the first time – thanks to the appropriate usage of a swear-word.

Frederic Morton's father Frank plays an important role in the thematic development of change of language. In the chapter 'The Bride in the Gym' the reader learns why the change of name from 'Mandelbaum' to 'Morton' occurred. When the now twenty-year-old Frederic invites his American friend Warren home for dinner, Frederic's father introduces himself as Frank Morton. He then explains to Warren (who is surprised by the American last name) that he gave up his original last name up in the hope for better chances at in the job market. Thus, Frank Morton was willing to renounce a constitutive part of his identity in the new country in order to achieve a new one. This can be seen as the father's first step towards assimilation and identification with America.

41 Cf. Henry Grunwald, How to Become an American, in: Walter Hölbling – Reinhold Wagnleitner (Eds.), The European Emigrant Experience in the USA, Tübingen 1992, 17–24.

42 Frederic Morton, Fritz! Es ist ein Traum!, http://diepresse.com/home/spectrum/zeichenderzeit/1305981/Fritz-Es-ist-ein-Traum, 23. February 2014.

43 Morton, Waltz, 67.

44 Cf. Grunwald, American. Besides Grunwald, Sokel also states dreaming in English as a sign for complete integration: 'Ich wollte auch denken und träumen lernen in Englisch, und als ich die ersten Träume auf Englisch hatte, wusste ich, ich habe die Sprache gemeistert'. [I also wanted to learn how to think and dream in English. When I had dreams in English I knew that I had mastered the language.] Cf. Müller-Kampel, Lebenswege, 51.

45 Morton, Waltz, 42.

The new language as a means of assimilation exceeds the change of name and finds its way into the intra-familial relationship between father and son. More and more often they are having conversations in English. Frederic uses the new language as a way to please his father: 'Stop worrying! Will you, Dad, please?' The 'Dad' is to Americanize and thus to please him.'[46] In the same chapter, the reader is also informed that Frederic is secretly working on two novels instead of studying for his Chemistry exam.[47] The language of these works of fiction is English. It therefore becomes clear that new language plays a central role both in Morton's professional career as well as in his private life.

Although English serves as a means of convergence between father and son in certain situations (as mentioned above), the usage of the new language mostly evokes the opposite effect. A formal distance is created by speaking English in the family. Frank Morton uses English when he wants to implicitly criticize his son's lifestyle and profession, for instance. In the chapter '1960 – Christmas with the Rothschilds' the autobiographer elaborates on the subject at hand: 'Now, talking to me in English always imposes a certain formal distance between us, a stiff space, a withholding of our familiar German by way of a rebuke.'[48] On the contrary, the familiar German serves as a private code that ties the family together. Nevertheless, the Morton family uses English as a means of communication among themselves more and more often over the years.[49] Seven years later, Frederic notices that his father now uses English as the predominant language: '[He] hardly talks German with me anymore.'[50]

Summing up, it can be said that Frederic Morton owes both his academic career as well as his career as a writer largely to the perfection of the English language. While his relationship to the new culture and the 'American way of life' is rather critical, he fully arrived in linguistic terms, developing passion and love for English.[51] This passion was Morton's entry ticket to conventional success as well as a save safe haven for the troubled and unmoored *émigré*. Morton described his verbal assimilation as extremely intense:

---

46 Morton, Waltz, 50.

47 Interestingly both English drafts (which have never been published) have German titles. The draft of the first novel, 'Frosch', is about a physician who is forced into exile and then works in a bakery. The second one, 'Wien', centers on an adolescent who gets caught up in machine. These works of autobiographical fiction can be understood as the writer's first step towards coping with his past.

48 Morton, Waltz, 112.

49 In the next generation, German is not used to communicate anymore. Frederic Morton's daughter Rebecca only speaks broken German (a fact confirmed by the author in my interview).

50 Morton, Waltz, 150.

51 Cf. Frederic Morton's statement in my interview (when asked about his relationship to Vienna today): 'Meine andere große Liebe [neben der Liebe zu Wien] ist eben die englische Sprache. Nicht Amerika, sondern die Sprache.' Hofmann-Wellenhof, Identity Crises, 203. [My other big love (besides to love towards Vienna) is the English language. Not America, but the language.]

> 'Ich konnte nie genug Vokabeln lernen, hab mich vollkommen in die Etymologie und die Geschichte der englischen Sprache vertieft, die ist ja hochinteressant, weil sie so vielseitig ist. Ich habe mich also sozusagen in die Sprache geflüchtet.'[52]

Frederic Morton suffered a severe identity crisis not only by being forced to leave his home country, but much rather by feeling overwhelmed by the challenges and ruthless individualism of the modern western society. His inability to assimilate on a profound intellectual level and to grow roots in America is accompanied by his restlessness. Even though the author found refuge in the English language, he sees himself as an eternal wanderer 'neither fit nor fated to be tied down, who'd lose his purpose if he reached a terminus.'[53] Perhaps the English language is the sole terminus where he is able and willing to remain.

52 Cf. *Ibid.*, 208: 'I could never study enough vocabulary. I totally immersed myself in the etymology and history of the English language which is highly interesting because it is so versatile. I basically escaped into the language.'

53 Morton, Waltz, 98.

Martina Bartečková Nováková

Franz Spina – A Personality of German-Czech Dialogue. A Biographical Sketch

Palacký University Olomouc

> 'We have lived with the Czechs for 1000 years, and we are so closely connected with them through economic, social, cultural and even racial relations that together we represent a unity. We constitute, to give an example, the diverse patterns of a homogenous carpet. Certainly, you can cut up a carpet, but you cannot divide the weaved-in flowers from each other. We live in a state of symbiosis with the Czechs, we entered a marriage of convenience with them, and nothing can separate us.'[1]

These are the words of Franz Spina included in his speech before the parliament of 19 November 1921, which was printed five years later in the Parisian newspaper *Le Matin* [The Morning]. Words, in which Spina declared his political course – namely one of German activism – of which he became the most prominent proponent in the First Czechoslovak Republic. Words, which made it clear that the German Czech studies in Prague had lost their first professor for the benefit of politics.

Abundant answers can be found to the question of 'Who was Franz Spina?' – a farmer, a grammar school teacher, local history researcher, university professor, a Member of Parliament, a minister of German origin in nine Czechoslovak governments, and, finally, a forgotten German activist who died 'at the right time'. His personality and his work only found little approval in Czechoslovakia and later in the Czech research of history or in German studies. With the exception of isolated articles, comprehensive research concerning the figure of Spina and his

1 'Wir haben 1000 Jahre mit den Tschechen gelebt, und wir sind mit den Tschechen durch wirtschaftliche, soziale, kulturelle, sogar rassische Beziehungen so eng verbunden, daß wir mit ihnen eine Einheit darstellen. Wir stellen, um ein Beispiel zu gebrauchen, die verschiedenen Muster eines einheitlichen Teppichs dar. Natürlich kann man einen Teppich zerschneiden, aber man kann die eingewebten Blumen nicht voneinander trennen. Wir leben mit den Tschechen in einem Zustand der Symbiose, wir sind mit ihnen eine Vernunftehe eingegangen, und nichts vermag uns zu separieren.' Cited in Johann Wolfgang Brügel, Tschechen und Deutsche. 1918–1938, München 1967. Translated from German by Karolína Cohen.

life has not been undertaken.[2] This deficiency is being made up for very slowly. The first step was a conference in Prague in 2010 devoted to Spina, the outcomes of which were published in an edited volume two years later.[3] The presented study is an introductory exposé to a dissertation thesis, which intends to evaluate the reception of Franz Spina (especially as a politician) in Czech and German press in the period of the First Czechoslovak Republic. The author sees it as her goal to compare Spina's reception not only across available periodicals – be it official state periodicals, regional or factional periodicals, but also on the chronological level – from the politically favorable years (1925–1929) to the end of his public career (1935–1938).

Franz Spina was born on 5 October 1868 to the German family of a farmer and butcher also named Franz Spina and his wife Marie Frieb. The family lived in Městečko Trnávka [Markt Türnau] on the border of Bohemia and Moravia. The village – which was important for Spina's development – is located in the Schönhengstgau region, in a German speaking linguistic enclave considered to be a part of what was historically referred to as the 'Sudetenland'. In Městečko Trnávka, where Spina attended the Utraquist, *i.e.* German-Czech primary school, at the time of his childhood years, the majority of the population was Czech[4], which means that he actually grew up bilingual. From 1879, Spina studied at the Piarist grammar school in nearby Moravská Třebová [Mährisch Trübau], where he took his final exams in 1887. Supported by his parents, he simultaneously enrolled for military service and at the University of Vienna to study German Philology, Classical Philology and Philosophy. In the capital of the Habsburg Empire, Spina also frequented the lectures of the founder of modern Slavic Studies, Vatroslav Jagić[5],

2 Only the following studies shall be mentioned: Jiří Pešek, Franz Spina – sudetoněmecký bohemista a československý ministr [Franz Spina – A German Czech Studies Scholar and Czechoslovak Minister from Sudetenland], in: Dějiny a současnost 20, Praha 1998, 19–23; Miloš Trapl, Profesor Franz Spina, německý agrární aktivistický politik [Professor Franz Spina, a German Agrarian Activist Politician], in: Osobnosti agrární politiky 19. a 20. století, Studie Slováckého muzea H 11, Uherské Hradiště 2006, 89–95.

3 German as well as Czech scientists participated at the conference. Steffen Höhne – Ludger Udolph (Eds.), Franz Spina (1868–1938). Ein Prager Slavist zwischen Universität und politischer Öffentlichkeit [Franz Spina. (1868–1938). A Slavist from Prague between University and Political Publicity], Köln/Weimar/Wien 2012.

4 The Markt Türnau originated through the fusion of two towns, namely Neu-Türnau [New Türnau] and Alt-Türnau [Old Türnau] in 1918, whereas the name Türnau was used until 1929. In Neu-Türnau, where Spina was born, 421 Czechs and 205 Germans lived in 1880. In 1910, this amounted to 494 Czechs and 108 Germans. See Josef Bartoš – Jindřich Schulz – Miloš Trapl, Historický místopis Moravy a Slezska v letech 1848–1960 [A Historical Topography of Moravia and Silesia in 1848–1960], 5 vols., Ostrava 1976, 258f. In the united village in 1921, from a total of 914 inhabitants, 661 registered as inhabitants of Czech nationality and 250 of German nationality (3 inhabitants belonged to a different nationality). See Moravskotřebovsko. Svitavsko [The Moravská Třebová Region. The Svitavy Region], Brno 2002, 631.

5 Vatroslav Jagić (6 July1838 – 5 August 1923), who was born in the Croatian Varaždin, gained his reputation thanks to pivotal work in the field of history of Slavic languages and literature. He held positions at departments in Odessa (comparative linguistics), Berlin (Slavic languages), Sankt Petersburg (Old Slavic languages and Russian language) and Vienna (Slavic philology). It

which provided him the first impulse in his profiling as a Slavicist. Due to his father's death, he returned to Moravia, and in 1888, he enrolled at the Charles-Ferdinand University in Prague to study German Philology, Classical Philology, Philosophy, and Slavic Studies. In 1901, Spina obtained the degree of Doctor of Philosophy under the guidance of his teacher and mentor August Sauer, who essentially influenced his professional evolvement. The years of waiting for his doctorate were filled with pedagogical activities at grammar schools in Bohemia and Moravia, on the one hand, and with his research in the field of local history, supported by Sauer, on the other.[6] He began his teaching career in 1893 as a substitute teacher at the Broumov [Braunau] Abbey Grammar School of the Benedictines, and in 1896, he was transferred (already as a proper grammar school teacher) to the Grammar School in Uničov [Mährisch Neustadt].

1901 was a lucky year for Franz Spina, who had just turned 33. The young educator successfully passed his graduation exams under August Sauer, dealing in his dissertation with the verse in the dramas of Andreas Gryphius.[7] Shortly after, he was able to return to his native region and taught at the Grammar School in Moravská Třebová. Alongside his scientific and professional life, his private life was fulfilled as well. Spina married Valerie Weigel, the stepdaughter of the Ger-

---

is not without interest for Czech recipients that he published the correspondence between Josef Dobrovský and Jernej Kopitar. See Österreichisches Biographisches Lexikon 3, Wien 1965, 59f.

6 In his rector's inaugural address, Sauer urged his fellow scholars to foster and research cultural anthropology. He particularly praised Spina: 'The German culture in Moravia and Silesia, in Upper and Lower Austria is not always cared for with the same persistent vigilance and industriousness that became second nature to us Germans here in Bohemia. Would these countries not require a national journal of high style, the way we have here? The promising beginnings of cultural anthropological research in Moravia that we especially owe to our colleague Franz Spina deserve to be continued and emulated […].' In: August Sauer, Literaturgeschichte und Volkskunde. Rektoratsrede gehalten in der Aula der k. k. deutschen Karl-Ferdinands-Universität in Prag [Literary History and Folk Studies. Rector's speech in the assembly hall of the imperial and royal German Charles-Ferdinand University in Prague], Prag 1907, 20–22. Spina devoted his cultural anthropological studies to his native region, the Schönhengstgau region. In 1905, together with Alois Czerny (6 February 1847 – 28 April 1917), he founded the cultural anthropological journal 'Mitteilungen zur Volkskunde des Schönhengster Landes' (later 'Mitteilungen zur Volks- und Heimatkunde des Schönhengster Landes' ['Notes on the Natural History and Geography of the Hřebeč Ridge Region']), which was published until 1941. The regional researcher Alois Czerny worked as the director of the secondary school in Mährisch Trübau, and later he was the director of the local museum.

7 Spina's work 'Der Vers in den Dramen des Andreas Gryphius' [Verse in the dramas of Anreas Gryphius] was previously published in 1895 in Broumov in Bohemia. Researchers are not in agreement about the date of the doctoral exam, and indications oscillate between the years 1896 (Wilhelm Zeil, Franz Spina, in: Ernst Eichler (Ed.), Slawistik in Deutschland von den Anfängen bis 1945. Ein biographisches Lexikon, Bautzen 1995, 474–476), 1897 (Václav Petrbok, Franz Spina, in: Lexikon české literatury 4/1, Praha 2008, 297–300), and 1901 (Harald Bachmann, Franz Spina, in: Karl Bosl (Ed.), Lebensbilder zur Geschichte der Böhmischen Länder [Life Images Reflecting the History of the Bohemian Lands], 2 vols., München/Wien 1976, 169–185, Meds Ole Balling, Franz Spina, in: Von Reval nach Bukarest. Statistisch-Biographisches Handbuch der Parlamentarier der deutschen Minderheiten in Ostmittel- und Südosteuropa 1919–1945, 2 vols., Kopenhagen 1991, 290).

man-Austrian compatriot minister and Member of Parliament Franz Peschka.[8] Two children were born in this marriage – his son Herbert and daughter Margarete. To the teacher and local history researcher, this marriage opened up a new horizon, namely the one of politics, through his father-in-law, a prominent agrarian politician.

In 1905, the young family moved to Prague, where Spina became employed at the German Grammar School in Prague-Vinohrady, but by the autumn of 1906, he was already working as a lecturer for Czech language at the Department of Slavic Studies at the German University.[9] Three years later, in 1909, Spina managed to achieve his habilitation[10] in the field of Czech language and literature with his work on 'Frantova práva' and began teaching as an associate professor. In 1917, he became a non-tenured professor. However, his appointment as 'a full/tenured professor of Czech language and literature with regard to other west-Slavic languages and literatures' came later with the establishment of the new Czecho-

8 The agriculturalist Franz Peschka (14 August 1856 in Opatov [Abtsdorf] – 30 April 1908 in Vienna) asserted himself, while relatively young, in politics, and in 1891, he became a Reichstag deputy (Reichstagsabgeordneter), and from 1895, he held the position of a Landtag deputy (Landtagsabgeordneter). He was very engaged in the questions of agriculture and was one of the founding fathers of the German Agrarian Party in Bohemia (1905). From November 1907 he occupied the position of national representative (Landsmannminister) in the Beck cabinet, until his death prematurely ended his activities.

9 The state of Slavic Studies at the German University at the turn of the century was not gratifying and was closely related to Czech studies and Czech education, which was introduced as mandatory by the so-called 'Badenische Sprachverordnungen' 1897 ['Baden Language Regulations']. The attitude of the academic staff towards these language regulations was rather reluctant, if not directly negative. Only after the petition of the students and upon the initiative of the comparative linguist Erich Berneker, the Ministry of Education and Cultural Affairs allowed the establishment of a department for the teaching of Czech language. Franz Spina was appointed a lecturer at this department on 13 September 1906. The speculations that his father-in-law Peschka had supposedly intervened in this matter were denied by Franz Jesser. When the faculty decided to choose Spina from three candidates, it was most likely his dedication that played an important role. Spina systematically argued the case for intensified teaching of Czech language at German schools. In 1906, his article was published in "Deutsche Arbeit" with the warning summons: 'Learn the second language of the country, for you can only dominate a nation if you speak its language!' ['Lernen Sie die zweite Landessprache, denn man kann ein Volk nur dann beherrschen, wenn man dessen Sprache versteht!'] Translated from German by Karolína Cohen. For more information about this topic, see Zdeněk Šimeček, Počátky slavistických studií na Německé univerzitě v Praze a zápasy o jejich charakter [Beginnings of Slavic Studies at the German University in Prague and Struggles over their Nature], in: Slovanské historické studie 17, Praha 1990, 31–61; Ludger Udolph, Franz Spina als Bohemist [Franz Spina as a Czech Studies Scholar], in: Steffen Höhne – Ludgar Udolph (Eds.), Franz Spinna (1868–1938). Ein Prager Slavist zwischen Universität und politischer Öffentlichkeit, Köln/Wien/Weimar 2012, 39–66, here 41f.

10 The habilitation process went smoothly, and three months after the habilitation application (submitted on 23 January 1909), on 16 April 1909, the candidate was awarded the title of docent. The thesis was published in the same year with the title 'Beiträge zu den deutsch-slawischen Literaturbeziehungen. I. Die alttschechische Schelmenzunft "Frantova práva"' ['Contributions to German-Slavic Literary Relationships. I. The Old Czech Picaresque Guild "Frantova práva"']. Comprehensive information in Šimeček, Počátky, 50–52.

slovak Republic in 1921.[11] An 'exemplary pioneer of the new and better German Slavic studies'[12], as his students (among them Paul Eisner and Roman Jakobson) referred to Spina[13], was already fifty-three years old. His keen, broadly defined activity of a university professor and researcher culminated in the beginning of the 1930s, when he co-founded and published the subject-oriented *Slawische Rundschau* [Slavic Review][14] and *Germanoslavica*.[15]

Along with his academic career, Spinas's political engagement started developing after the new Czechoslovak Republic had been established. Under the influence of his father-in-law, he placed his abilities and knowledge in the service of the agrarian movement.[16] Already in 1920, he was elected into the National Assembly

---

11 A full expansion of the Prague German Slavic Studies came with the establishment of the Czechoslovak Republic, when Spina was installed in the position of a tenured professor (1921) and Gerhard Gesemann (1922) and Friedrich Slotty (1924) as non-tenured professors. The foundation for this development was previously laid owing to the influence of the constituting personalities. Besides August Sauer, Erich Berneker has to be mentioned, who also co-shaped Spina's pedagogical and scientific orientation as a Bohemist. He smoothed Spina's way towards his habilitation before he left for Wrocław and thus reinforced the future of the field. For more about this topic, see Šimeček, Počátky, 45–61; Ota Konrád, Dějepisectví, germanistika a slavistika na Německé univerzitě v Praze 1918–1945 [Historiography and German and Slavic Studies at the German University in Prague in 1918–1945], Praha 2011, 177–195.

12 Cited from the Paul Eisner's greeting, Pavel Eisner, Der Pionier einer neuen deutschen Slawistik [The Pioneer of New German Slavic Studies], in: Hugo Scholz, Franz Spina als Politiker, Wissenschaftler und Mensch, Braunau in Böhmen 1928, 27–29, here 27f.

13 Spina continued Sauer's and Berneker's efforts. He designed his Czech courses according to the orientation of the attendees (philologists, lawyers, beginners, advanced students), *e.g.*, in the courses for philologists, he made sure to convey the mutual relationship between German and Czech literature. From the middle of the first decade of the 20th century, he managed to educate numerous graduates – German teachers – who not only were able to use the Czech language, but who were also knowledgeable in Czech history, literature, and culture.

14 *Slavische Rundschau* was intended as a monthly magazine. The aim of this critical magazine, founded by Spina and Gesemann, was to report on the intellectual life of the Slavic nation. From February 1929, it was supposed to inform the German readers in a journalistic way about the contemporary cultural and intellectual life of the Slavic nations. Among the cooperators were also other colleagues from the faculty, *e.g.*, Eugen Rippl, Stanislav Antonín Mágr, Roman Jakobson, Edmund Schnneweis, and Isa Šaun. For the project, Spina managed to win the financial support of the Ministry of Education, which would allow it to function well until the middle of the 1930s. In addition to the uncertain financial situation, there was the ever more polarizing political situation. The magazine was ready to be published by 1940. See Konrád, Dějepisectví, 82f.

15 In 1931, '*Germanoslavica*. A Quarterly for the Research of Germanic-Slavic Cultural Relationships' was likewise founded by the scientific tandem of Spina – Gesemann. The goal of this journal was to explore the cultural relationships of the Germanic and Slavic people in the course of history, among others in the areas of literary history, historical linguistics, economic history, political history, and history of art. *Germanoslavica* shared a similar fate as *Slavische Rundschau*. Apart from economic trouble, it had to struggle with attempts at being exploited by nationalist propaganda. It was discontinued in 1938. Konrád, Dějepisectví, 182f.

16 When, in November 1914, F. Peschka's heir, his son Rudolf, fell in World War I, the academic Spina took over the management of the estate in Opatov for the still minor nephew. Spina did not risk any fertilization and seed experiments and proved to be a successful farmer in the difficult years of controlled economy. This ensured respect and acknowledgement among his countrymen, who saw in him their voice and supporter.

in the election district Pardubice [Pardubitz] as a representative of his party, the 'Bund der Landwirte' (BdL ['Association of Agrarians']).[17] He was active there as a deputy until 1938.[18] In the year 1926, the 58-year-old was appointed by Prime Minister Antonín Švehla into the ninth Czechoslovak administration, much to the joy of President Tomáš Garrigue Masaryk.[19] Spina then acted as Minister of Public Works (1926–1929), Minister of Public Healthcare (1925–1935) and, last but not least, as a minister without portfolio until 1938, when his political engagement – from the perspective of the approaching disaster – failed.[20]

With the arrival of National Socialism in Germany and the ever-increasing radical atmosphere among the German speaking population in Czechoslovakia, Spina was exposed to harsh criticism and a rabble-rousing campaign (especially on the part of the Henlein movement). Disappointed and seriously ill, Spina resigned in March 1938 from his ministerial office and public life altogether. He died of pneumonia on 17 September 1938 in Prague, three weeks before his seven-

17 The 'Bund der Landwirte' was founded in November 1918 in Česká Lípa [Böhmisch-Leipa] as a national party 'which set the national and economic interests of the entire German rural population as its objective'. Norbert Linz, Der Bund der Landwirte in der Ersten Tschechoslowakischen Republik [The Association of Agrarians in the First Czechoslovak Republic], München/Wien 1982, 331f. In its political program, the party demanded the right for the autonomy of all nations, progressive taxation of the rich, tax abatement for meager assets and full civil rights for women. Under the leadership of Franz Křepek and Franz Spina, the party very soon diverged from the idea of the German *Irredenta*.

18 President Masaryk previously wished for the participation of the representatives of the German minority in the government in the earlier years, and Švehla negotiated this possibility with Spina in the fall 1922. See Jiří Kovtun, Republika v nebezpečném světě. Éra prezidenta Masaryka 1918–1935 [Country in a Dangerous World. The Era of President Masaryk 1918–1935], Praha 2005, 235f. Masaryk was very pleased when, on 13 October 1926, the German consented to participate in Švehla's third administration. The President wrote about this in a letter to the Prime Minister Švehla on the day after the appointment of the new government: 'Colleague Švehla, I constantly have the Germans in front of my eyes: a great and a fine thing! And how happy I am that I am not the only one, that they have attended to the matter so well and with such earnestness – we are going to see it through and successfully! I can feel the first effects on myself since yesterday: I felt embittered and weary of all the attacks – it all has vanished. I want to invite Křepek as soon as I arrive in Prague [it means on the 26th or 27th]; Spina reinforced my decision by delivering a special and very cordial salute and a promise of loyalty all along the line […].' Eva Broklová – Vlasta Quagliatová (Eds.), Korespondence T. G. Masaryk – Antonín Švehla [T. G. Masaryk – Antonín Švehla: Correspondence], Praha 2012, 200.

19 Spina was active in altogether nine administrations from 1926 to 1938 and was thus the only minister in the First Czechoslovak Republic to hold his office for such a long period. Similarly successful with regard to the continuity of functioning in upper political circles was, besides several Czech politicians, the chairman of the social-democratic labor party of Czechoslovakia, Ludwig Czech. Despite the frequent change of administrations, the stability of the state was preserved due to this continuity of personnel. Josef Harna, Konsenzus a kompromis. Budování politického systému první ČSR [Consensus and Compromise. Building the Political System in the First Czechoslovak Republic], Praha 2013, 43.

20 It was the irony of fate that in the early summer 1934, when the BdL was negotiating possible cooperation with the 'Sudetendeutsche Heimatfront' ['Sudeten German Home Front'], Spina was still convinced that Heinlein was trustworthy. Kovtun, Republika, 765.

tieth birthday[21], just in time before the invasion of the Nazis. Upon his wish, his remains were laid to rest in Městečko Trnávka.

The title of this article announces Franz Spina as THE personality of German-Czech dialogue, as a politician-researcher, who was convinced about German-Czech coexistence and togetherness, about the inseparable interlacement of both nations and cultures. The aforementioned citation, Spina's speeches to parliament, newspaper articles and his enormous correspondence with the intellectual, cultural and political elite across the national spectrum of the First Czechoslovak Republic all give evidence of this lifelong attitude. When concerning oneself with Franz Spina, another question, almost a heretical one, must be raised: How deeply did Spina himself identify with his statement/conviction? When and why did Spina become a 'Symbiotiker?'[22] There are letters available that include different tones. In a letter to Hugo Hofmannsthal from 26 January 1918, he wrote:

> 'Today, the lever of the possible ruin of Austria seems to be in Czech hands. [...] The internally Germanized nation seems to be given only one truly Slavic attribute – the exorbitance of their goals, the overestimation of the achievable and of their own powers and the inability to learn from history and reality. The development of the psychosis since the return of Kramář, a politician of passion, suggests a deliberate isolation of the nation (the state after the Hussite Wars), a radical disengagement of Czech culture from the German element, which is, however, entirely inorganic and pragmatically not at all possible.'[23]

What was unthinkable and unacceptable for Spina became reality. On 28 October 1918, the Republic of Czechoslovakia was proclaimed. Not even two years after the exchange of the letter with Hofmannsthal, Spina lunged into the political life of a new republic that was burdened with national traumas. In this atmosphere of change, he belonged to the part of the German population that was able

---

21 Spina had been suffering from cancer for quite some time, as is clear from the statement of his granddaughter Ingeborg Götz. See Proč by měli být Češi lepší než Němci? Vzpomínky ministrovy vnučky [Why Should Czechs Be Better than Germans? Memoirs of a Minister's Granddaughter], in: Listy 2009/2, Olomouc 2009, 41–47.

22 As reported by Michael Havlin, Spina used the scientific term 'symbiosis' for the first time in 1907 in his article in 'Deutsche Arbeit'. For the second time, he used it in his speech to parliament in November 1921, when he described the geographically determined 'century-long community of fate' between the Germans and Czechs. A wave of outrage came much later in 1926, when Spina, just newly settled in his ministerial office, was interviewed by the Parisian magazine *Le Matin* (see citation on page 1). For many long months, Spina received critical reactions from the German national press and negativist politicians, which were also reflected in the title 'Symbiotiker' (at that time still with a negative connotation). Michael Havlin, Eine Begriffsgeschichte der deutsch-tschechischen 'Symbiose' nach Franz Spina [History of Franz Spina's Concept of Czech-German 'Symbiosis'], in: Steffen Höhne – Ludgar Udolph (Eds.), Franz Spinna (1868–1938). Ein Prager Slavist zwischen Universität und politischer Öffentlichkeit, Köln/Wien/Weimar 2012, 261–280.

23 Cited after Martin Stern (Ed.), Hofmannstahl und Böhmen [Hofmannstahl and Bohemia], in: Hofmannstahl Blätter 1, Frankfurt am Main 1968, 203.

to accept the new statehood. Spina was equipped with the best requirements for the overcoming of the national trauma of the German population – the change of status from a majority in the Austrian Monarchy to the minority in Czechoslovakia. These requirements were – firstly – perfect knowledge of the Czech language and a longstanding occupation with Czech culture, literature, and history; secondly, it was his background, the bilingual environment in the German linguistic enclave in Moravia, where, in comparison to Bohemia, the national edges were not as sharp. It was Spina who in numerous newspaper articles since 1906 urged Germans to learn Czech, and he was the one who systematically strived for the introduction of Czech lessons at German schools to make it possible for Germans to understand Czechs and their culture and to be able to compete with them.

Even though Spina was a 'Czechophile', he was primarily a German, and more precisely a German Moravian. Furthermore, he was a realist and pragmatist. In the first months of the existence of the new statehood and at the time of its birth, the Germans in Bohemia, Moravia and Silesia had hardly any voice in the decision-making. Their affiliation to the unwanted republic was definitely sealed by the Treaty of Saint-Germain. Spina realized that the situation had to be accepted and that it brought about new challenges. He applied his experience, authority, and reputation in the service of 'Germanness'. The instrument in this case was no longer science and the analysis of old Czech literature – it was politics.

In 1919, Spina, as a university professor and still an active agriculturalist himself, joined the 'Bund der Landwirte', a party of medium and small German farmers[24], and rapidly rose in the party hierarchy all the way to the top. Together with Franz Křepek[25], they formed an exposed tandem which determined the orientation of the party. The enforcement of so-called economic activism played a key role in Spina's political activity. This activism was interpreted as a readiness to take part in the economic and political life of the new republic, but with the goal to achieve the acknowledgement of national autonomy and to win the maximum

24 The party had approximately 150,000 members, and about 60% of these owned and farmed their lands. Mostly they were small farmers with up to 20 acres of land. According to the calculations of Kubů und Šouša, the members of the 'Bund der Landwirte' cultivated 16.06% of the agricultural areas in the Czech lands. Eduard Kubů – Jiří Šouša, Franz Spina und der deutsche Agrarismus in den böhmischen Ländern der ersten Jahrzehnten des 20. Jahrhunderts [Franz Spina and the German Agrarian Policy in the Czech Lands in the Early 20th Century], in: Steffen Höhne – Ludgar Udolph (Eds.), Franz Spinna (1868–1938). Ein Prager Slavist zwischen Universität und politischer Öffentlichkeit, Köln/Wien/Weimar 2012, 141–168, here 154. The party, however, focused on a wider spectrum of rural layers, such as tradesmen, workers, teachers and others. Kubů – Šouša, Franz Spina, 152.

25 At the time of the establishment of the Czechoslovak Republic, Franz Křepek (15 January 1855 Dolní Nezly [Nieder Nösel] – 28 April 1936 Svor [Rörsdof]) was already an experienced agrarian politician. In 1886–1899, he represented the Litoměřice [Leitmeritz] rural community district as a deputy of the Landtag in Vienna and was also known as an agricultural leader. From this time, he knew not only Spina's father-in-law F. Peschka, but also Masaryk and Švehla. Křepek was regarded as the political brain of the party. Spina and he were in agreement with respect to the question of German-Czech rapprochement. This made it possible to continue an activist direction in the 'Bund der Landwirte' until the middle of the 1930s.

of what was real and possible for the German population. His thoughts were clearly expressed in his speech to parliament from November 1921:

> 'In this hour, we become aware of the character of our opposition, which is not directed against the existence of the state, but against the manner of government and administration. […] We are included in this state through our economy and work; in this state, which is a real given quantity, we have to claim not only our duties, but also our rights, and we demand, according to the basic principles of democracy, for every single German and for our part of the nation', such a position that is necessary for a viable preservation of our part of the nation.'[26]

With this in mind, he acted as a representative, while applying himself not only in the question of agriculture. His special focus was directed at the issues of the school system. The wave of success of the party culminated with the election result in 1925, when the 'Bund der Landwirte' achieved 24 mandates, equivalent to 571,765 votes. For Spina, his appointment in the new administration meant that he had to abandon his oppositional attitude. He actively participated in the formation and the orientation of the new statehood. His activist politics came to fruition – gradually, cooperation across the national spectrum was built not only on the level of the parliament, but also on the economic level. The relatively stable situation towards the end of the 1920s let Spina believe that due to 'Masaryk's conception, Czechoslovakia was a generally consolidated central European state.'[27]

With the arrival of the 1930s, the republic had to struggle with more problems than just the economic crisis. It became apparent that the growing influence of National Socialism in Germany would prove disastrous in Czechoslovakia. Through Henlein's 'Sudetendeutsche Partei' ['Sudeten German Party'][28] and its

26 'Wir werden uns in dieser Stunde des Charakters unserer Opposition bewußt, die sich nicht gegen den Bestand dieses Staates richtet, sondern gegen die Art uns Weise, wie hier regiert und verwaltet wird. […] In diesem Staate sind wir eingeschlossen mit unseren Körpern, mit unserer Wirtschaft, mit unserer Arbeit, in diesem Staate als einer gegebenen realen Größe müssen wir nicht nur Pflichten, sondern auch Rechte in Anspruch nehmen, und wir verlangen nach den Grundsätzen der Demokratie für den einzelnen Deutschen und für unseren ganzen Volksteil jene Stellung, deren wir zur lebensfähigen Erhaltung dieses unseres Volksteiles bedürfen.' Translated from German by Karolína Cohen. See Stenographical protocol of the House of Deputies of the Czechoslovak Republic. The attachment to the stenographical protocol. The speech of the deputy Dr. Spina, Prague 16 November 1921, http://www.psp.cz/eknih/1920ns/ps/stenprot/091schuz/prilohy/priloh01.htm, 9 October 2013.

27 Spina said these words in 1929 in connection with the debates about Masaryk's possible successor in office. It should be mentioned that for Spina, it was Beneš who was qualified as the only statesman able to lead the state. According to Spina, Beneš 'was capable of solving the national issue'. Kovtun, Republika, 605.

28 The 'Sudetendeutsche Partei' was founded by Konrad Henlein in 1933 as the 'Sudetendeutsche Heimatfront' ['Sudeten German Home Front']. After the election success in May 1935 (1,249,530 votes won), the party intensified its demands for autonomy all the way to the moment of the 'Anschluss' to the German Reich. After the Munich Agreement, the party was incorporated into the NSDAP (National Socialist German Workers' Party).

aggressive and populist politics, it soon gained foothold. Spina, who in 1928 was still supposed to be 'the only true leader and savior'[29] of the German nation, was now frowned upon as a collaborator and 'Symbiotiker'. His mission at the top of the politic ladder lasted for twelve years, which was a period too short to reach the desired symbiosis and to prevent the tragedy of the Munich Agreement. His end was symptomatically. The collective volume planned in honor of his seventieth birthday was completely ignored by his German colleagues from political, intellectual, and academic circles. There were only a handful of Czech admirers to still appreciate him.[30] After the Second World War, even these fell silent.

29 Cited from an anonymous message of greetings to Spina on the occasion of his sixtieth birthday. In: Scholz, Franz Spina, 3.

30 Slavische Rundschau 10/6, Sonderband: Arbeiten zur älteren Geistesgeschichte der Westslawen. Franz Spina zum Gedächtnis, Leipzig/Prag 1938.

III. Regulating Mind and Memory

Markus P. Beham

Genocide and Crimes Against Humanity: Siamese Twins or Separated at Birth?

University of Vienna

A. Introduction

The following paper will focus on one of the main aspects underlying the research question of the author's doctoral thesis in history, which itself focuses on the use of 'borrowed concepts' in historiography, taking the prominent example of 'genocide'.[1] That aspect is the particularity of the term and concept 'genocide' as opposed to other international crimes such as war crimes or crimes against humanity. In consideration of the restraint of this present contribution as part of a conference volume, only one of these international crimes will be drawn upon to contrast genocide and make the case in point. After all, it is one of the most prominently discussed cases of genocide next to the Holocaust, the destruction of the Armenians during World War II, that brought forth the term[2]: crimes against humanity. Comparative preoccupation with genocide and crimes against humanity brings with it a catalogue of potential polemics: Are these two concepts indeed so similar, or – as current international legal scholarship would have us to believe – merely shades of the same thing? Is the concept of genocide inseparably laden with the collective memory of the Holocaust? Or is that merely its most heinous outgrowth in recorded history? Are crimes against humanity a lesser evil? Are the context and purpose of the commission of atrocities a reason to actually weigh the level of evil? Or may a parallel to the differentiation between murder and manslaughter be upheld in this context? What if it all comes down the perspective of the victim, the individual?[3]

1 The doctoral thesis, which is being pursued at the Institute of East European History of the Faculty of Historical and Cultural Studies of the University of Vienna and supervised by a.o. Univ.-Prof. Mag. Dr. Christoph Augustynowicz, carries the working title 'How We Come to Terms: Inherent Problems in Genocide Studies'. An outline of its methodology has been published in the proceeding of the last Austrian Centers meeting in Vienna in 2012: "Borrowed" Concepts: The Pitfalls of "Atrocity Labelling" in Contemporary Historiography', in: Marija Wakounig – Markus Peter Beham (Eds.), Transgressing Boundaries. Humanities in Flux, Europa Orientalis 14, Wien/Berlin 2013, 73–91.

2 See *infra* n. 8.

3 Cf. Boris Barth, Genozid. Völkermord im 20. Jahrhundert. Geschichte, Theorien, Kontroversen [Genocide. Genocide in the 20. Century. History, Theories, Controversies], München 2006, 43.

Rather than trying to emulate the infamous *Historikerstreit* of the late 1980s, the present contribution attempts on a more general level at aiming these questions in the direction of how such international crimes might translate into a terminology used within historiography and their actual analytical value therefore. In order to do this, it will be necessary to focus in particular on the emergence and respective development of each of these – one might again emphasize – legal concepts, before turning to the issue of comparative understanding within Genocide studies and international law. The main and final question will then be as to the approach historiography should take in joining the discourse or at least in applying or 'borrowing'[4] such legal terms.

B. Crimes Against Humanity: Never in Peacetime?

The historical development, as well as the scope of the legal concept were extensively deliberated upon by the International Criminal Tribunal for the former Yugoslavia (ICTY) in the *Tadić* case[5] and in even more detail by the International Criminal Tribunal for Rwanda (ICTR) in the *Akayesu* case.[6] However, it must be noted that it is a general trend, particularly in rather young fields of international law – such as international criminal law – to attempt at taking a number of prominent, yet not necessarily dependent and interrelated singular instances, and to strip them of their individual historical context, in order to establish a developmental narrative. Such efforts are to be seen in light of the urge to establish a customary international law basis for a norm or to bridge the gap of legal authority, in cases in which other legal principles might stand in the way.[7] In the present case, the instances of application are merely stated in order to construct a history and development of the term itself, notwithstanding any such implications.

The term 'crimes against humanity' first featured in the context of atrocities committed against the Armenian ethnicity within the Ottoman Empire in the joint declaration of 15 May 1915 by the Entente powers France, Great Britain and Russia:

> 'In view of those new crimes of Turkey against humanity and civilization, the Allied governments announce publicly to the Sublime-Porte that they will hold

4 See Beham, 'Borrowed' Concepts, 74.

5 Prosecutor v. Tadić, Opinion and Judgement, No. IT-94-1-T (7 May 1997) paras. 618–623.

6 Prosecutor v. Akayesu, Judgement, No. ICTR-96-4-T (2 September 1998) paras. 563–637. For an early detailed description of the development of the concept prior to Nuremberg see Eugen Schwelb, Crimes Against Humanity, British Yearbook of International Law 23, London 1946, 178–226, here 179–188.

7 Such as the legal principle *nullum crimen* or *nulla poena sine lege*, which stands in stark contrast to the natural law considerations inherent in international criminal law or expressed through the 'Radbruch formula', for example.

> personally responsible [for] these crimes all members of the Ottoman government and those of their agents who are implicated in such massacres.'[8]

For sake of the comparative argument delivered in the second after next part of this contribution, it is additionally interesting to keep in mind some of the wording used by contemporary voices such as the British historian Arnold Toynbee, who famously spoke of the 'murder of a nation'.[9] However, as far as analogies and the evolutionary narrative go, it is interesting to take into account what Genocide scholar Adam Jones points out in his 'Comprehensive Introduction' to genocide, namely that the original wording in the draft propagated by Russia would have been 'crimes [...] against Christianity and civilization'.[10] This does not keep Jones from holding that this declaration was the birthdate 'of the most potent concepts of human rights and, eventually, international law'.[11]

As a criminal provision it was first incorporated into the Nuremberg Charter[12]:

> 'CRIMES AGAINST HUMANITY: namely, murder, extermination, enslavement, deportation, and other inhumane acts committed against any civilian population, before or during the war; or persecutions on political, racial or religious grounds in execution of or in connection with any crime within the jurisdiction of the Tribunal, whether or not in violation of the domestic law of the country where perpetrated.'[13]

The same wording was also included used in the Charter of the International Military Tribunal for the Far East.[14] The subordinate clause 'whether or not in violation of the domestic law of the country where perpetrated' was included due to

8 See http://www.armenian-genocide.org/Affirmation.160/current_category.7/affirmation_detail.html, 13 October 2013. Cf. William A. Schabas, Crimes Against Humanity, in: Dinah L. Shelton (Ed.), Encyclopedia of Genocide and Crimes Against Humanity 1 [A-H], Detroit *et al.* 2005, 209f.

9 Arnold J. Toynbee, Armenian Atrocities. The Murder of a Nation, London/New York/Toronto 1915. Cf. John Quigley, The Genocide Convention. An International Law Analysis, Aldershot/Burlington 2006, 3.

10 See Adam Jones, Genocide. A Comprehensive Introduction, London/New York 2011, 538.

11 See Jones, Genocide, 538.

12 Cf. Bruno Simma – Andreas L. Paulus, The Responsibility of Individuals for Human Rights Abuses in Internal Conflicts. A Positivist View, in: American Journal of International Law 90/2, Washington 1999, 302–316, here 308.

13 Charter of the International Military Tribunal, Art. 6 (c).

14 Charter of the International Military Tribunal for the Far East, 19 January 1946, Article 5(c): 'Crimes against Humanity: Namely, murder, extermination, enslavement, deportation, and other inhumane acts committed against any civilian population, before or during the war, or persecutions on political or racial grounds in execution of or in connection with any crime within the jurisdiction of the Tribunal, whether or not in violation of the domestic law of the country where perpetrated. Leaders, organizers, instigators and accomplices participating in the formulation or execution of a common plan or conspiracy to commit any of the foregoing crimes are responsible for all acts performed by any person in execution of such plan.' Text avail-

the fact that as far as such crimes committed *vis-à-vis* German nationals went, they were to some extent even provided for by national German laws during the time of their commission.[15]

More importantly, the subordinate clause 'in execution of or in connection with any crime within the jurisdiction of the Tribunal' – *i.e.* 'crimes against peace' and 'war crimes'[16] – was interpreted by the judges as intended by the drafters to require a nexus between crimes against humanity and war.[17] The reason for this applicational *caveat* so to speak was the concern of states such as the US that it might be itself confronted with issues regarding the treatment of minorities within their own country.[18] This can at the same time be seen as the birth moment for the necessity of such a concept as was later introduced by the crime of genocide.[19] As prominent Genocide scholar William Schabas has argued

> '[h]ad Nuremberg affirmed the reach of international criminal law into peacetime atrocities, the Genocide Convention might never have been adopted. The term 'genocide' might then have remained a popular or colloquial label used by journalists, historians, and social scientists but absent from legal discourse.'[20]

Interestingly enough, in the domestic peace of legislation introducing crimes against humanity into German law, Control Council Law No. 10 did not include this nexus.[21]

Although there are singular indications towards a development away from this requirement[22], the legal *status quo* seems to have been reconfirmed as late as 1993 (and since then not amended) within the Statute of the ICTY:

---

able at http://http://www.jus.uio.no/english/services/library/treaties/04/4-06/military-tribunal-far-east.xml, 13 October 2013.

15 See Schabas, Crimes, 212.

16 See Charter of the International Military Tribunal, Article 6, http://avalon.law.yale.edu/imt/imtconst.asp, 13 October 2013, formerly also at Yale's Avalon Project, see now http://web.archive.org/web/19990222030537/http://www.yale.edu/lawweb/avalon/imtfech.htm, 13 October 2013.

17 Cf. Schabas, Crimes, 211f.

18 Cf. *ibid.*, 212. See in detail on the discussions of the London Conference William A. Schabas, Genocide in International Law. The Crime of Crimes, Cambridge/New York 2009, 38–42.

19 Cf. Schabas, Crimes, 212.

20 Schabas, Genocide, 128.

21 Control Council Law No. 10. Punishment of Persons Guilty of War Crimes, Crimes Against Peace and Against Humanity, 20 December 1945, http://avalon.law.yale.edu/imt/imt10.asp, 13 October 2013. The provision Article II(c) reads: 'Crimes against Humanity. Atrocities and offenses, including but not limited to murder, extermination, enslavement, deportation, imprisonment, torture, rape, or other inhumane acts committed against any civilian population, or persecutions on political, racial or religious grounds whether or not in violation of the domestic laws of the country where perpetrated'.

22 See Schabas, Crimes, 212, referring to the use of the term within the Convention on the Non-Applicability of Statutory Limitations to War Crimes and Crimes Against Humanity, 26 November 1968, entry into force 11 November 1970, 754 UNTS 73 and the International

> 'The International Tribunal shall have the power to prosecute persons responsible for the following crimes when committed in armed conflict, whether international or internal in character, and directed against any civilian population:
>
> (a) murder;
> (b) extermination;
> (c) enslavement;
> (d) deportation;
> (e) imprisonment;
> (f) torture;
> (g) rape;
> (h) persecutions on political, racial and religious grounds;
> (i) other inhumane acts.'[23]

There is an interesting contradictory passage relating to this in the UN Secretary General's Report on the establishment of the tribunal. In his comment on crimes against humanity after tracing the concept back to the Nuremberg Tribunal and Control Council Law No. 10, and before suggesting the provision as included in the statute he states:

> 'Crimes against humanity are aimed at any civilian population and are prohibited regardless of whether they are committed in an armed conflict, international or internal in character.'[24]

The ICTY, however, in its jurisprudence simply relied upon customary international law to overcome this nexus requirement.[25] As far as clear legal pronunciations are concerned, it took the Statute of the ICTR to finally do away with the requirement of the context of an armed conflict:[26]

Convention on the Suppression and Punishment of the Crime of Apartheid, 30 November 1973, entry into force 18 July 1976, 1015 UNTS 243.

23 Cited from the text of the Updated Statute of the International Criminal Tribunal for the former Yugoslavia as of September 2009, Article 4(2), http://www.icty.org/x/file/Legal%20Library/Statute/statute_sept09_en.pdf, 13 October 2013.

24 Report of the Secretary General pursuant to Paragraph 2 of Security Council Resolution 808 (1993), 3 May 1993, S/25704, 13, para. 47. Cf. Bruno Simma – Andreas L. Paulus, The Responsibility of Individuals for Human Rights Abuses in Internal Conflicts: A Positivist View, in: American Journal of International Law 90/2, Washington 1999, 302–316, here 310.

25 Prosecutor v. Tadić, Appeal on Jurisdiction, No. IT-94-1-AR72, para. 141; cf. Simma – Paulus, Responsibility, 310.

26 Cf. Simma – Paulus, Responsibility, 310, who also incorrectly state this with regard to the ICTY statute; with regard to the narrowness of the definition of crimes against humanity within the ICTY statute see Prosecutor v. Tadić, Appeal on Jurisdiction, No. IT-94-1-AR72, para. 141.

'Article 3: Crimes against Humanity
The International Tribunal for Rwanda shall have the power to prosecute persons responsible for the following crimes when committed as part of a widespread or systematic attack against any civilian population on national, political, ethnic, racial or religious grounds:
(a) Murder;
(b) Extermination;
(c) Enslavement;
(d) Deportation;
(e) Imprisonment;
(f) Torture;
(g) Rape;
(h) Persecutions on political, racial and religious grounds;
(i) Other inhumane acts.'[27]

The definition of the Statue of the ICTR is particularly interesting with regard to any comparative approach between crimes against humanity and genocide in that it adds a *mens rea* element, requiring that the attack occur 'on national, political, ethnic, racial or religious grounds'. This element is also included in the definition of the Extraordinary Chambers in the Courts of Cambodia (ECCC).[28]

Furthermore, it includes a subordinate clause, also referred to as the 'contextual elements'[29], the requirement that crimes in order to qualify as crimes against humanity must take place 'as part of a widespread or systematic attack'. This approach was then also taken in the Rome Statute of the International Criminal Court (ICC) in 1998:

'Article 7: Crimes against humanity
1. For the purpose of this Statute, 'crime against humanity' means any of the following acts when committed as part of a widespread or systematic attack directed against any civilian population, with knowledge of the attack:
(a) Murder;
(b) Extermination;
(c) Enslavement;
(d) Deportation or forcible transfer of population;
(e) Imprisonment or other severe deprivation of physical liberty in violation of fundamental rules of international law;

---

27 Cited from the Statute of the International Criminal Tribunal for Rwanda as of 31 January 2010, Article 3, http://www.unictr.org/Portals/0/English%5CLegal%5CStatute%5C2010.pdf, 13 October 2013.

28 The Law on the Establishment of the Extraordinary Chambers as Amended, 27 October 2004, Article 5, http://www.eccc.gov.kh/sites/default/files/legal-documents/KR_Law_as_amended_27_Oct_2004_Eng.pdf, 13 October 2013.

29 Cf. Schabas, Crimes, 212.

(f) Torture;
(g) Rape, sexual slavery, enforced prostitution, forced pregnancy, enforced sterilization, or any other form of sexual violence of comparable gravity;
(h) Persecution against any identifiable group or collectivity on political, racial, national, ethnic, cultural, religious, gender as defined in paragraph 3, or other grounds that are universally recognized as impermissible under international law, in connection with any act referred to in this paragraph or any crime within the jurisdiction of the Court;
(i) Enforced disappearance of persons;
(j) The crime of apartheid;
(k) Other inhumane acts of a similar character intentionally causing great suffering, or serious injury to body or to mental or physical health.' [30]

However, it adds a second criterion in its legal definitions contained in paragraph 2 of that same provision:

'2. For the purpose of paragraph 1:
(a) 'Attack directed against any civilian population' means a course of conduct involving the multiple commission of acts referred to in paragraph 1 against any civilian population, pursuant to or in furtherance of a State or organizational policy to commit such attack; [...].'[31]

Therein, not only is 'a widespread or systematic attack' of which it is further aware necessary, but also that such an attack must be part 'of a State or organizational policy'. However, it does away fully with the requirement of a discriminatory motive.[32] Still, though more of theoretical than practical importance, knowledge of the attack is included as necessity in order to meet the *mens rea* requirement. It has been commented that the significance of the definition of the Rome Statute lies within the fact that it was 'developed by multilateral negotiations among 160 states'.[33] Schabas says that the wording of the Rome Statute is 'really no more than the "expanded" definition of genocide that many have argued for over the years'.[34] Still, there are deficiencies to the protection against crimes against humanity under international law and the definitional frames do not fit 1:1 as most scholars would want one to believe. This has already been observed by the ICTR in the *Kayishema* case:

30 Rome Statute of the International Criminal Court, 17 July 1998, entry into force 1 July 2002, 2187 UNTS 3, Article 7(1).

31 Rome Statute of the International Criminal Court, 17 July 1998, entry into force 1 July 2002, 2187 UNTS 3, Article 7(2).

32 Darryl Robinson, Defining 'Crimes Against Humanity' at the Rome Conference, in: American Journal Of International Law 93/1, Washington 1999, 43–57, here 46f.

33 *Ibid.*, 56.

34 Schabas, Genocide, 12.

> 'The definition of the crime of genocide was based upon that of crimes against humanity, that is, a combination of "extermination and persecutions on political, racial or religious grounds" and it was intended to cover *"the intentional destruction of groups in whole or in substantial part"* (emphasis added). The crime of genocide is a type of crime against humanity. Genocide, however, is different from other crimes against humanity. The essential difference is that genocide requires the aforementioned specific intent to exterminate a protected group (in whole or in part) while crimes against humanity require the civilian population to be targeted as part of a widespread or systematic attack. There are instances where the discriminatory grounds coincide and overlap.'[35]

In 2008, an expert group calling itself the 'Crimes Against Humanity Initiative' of the Whitney R. Harris World Law Institute at the Washington University in St. Louis School of Law was established in order to propagate the creation of treaty similar to the Genocide Convention in order to create not only individual international criminal responsibility, but also state responsibility with regard to crimes against humanity.[36] It is further reported that by vote of 30 July 2013 the ILC took up the agenda into its long-term work plan.[37]

Article 1 of its 'Proposed International Convention on the Prevention and Punishment of Crimes Against Humanity' brought forth in 2010 reads as follows:

> 'Crimes against humanity, whether committed in time of armed conflict or in time of peace, constitute crimes under international law for which there is individual criminal responsibility. In addition, States may be held responsible for crimes against humanity pursuant to principles of State responsibility for internationally wrongful acts.'[38]

The further definition basically follows that of the Rome Statute.[39]

35 The Prosecutor v. Clément Kayishema and Obeḍ Ruzindana, Judgement, Case No. ICTR-95-1 (21 May 1999), 41f., para. 89.

36 See their online presence http://crimesagainsthumanity.wustl.edu/, 13 October 2013. The list of directors reads like a who-is-who of prominent scholars of international criminal law: Nadya Sadat, M. Cherif Bassiouni, Hans Corell, Richard Goldstone, Juan Méndez, William Schabas, and Christine Van den Wyngaert. See http://law.wustl.edu/harris/crimesagainsthumanity/?page_id=1301, 13 October 2013.

37 See http://law.wustl.edu/news/pages.aspx?id=9778, 13 October 2013.

38 Proposed International Convention on the Prevention and Punishment of Crimes Against Humanity, August 2010, as of 17 February 2012, Article 1, http://law.wustl.edu/harris/cah/docs/EnglishTreatyFinal.pdf, 13 October 2013.

39 See Proposed International Convention on the Prevention and Punishment of Crimes Against Humanity, August 2010, as of 17 February 2012, Article 3, http://law.wustl.edu/harris/cah/docs/EnglishTreatyFinal.pdf, 13 October 2013. Cf. Rome Statute of the International Criminal Court, 17 July 1998, entry into force 1 July 2002, 2187 UNTS 3, Article 7.

C. Genocide: The Crime of Crimes?

The term 'genocide' was coined by Polish jurist Raphaël Lemkin and popularized through his study 'Axis rule in occupied Europe'.[40] As opposed to other forms of atrocity, the term genocide was to 'convey the racial and national motivation of the crime'.[41] It is Lemkin's frequently quoted introduction to the concept, in which he not only meticulously explains the composition of the term but also outlines its scope of application:

> 'New conceptions require new terms. By "genocide" we mean the destruction of a nation or of an ethnic group. This new word, coined by the author to denote an old practice in its modern development, is made from the ancient Greek word *genos* (race, tribe) and the Latin *cide* (killing), thus corresponding in its formation to such words as tyrannicide, homocide [sic], infanticide, etc. Generally speaking, genocide does not necessarily mean the immediate destruction of a nation, except when accomplished by mass killings of all members of a nation. It is intended rather to signify a coordinated plan of different actions aiming at the destruction of essential foundations of the life of national groups, with the aim of annihilating the groups themselves. The objectives of such a plan would be disintegration of the political and social institutions, of culture, language, national feelings, religion, and the economic existence of national groups, and the destruction of the personal security, liberty, health, dignity, and even the lives of the individuals belonging to such groups. Genocide is directed against the national group as an entity, and the actions involved are directed against individuals, not in their individual capacity, but as members of the national group.'[42]

The term makes its first official appearance[43] in 'Count Three' of the indictment of the major Nazi war criminals International Military Tribunal's (IMT or 'Nuremberg Tribunal')[44], probably 'the first formal recognition of the crime of genocide'.

40 Raphaël Lemkin, Axis Rule in Occupied Europe. Laws of Occupation, Analysis of Government, Proposals for Redress, Washington 1944. Parts of the following description of the genesis of the concept of genocide have been published as part of a more detailed account in Beham, 'Borrowed' Concepts, see *supra* n. 1.

41 Memorandum from Raphaël Lemkin to R. Kempner, 5 June 1946, United States Holocaust Memorial Museum, R. Kempner Papers (RS 71.001), quoted from A. Dirk Moses – Raphael Lemkin, Culture, and the Concept of Genocide, in: Donald Bloxham – A. Dirk Moses (Eds.), The Oxford Handbook of Genocide Studies, Oxford/New York 2010, 19–41, here 28. In this context it is not clear why Cathie Carmichael writes that Lemkin 'was creating a neologism rather than simply forging a juridical concept', see Cathie Carmichael, Genocide before the Holocaust, New Haven 2009, 9.

42 Lemkin, Axis Rule, 79.

43 Cf. Leo Kuper, Genocide. Its Political Use in the Twentieth Century, New Haven/London 1982, 22.

44 International Military Tribunal, Indictment, The United States of America *et al.* against Herman Wilhelm Göring *et al.*, reprinted in: John C. Watkins – John Paul Weber (Eds.), War

However, there was no consecutive reference by the ITM itself to the term or the concept.[45] It has been commented that the terms 'crimes against humanity' and 'genocide' were used as if synonymous.[46]

It did not take long for the newly established United Nations to address the issue. After passing a resolution reaffirming the so-called 'Nuremberg Principles'[47], there followed the unanimous adoption of the resolution addressing the 'The Crime of Genocide', requesting the Economic and Social Council (ECOSOC) to draw up 'a draft convention on the crime of genocide to be submitted to the next regular session of the General Assembly'.[48] That same resolution is the cause for many a confusion and discussion regarding the scope of the crime. In its preambular paragraphs it defines the concept as

> 'a denial of the right of existence of entire human groups, as homicide is the denial of the right to live of individual human beings. [...] Many instances of such crimes of genocide have occurred when racial, religious, political and other groups have been destroyed, entirely or in part.'[49]

It goes on to affirm in its operative paragraphs

> 'that genocide is a crime under international law which the civilized world condemns and for the commission of which principals and accomplices – whether private individuals, public officials or statesmen, and whether the crime is committed on religious, racial, political or any other ground – are punishable.'[50]

In contrast to any following definition under international law, this resolution includes 'political and other groups'. Interestingly enough, the preambular paragraphs of the Genocide Convention – with its more restrictive definition[51] –, which followed only two years later, recall General Assembly Resolution 96.[52] However,

---

Crimes and War Crime Trials. From Leipzig to the ICC and Beyond. Cases, Materials and Comments, Durham 2006, 127–143 [Göring misspelt 'Göering' here], and also available at The Avalon Project, Documents in Law, History and Diplomacy, http://avalon.law.yale.edu/imt/count.asp, 28 February 2013.

45 Kuper, Genocide, 22.

46 William A. Schabas, The Law and Genocide, in: Donald Bloxham – A. Dirk Moses (Eds.), The Oxford Handbook of Genocide Studies, Oxford/New York 2010, 123–141, here 125.

47 UNGA – Res. 95 (I), Affirmation of the Principles of International Law recognized by the Charter of the Nürnberg Tribunal, 11 December 1946, 1 UN – GAOR, 188, UN Doc. A/64/Add. 1.

48 UNGA – Res. 96 (I), The Crime of Genocide, 11 December 1946, 1 UN – GAOR, 188, UN Doc. A/64/Add. 1.

49 Ibid.

50 Ibid.

51 See *infra*.

52 Convention for the Prevention and Punishment of the Crime of Genocide, 9 December 1948, entered into force 12 January 1951, 78 UNTS 277, preamble.

describing genocide as a crime against humanity, as propagated by France during the drafting process of the Charter, was rejected.[53]

In 1948, four years after Lemkin's treatise had been published, the General Assembly of the United Nations adopted the Genocide Convention.[54] Its Articles II and III – which are in legal doctrine also held to represent customary international law[55] or even *ius cogens*[56], placing it atop of the hierarchical pyramid of sources of international law – define the act of genocide, which is applicable up until today:

> 'Article II
> In the present Convention, genocide means any of the following acts committed with intent to destroy, in whole or in part, a national, ethnical, racial or religious group, as such:
> (a) Killing members of the group;
> (b) Causing serious bodily or mental harm to members of the group;
> (c) Deliberately inflicting on the group conditions of life calculated to bring about its physical destruction in whole or in part;
> (d) Imposing measures intended to prevent births within the group; (e) Forcibly transferring children of the group to another group.
> Article III
> The following acts shall be punishable:
> (a) Genocide;
> (b) Conspiracy to commit genocide;
> (c) Direct and public incitement to commit genocide;
> (d) Attempt to commit genocide;
> (e) Complicity in genocide.'[57]

Doctrine has often called for a broadening of the scope of application of the Genocide Convention, such as the inclusion of political groups[58], which indeed

53 See Schabas, Genocide, 73.

54 Convention for the Prevention and Punishment of the Crime of Genocide, 9 December 1948, entered into force 12 January 1951, 78 UNTS 277.

55 See, for example, Schabas, Genocide, 6, 648; Simma – Paulus, Responsibility, 308f., in particular also ns. 36–39.

56 For example Ian Brownlie, Principles of Public International Law, Oxford/New York 2008 508–511. See also the judgment by the ICJ in Armed Activities on the Territory of the Congo (New Application: 2002) (Democratic Republic of the Congo v. Rwanda), Jurisdiction and Admissibility, Judgment (3 February 2006), ICJ Reports 2006, 6, here 32, para. 64.

57 Convention for the Prevention and Punishment of the Crime of Genocide, 9 December 1948, entered into force 12 January 1951, 78 UNTS 277, Articles II and III.

58 Cf. Boris Barth, Genozid. Völkermord im 20. Jahrhundert. Geschichte, Theorien, Kontroversen [Genocide. Genocide in the 20th Century. History, Theories, Controversies], München 2006, 19. For a list of further examples see Schabas, Genocide, 161.

some national legislations have followed.[59] Notwithstanding such voices, the 'final'[60] definition of Article II of the Genocide Convention has found its *verbatim* inclusion in the statutes of the International Criminal Tribunal for the former Yugoslavia (ICTY)[61], the International Criminal Tribunal for Rwanda (ICTR)[62] and the International Criminal Court (ICC)[63] as well as numerous national legislations.[64] Furthermore, the elements of genocide are legally now even more clearly outlined in the ICC's Elements of Crimes list.[65]

D. Siamese Twins?

Article I of the Genocide Convention specifies that genocide constitutes an international crime in times of war as well as in times of peace[66], seeing as crimes against humanity at the time were only deemed international crimes when occurring in connection with an armed conflict.[67] As has been mentioned above, this was one of the main motivators for establishing genocide as an international crime.[68] The conception of this relationship has since shifted. The nexus requirement between crimes against humanity and internal or international armed conflict is held to no longer exist.[69] The legal view – at least in doctrine – makes geno-

59 On the French implementation of the Genocide Convention see Schabas, Genocide, 6, 131. On the Canadian implementation of the Rome Statute (see *infra* n. XX) see Schabas, Genocide, 6, 151 and 161f. for further examples, including Bangladesh, Costa Rica, Lithuania, Panama, Peru and Slovenia.

60 On the status of the discourse on inclusion of political groups in international law see Schabas, Genocide, 163f.

61 Statute of the International Criminal Tribunal for the former Yugoslavia, Article 4(2), http://www.icty.org/x/file/Legal%20Library/Statute/statute_sept09_en.pdf, 28 February 2013.

62 Statute of the International Criminal Tribunal for Rwanda, Article 2(2), http://www.unictr.org/Portals/0/English%5CLegal%5CStatute%5C2010.pdf, 28 February 2013. See, however, its jurisprudence, Schabas, Genocide, 151–153.

63 Rome Statute of the International Criminal Court, 2187 UNTS 3, 17 July 1998, entered into force 1 July 2002, Article 6, http://www2.icc-cpi.int/NR/rdonlyres/ADD16852-AEE9-4757-ABE7-9CDC7CF02886/283503/RomeStatutEng1.pdf, 28 February 2013. While drafting the Rome Statute, only Cuba argued for the inclusion of political groups: 'Ms. Cueto Milian (Cuba), while agreeing that the provisions on genocide in the draft Statute were generally acceptable, thought that they could be expanded by the inclusion of social and political groupings and a reference to intentional conduct.' See United Nations Diplomatic Conference of Plenipotentiaries on the Establishment of an International Criminal Court, Rome, Italy, 15 June – 17 July 1998, 3rd meeting of the Committee of the Whole, UN Doc. A/CONF.183/C.1/SR.3, 151. Cf. Schabas, Law, 130f.

64 See Schabas, Genocide, 6.

65 International Criminal Court, Elements of Crimes, ICC-ASP/1/3(part II-B), 9 September 2002, http://www2.icc-cpi.int/NR/rdonlyres/336923D8-A6AD-40EC-AD7B-45BF9D-E73D56/0/ElementsOfCrimesEng.pdf, 28 February 2013.

66 Genocide Convention, Article I.

67 Schabas, Genocide, 12f., 645. See the elaboration on the evolution of crimes against humanity as a legal concept *supra* under point B.

68 See *supra* n. 22 and the foregoing text.

69 See Schabas, Crimes, 216.

cide a subset, or *lex specialis* if one will, of crimes against humanity.[70] The ICTY in *Tadić* put genocide next to apartheid 'as two of its [crimes against humanity's] most egregious manifestations'.[71] According to Schabas, the latter may 'be usefully viewed as the most extreme form of crimes against humanity'.[72] He further observes that the approach of international criminal tribunals has shifted its view to consider the three core crimes, genocide, crimes against humanity, and war crimes to be 'of equal gravity'.[73]

Even if genocide may now be safely viewed as an 'under-category' of crimes against humanity, there are still also differences in the level of legal enforceability. While the Genocide Convention allows for jurisdiction of the International Court of Justice, there is no convention putting the same level of obligations upon states with regard to crimes against humanity.[74] Schabas argues though that 'the obligations upon States found in the Genocide Convention now apply *mutatis mutandis*, on a customary basis, in the case of crimes against humanity'.[75]

Yet somehow, public opinion still perceives crimes against humanity as something less severe, not calling for the same form of resolute action by the international community.[76] Accusation of genocide serves as a weapon in conflict, with which an enemy can easily be made to be seen as a pariah against whom mobilization is sought from other actors[77], and being brought in connection with it may create an almost impervious stigma upon a person, an organization or a state.[78] This does not seem to be the case for crimes against humanity. For example, the International Commission of Inquiry on Darfur to the United Nations Secretary-General to include the following passage in its 2005 report:

> 'The conclusion that no genocidal policy has been pursued and implemented in Darfur by the Government authorities, directly or through the militias under their control, should not be taken in any way as detracting from the gravity of the crimes perpetrated in that region. International offences such as the crimes

70 See Schabas, Genocide, 14f. Steven R. Ratner differentiates between a customary law crime, being crimes against humanity, and a treaty-based law, genocide; Steven R. Ratner, Labeling Mass Atrocity. Does and Should International Criminal Law Rank Evil?, in: Wayne Law Review 54, Detroit 2008, 569–575, here 569. From a legal dogmatic point of view, this does not really make sense, seeing as genocide may also constitute customary international law, while crimes against humanity have now found inclusion in a number of statutes, including the Rome Statute of the ICC.

71 Prosecutor v. Tadić, Opinion and Judgement, No. IT-94-1-T (7 May 1997) para. 622.

72 Schabas, Crimes, 216.

73 Schabas, Genocide, 652f.

74 Cf. Schabas, Crimes, 216.

75 Schabas, Genocide, 14.

76 Cf. Ratner, Labeling, 570.

77 Cf. Barth, Genozid, 44f., who also gives a list of practical examples.

78 Cf. Schabas, Genocide, 10.

against humanity and war crimes that have been committed in Darfur may be no less serious and heinous than genocide.'[79]

And further:

> 'As stated above genocide is not necessarily the most serious international crime. Depending upon the circumstances, *such international offences as crimes against humanity or large scale war crimes may be no less serious and heinous than genocide.*'[80]

The awareness factor may be easily illustrated by a simple Google search: While there are around 25,300,000 hits for the term 'genocide', a search for 'crimes against humanity' in inverted commas brings up (merely) approximately 16,000,000 hits, the second one following the obligatory Wikipedia entry being for an independent music record label by the name of 'Crimes Against Humanity Records'.[81]

But are these facts indeed contrary to the agendas of Genocide studies or international legal scholarship? The actual goal setting by Genocide studies seems clear though. While crimes against humanity should function as the legal *chapeau*, genocide should remain mainly as a tool of agenda. Jones observes 'a subtle but noticeable shift in international tribunals away from genocide and toward crimes against humanity as the preferred legal framework'.[82] He clearly lays out his view at the outset of his 'Comprehensive Introduction' to the subject:

> 'The reader should keep in mind throughout, however, that there is just one international-legal definition of genocide. When I touch on legal aspects of genocide, I highlight the UN Convention definition; but I deploy it and other legal framings instrumentally, not dogmatically. I seek to convey and understanding of genocide in which international law is a vital but not a dominant consideration. In part, this is because at the level of international law, genocide is perhaps being displaced by the framing of "crimes against humanity", which is easier to prosecute and imposes much the same punishments as for genocide convictions. The result may be that "genocide", in the coming years and decades, will prove more significant as *an intellectual and scholarly framework* (a heuristic device, for the jargon-inclined), and as *a tool of advocacy and mobilization*.'[83]

---

79 Report of the International Commission of Inquiry on Darfur to the United Nations Secretary-General, Pursuant to Security Council Resolution 1564 of 18 September 2004, Geneva, 25 January 2005, S/2005/60, 4.

80 *Ibid.*, 132, para. 522.

81 Search for the terms 'crimes against humanity' and 'genocide' on http://www.google.com/, 13 October 2013. The website referred to is http://www.cahrecords.com/, same date as the search.

82 See Adam Jones, Genocide. A Comprehensive Introduction, London/New York 2011, 540.

83 See *ibid.*, 25.

He continues later further on in his book, laying out these functions in more detail:

> 'The growing prominence of crimes against humanity in legal and public discourse also points to something I have long sensed: that the most significant deployment of "genocide" may *not* be as a legal-prosecutorial device, but as an intellectual concept and – recognizing the term's unequalled rhetorical power – an advocacy tool to arouse public concern, shame perpetrators, and press for intervention. This may also free the term form its unnecessarily restrictive framing in the UN Genocide Convention, with its limited target groups and high evidentiary requirement of genocidal intent.'[84]

Schabas comments on the subject seem more differentiated:

> 'If labelling genocide the "crime of crimes" has contributed to the difficulty in explaining the terrible seriousness of crimes against humanity which, after all, formed the basis of the 1915 allegations against the Ottomans as well as the judgments at Nuremberg, then there are solid grounds to abandon the expression.'[85]

However, this does not keep him from holding on to the relevance of genocide and its inherent symbolism for public debate and perception:

> 'International lawyers seem sometimes to insist in vain that the distinction between genocide and crimes against humanity is of little or no importance. The argument is not about the state of the law: it is one of symbolism and semantics. If the result of the terminological quarrel is to insist upon the supreme heinousness of "racial hatred", for want of a better term, and to reiterate society's condemnation of the mass killings of Jews, Tutsis and Armenians, to cite the primary historical examples of the past century, the distinction retains and deserves all of its significance. From this perspective, genocide stand to crimes against humanity as premeditated murder stand to intentional homicide. Genocide deserves its title as the "crime of crimes".'[86]

And in even stronger terms, with regard to state commitment to atrocity prevention, he argues against hampering with the current legal definition of genocide:

> 'It has become apparent that there are undesirable consequences to enlarging or diluting the definition of genocide. This weakens the terrible stigma associated with the crime and demeans the suffering of its victims. In its also likely to en-

84 See *ibid.*, 540f.

85 Schabas, Genocide, 653.

86 Schabas, Genocide, 15.

feeble whatever commitment States may believe they have to prevent the crime. The broader and more uncertain the definition, the less responsibility States will be prepared to assume.'[87]

Conclusion

While both concepts came to life in the context atrocious historical events, with the purpose of describing or penalizing such acts, the politically compromised definition of crimes against humanity used at the Nuremberg trials made it necessary to come up with a distinct concept in order to penalize atrocity crimes during peacetime. Following a brief synonymous life within the Nuremberg indictments, both international crimes went their separate ways, with the Rome Statute of the ICC seemingly bringing them back together. As opposed to genocide, a legal term that may be used within other field of humanities or social science for the benefit of capturing the element of intent focused against the destruction of a particular group, it is difficult to assert such a purpose for crimes against humanity considering what has been said above on the broadness of its scope and acts falling within the definition. In a legal sense, the evolution of the concept of crimes against humanity has at least been able to catch up with genocide in the sense of peacetime applicability.

However, it seems that the causal connection between the Holocaust and the term genocide has endowed the latter with the necessary collective memory that elevates its impact on the public conscience to an almost unrivaled level. Additionally, on a very semantic level, the neologism 'genocide' has proven the catchier term as opposed to crimes against humanity, often awkwardly abbreviated CAH. This is made particularly evident in such statements as the before mentioned assessments by prominent scholars such as Adam Jones or William Schabas. Unfortunately, this position exacerbates what I have called in my previous contribution the 'meta effect'[88], namely that any acts not fitting the genocide definition are out of hope of meeting its impact threshold. Circumstances may arise, in which atrocities are considered to be of a lesser moral gravity, even though they might entail the systematic and widespread killing of dozens, hundreds, thousands, or even millions of innocent civilians through government forces. (One might mention the discussion on Stalinist crimes, recently popularized again through a contribution by Norman Naimark.) The consequence of this is usually inaction by the international community, accompanied by at best short-term media coverage and inexistence of a public conscience of the events in the long-term.[89]

---

87 *Ibid.*, 10.

88 See, Beham, 'Borrowed' Concepts, 88–91.

89 See, *e.g.*, the above mentioned need to clarify the point with regard to the situation in Darfur *supra* n.

While Genocide studies, governments, NGOs and private interest groups fight the war of the words, historiography should briefly consider, take a deep breath, and establish a best practice of terms, not contributing to the will for action bias – atrocities, not laden with the burden of legal definition, might serve as such a term, still conveying the extent and gravity of acts committed. It should rely on legal terminology only where it serves an added value purpose to the respective analysis as has been argued for the legal definition of genocide in the previous contribution.[90]

90 See, Beham, 'Borrowed' Concepts, 91.

Henriett Éva Dinók

Questions of Hate Crimes with Special Regard to Austrian and Hungarian Case Law

University of Alberta

The doctoral project focuses on bias-motivated crimes. Bias crimes, including, but not limited to racially motivated hate crimes differ from other criminal activities in several regards. In Hungary, similarly to other Central-European post-communist countries in the region, despite the fact that the legislative framework sets forth a number of bias-crime provisions, authorities often fail to apply them. While in the UK the number of cases is around 40,000 annually for a population of 63 million, in Austria, for a population of 8.4 million, about one hundred cases, in Hungary, with a population of 10 million, only a dozen cases are prosecuted. The paper provides an overview of the general approaches to hate crimes through examples from the Austrian and Hungarian legislation, cases and statistics, explains the above mentioned differences, points out the reasons of the differences between the official and civil statistics, and gives examples of good practices from North America where I am currently doing my research. Finally, it highlights the most important questions in addressing hate crimes.

Definition of Hate Crime

The first question is what hate crime is. Hate crimes are criminal acts committed with a bias motive. The first element of a hate crime is the act that constitutes an offence under criminal law. Common offences are assaults, threats, arson, murders, and property damage. The second element is the hate or bias motivation. The term 'bias' is more appropriate, because in several cases the offender might not hate the victim, but is motivated by bias, by some negative attitude towards the victim.[1] The negative attitude is based on the personal characteristics of the victims; the perpetrator intentionally chooses the victim because of particular characteristic, such as race, ethnicity, national origin, religion, sexual orientation, or disability. There is no shared global approach to who/which groups should be

1 Frederick M. Lawrence, Punishing Hate. Bias Crimes under American Law, Cambridge 1999, 9–28; Tim J. Berard, Hate Crimes and their Criminalization, in: Research in Social Problems & Public Policy 17, Bingley 2010, 15–40, here 16f.

protected by hate crime laws. Therefore, specific definitions of hate crime differ under domestic laws. The Office for Democratic Institutions and Human Rights (ODIHR) of the Organization for Security and Co-operation in Europe (OSCE)[2] gives one of the most comprehensive definitions:[3]

> 'A) Any criminal offence, including offences against persons or property, where the victim, premises, or target of the offence are selected because of their real or perceived connection, attachment, affiliation, support, or membership with a group as defined in Part B.
>
> B) A group may be based upon a characteristic common to its members, such as real or perceived race, national or ethnic origin, language, colour, religion, sex, age, mental or physical disability, sexual orientation, or other similar factor.'

This negative attitude may not necessarily be rooted in the perception of the perpetrator, but may be rooted in the social prejudices.[4] The distinction is thereby made between prototypical and opportunistic hate crimes. The prototypical hate crime is an act, where the perpetrator targets the victim because of the victim's group membership. Opportunistic hate crimes are not motivated by a perpetrator's hostility towards a particular group. Rather, the perpetrator intentionally selects a (supposedly) vulnerable[5] victim for gaining 'easy money' or 'respect' within his peer group.[6]

---

2 The OSCE is the world's largest regional security organization with 57 States (Austria and Hungary are among the participating States). The Organization has a long history of dealing with hate crimes. The OSCE Ministerial Council has established the ODIHR, which serves as a collection point for information and statistics on hate crimes and makes this information publicly available.

3 Hate Crimes in the OSCE Region: Incidents and Responses, Annual Report for 2006, 9, http://www.osce.org/odihr/26759, 10 October 2013.

4 'In 2006, Michael Sandy, a gay man, was attacked by three men who were trying to rob him, he fled for his life across a highway, he was struck by a car and killed. The men testified at trial that they did not actually hate Michael because he was gay, but they targeted him because he was gay and they thought a gay man would be less likely to fight back. The court rejected this defense. The Court interpreted the New York hate crime law to require nothing more than the intentional selection of the victim because of a particular attribute – in this case his sexual orientation.' Allison Jernow, A Human Rights Approach to Hate Crimes. Closing Conference of Working with the Police and Challenging Hate Crimes in Europe 2008–2011, 8 and 9 December 2011 in The Hague, The Netherlands, http://www.ilga-europe.org/home/issues/hate_crime_hate_speech/projects/ilga_europe_hate_crime_project/closing_conference, 31 January 2014.

5 Jordan Blair Woods, Taking the 'Hate' Out of Hate Crimes. Applying Unfair Advantage Theory to Justify the Enhanced Punishment of Opportunistic Bias Crimes, in: UCLA Law Review 56/2, Los Angeles 2008, 489–521, here 491.

6 Consider a man who is looking to prove his masculinity to his friends and chooses to assault an Amish man because he believes that the Amish will not fight back by virtue of their pacifist commitments.

Significance

Hate crimes differ from other criminal acts in several regards. Firstly, their impact on individual victims is more serious. One of the most comprehensive studies in the field of hate crime victimization was conducted by McDevitt, Balboni, Garcia, and Gu in 2001. The study takes a comparative look into the experience of bias and non-bias victims. The study surveys a comparable group of violent bias and non-bias assault victims identified from law enforcement and advocacy agency legal records. The victims of bias crimes recorded statistically significant higher level of depression, nervousness, lack of concentration, and unintentional thinking of the incident. They also asked how safe the victims feel after the crime. Bias crime victims are significantly less likely to feel safe.[7] According to the British Crime Survey, higher proportions of victims of racially motivated crime, compared with victims of non-racially motivated crime, reported being 'worried' or 'very worried' about future victimization (worry about rape provides the exception to the trend, as equal proportions of minority ethnic respondents were worried about future victimization, irrespective of whether or not they were victims of racially motivated crime.).[8]

Secondly, hate crimes affect the whole group and not just the victim. The victim experiences the incident as a message that his or her group is of inferior value.[9] Many scholars[10] emphasize that hate crimes are 'message crimes' that emit a warning to all members of the victim's community.[11] Consequently, such crimes send a message to the victim and the entire community that they are not welcome, they do not belong to society, and every member of the community could equally be a target.[12]

Finally, patterns of violent hate crime can also serve as indicators and (somewhat) early warning signals for social or ethnic conflict, because hate crimes might escalate to intergroup aggression. Hate crimes, therefore, can damage the fabric of society and fragment communities.[13] Therefore, hate crimes call into question the basic concept and self-understanding of modern pluralist societies, which is based

7 Jack McDevitt – Jennifer Balboni – Luis Garcia – Joann Gu, Consequences for Victims. A Comparison of Bias and Non-bias Motivated Assaults, in: American Behavioral Scientist 46/1, Thousand Oaks 2001, 27–50, here 32.

8 Paul Iganski – Sporidoula Lagou, How Hate Crimes Hurt More: Evidence from the British Crime Survey, in: Barbara Perry – Paul Iganski (Eds.), Hate Crimes. The Consequences of Hate Crime, Westport/London 2009, 1–13, here 9.

9 Iganski – Lagou, Hate, 12.

10 See, *e.g.*, Kellina M. Craig-Henderson, The Psychological Harms of Hate: Implication and Interventions, in: Barbara Perry – Paul Iganski (Eds.), Hate Crimes. The Consequences of Hate Crime, Westport/London 2009, 15–30; Barbara Perry – Patrik Olsson, Hate Crime as a Human Rights Violation, in: Barbara Perry – Paul Iganski (Eds.), Hate Crimes. The Consequences of Hate Crime, Westport/London, 2009 175–191.

11 Perry – Olsson, Hate, 179.

12 ODIHR, Hate Crime Laws. A Practical Guide, Warsaw 2009, 17, http://www.osce.org/odihr/36426?download=true, 22 January 2014.

13 *Ibid.*

on the notion of individual human dignity. A related area is that anxiety triggered by the victimization of one's group can easily erupt into periods of retaliatory violence. For instance, in the United States, Chief Justice Rehnquist acknowledged this in the widely cited *Wisconsin v. Mitchell* (1993).[14] He argued for the recognition of hate crime as a special class of offence because of the likelihood that it would, in fact, initiate yet more violence.[15]

Legal Framework

Three main approaches may be identified in the field of hate crime laws in different countries. The least common approach is that acts committed with hate-based motivation constitute a specific category of offences, by redefining the conduct that is already a criminal act as a specific crime.[16] The second approach is the most common, the sentence enhancement type, where the perpetrator might be sentenced to a more severe penalty due to the hate/bias motivation; these laws increase the penalty for a particular crime. There are two possible ways of penalty enhancement: the specific[17] and the general[18] penalty enhancement. A specific penalty enhancement applies an increased sentence to specific crimes committed with bias motivation. The general penalty enhancement applies to nearly all crimes in the criminal code. It usually sets out aggravating circumstances and can include bias motivation against certain protected characteristics.[19] The bias motive may be considered an aggravating circumstance in an 'ordinary' crime, requiring a stronger penalty. Third, some hate crime laws make no amendments to the criminal law, but require administrative agencies to collect hate crime statistics. Furthermore, we can find a combination of these approaches.[20] Whether a hate crime law takes the first (substantive offence) or second (sentence enhancement) form, the result is the same – more severe punishment.

The Austrian (StGB – Strafgesetzbuch) and Hungarian (Btk – Büntető törvénykönyv) Criminal Codes combine the different ways of regulation.

---

14 On the evening of October 7, 1989, a group of young black men and boys, including Mitchell, gathered at an apartment complex in Kenosha, Wisconsin. Several members of the group discussed a scene from the motion picture 'Mississippi Burning', in which a white man beat a young black boy who was praying. The group moved outside and beat the first white boy severely, and stole his tennis shoes. The boy was rendered unconscious and remained in a coma for four days. http://www.law.cornell.edu/supct/html/92-515.ZO.html, 26 January 2014.

15 Perry – Olson, Hate, 179.

16 If, for instance, the Criminal Code creates new offences of 'racially-aggravated' assault.

17 If, for instance, the Criminal Code provides that murder committed on racial motive is punishable by a minimum term of 10 years' imprisonment; without the penalty enhancement the minimum period is five years.

18 If the Criminal Code provides an aggravating circumstance, *e.g.*, racist and xenophobic motives that courts consider when it impose the punishment in the case of assault, murder, harassment or other crimes.

19 ODIHR, Prosecuting Hate Crimes. A Practical Guide, Working Draft, March 2010, 4.

20 ODIHR, Hate, 80.

A. Aggravating Circumstance/Sentence Enhancement

In the Austrian Criminal Code, bias motive is considered as an aggravating circumstance to the 'ordinary' crimes, and requires a more severe penalty. One of the aggravating circumstances that is considered by courts when imposing punishment under Article 33 is 'when the perpetrator [...] 5. has acted out of a racist, xenophobic or other particularly reprehensible motive; [...]'.[21]

In the Hungarian Criminal Code, the provisions of assault (Article 164) and homicide (Article 160) include an aggravating circumstances called malicious motive (when somebody commits a crime with a base reason or with a base purpose).

B. Substantive offence

Austria's hate crime legislation does not create a specific category of offences based on motivation.[22] The only provision is the 'incitement to violence'. Pursuant to Article 283 (1) 'In a manner likely to jeopardize public order, incites to hostile action against a church or religious community established in the country or a group defined by their affiliation to such a church or religious community or to a race, nation, ethnic group or state is punishable with up to two years imprisonment; [...]'.[23]

However, hate crimes are different from laws that penalize public expression of hate, also known as hate speech or incitement to hatred laws. These laws do not have the element of a common crime (*i.e.* assault, threat, vandalism, etc.), but criminalize certain forms of expression.[24]

The Hungarian Criminal Code contains a *sui generis* hate crime provision on 'violence against a member of a community', prescribing more severe punishment than similar acts of violence without a hate motivation. Under Article 216, any person who displays an ostensively anti-communal conduct against a member of a community, which is suitable for inducing indignation or alarm in the members

21 The translation is based on an online legislative database. Legislationline was created in 2002 to assist OSCE participating States in bringing their legislation into line with relevant international human-rights standards. It is the most comprehensive database on legislation related to hate crime in English. The above used text is an excerpt. Legislationline, Austria, Hate Crime Laws, http://legislationline.org/topics/country/44/topic/4/subtopic/79, 26 January 2014.

22 There are a number of concepts which are closely related to hate crime which are not included within my research.
Although genocide is a crime motivated by bias it has been excluded from the research, because it has certain special characteristics which make it different from 'ordinary' crimes. Although national legislations may prohibit genocide and other related crimes, they are not, in this context, described as hate crime laws. Genocide requires an intention to destroy — in whole or in part – a national, ethnic, racial or religious group. This is qualitatively and quantitatively different from hate crimes, as are all crimes under international law that require widespread, systematic acts of violence. The legislative, investigative and prosecutorial issues arising from such international crimes are very different from those which arise in hate crimes. All such crimes are therefore outside the scope of this paper.

23 Legislationline, Austria, Hate Crimes Laws, http://legislationline.org/topics/country/44/topic/4/subtopic/79, 26 January 2014.

24 ODIHR, Prosecuting, 3.

of the community, or assaults another person for belonging to, whether in fact or under presumption, of a national, ethnic, racial, [or] religious group, or certain groups of the population, especially their disability, sexual identity or gender identity, or compels him by applying coercion or duress to do, not to do, or to endure something [...]. Pursuant to Article 216(2), the punishment shall be imprisonment between two to eight years if the act of crime is committed: (a) by force of arms; (b) with a deadly weapon; (c) causing a considerable injury of interest; (d) with the torment of the injured party; (e) in groups; (f) in criminal conspiracy. Finally, any person who engages in preparations for violence against member of community is guilty of a misdemeanor punishable by imprisonment for up to two years.[25]

Official Statistics

Most states collect some form of data on hate crimes by the police and/or public prosecutors and the judiciary, just as in Austria and Hungary (Figure 1). The report of ODIHR provides a brief overview of the hate crime data-collection systems and results, including a comparative table with the number of reported hate crimes from the years 2010 through 2012.[26]

Year	Austria*	Hungary**
2010	99	19
2011	57	35
2012	90	36

Figure 1: Cases recorded by the police in Austria and Hungary

* Data include crimes of incitement to hatred, in addition to hate crimes.

** Data include crimes of incitement to hatred and of discrimination, in addition to hate crimes.

Figure 1 and 2 present a summary of the number of hate crimes recorded in these countries above. However, the number of cases needs to be analyzed with great caution, because some states record hate crimes specifically, while others look at the crime statistics for general figures. The number of recorded cases of hate crimes simply indicates incidents acknowledged by the authorities as hate crimes

25 These are examples for the Austrian and Hungarian regulation. The following offences in the Hungarian Criminal Code are to be considered as hate crimes: 'incitement against a community' (Btk. Art. 332), 'violation of the freedom of conscience and religion' (Btk. Art. 215.), 'use of totalitarian symbols' (Btk. Art. 335), 'theft or criminal damage against religious or consecrated objects or cemeteries and other burial sites' (Btk. Art. 370(3) b; Art. 371(3)(bb)), 'public denial of the sins committed by the national socialist and communist systems' (Btk. Art. 333). The Btk. Art. 216 is based on the author's translation.

26 ODIHR, Hate Crimes in the OSCE Region, Incidents and Responses, Annual Report for 2012, 25–30, http://tandis.odihr.pl/hcr2012/, 27 January 2014.

or reported by victims.[27] When hate crimes are enacted, for instance, as substantive offences, the crime usually has greater visibility and hate crime data is easier to collect. States that do not have any express provisions to address bias motivation, general sentencing principles can be applied to impose a greater sentence for hate crimes, but the statistics may not appear all of the hate crimes. For instance, there are two main official sources for the number of hate crime offences in England and Wales: the Crime Survey for England and Wales (CSEW) and police recorded crimes.[28]

Country	Recorded Cases
United Kingdom	41,204
Sweden	5,518
Germany	4,514
Belgium	(first semester) 614
Switzerland	181
Ireland	98

Figure 2: Cases recorded by the police (OSCE 2011)

Consequently, the low numbers of registered hate crimes in Austria and Hungary cannot be explained by the low level of actual prevalence, rather with the limited data collection, as the hereunder victim survey indicates it. Besides, there are a number of differences in the coverage of the victimization surveys and police recorded crimes. In a report on racist violence in 15 EU Member States, the Vienna-based European Monitoring Centre on Racism and Xenophobia concluded that no data are available that can reliably be used to assess the extent of the phenomena of hate crimes in the Member States. In several countries, no official data on 'hate crimes' is collected at all. In the European Survey on Crime and Safety (EUICS) 2005 respondents in the 15 old EU Member States were asked whether they had fallen victim to any crime because or partly because of their nationality, race, or color, religious belief or sexual orientation in 2004. The results allow a first rough assessment in comparative perspective of the extent of such 'hate crimes' in the EU as perceived by respondents (see Figure 3).[29]

27 ODIHR, OSCE, 23.

28 Home Office, Office for National Statistics and Ministry of Justice, An Overview of Hate Crime in England and Wales, London 2013, https://www.gov.uk/government/uploads/system/uploads/attachment_data/file/266358/hate-crime-2013.pdf, 27 January 2014.

29 The Burden of Crime in the EU, Research Report, A Comparative Analysis of the European Crime and Safety Survey (EUICS) 2005, 52, http://www.europeansafetyobservatory.eu/downloads/EUICS%20-%20The%20Burden%20of%20Crime%20in%20the%20EU.pdf, 11 October 2013.

Country	%
United Kingdom	4.2
Sweden	3.0
Germany	2.6
Belgium	4.1
Ireland	2.3
Austria	1.8
Hungary	1.1

Figure 3: Percentages of population victimized by hate crime in 2004

Differences between victimization surveys and police statistics, as well as the obstacles to monitoring and latency in general are to be explained by two sets of factors: those that discourage victims from reporting crimes to the police, and those that result in offences not being recorded as having hate motivation. These factors result in both underreporting and under-recording of hate-motivated crimes.[30]

The reasons of differences in the statistics, with special regard to Hungary, are the following: the first is underreporting, which may derive from the victim's previous negative experience of the police, or the victims may believe that nothing will happen, the police will not take the report seriously, police officers and prosecutors will not take appropriate action to respond to the incident, either as an ordinary crime or as a hate crime. Research shows that there is a low level of general trust in the police among members of minority groups.[31] A common reason is the fear of hostility or prejudice by the police (secondary victimization) or fear of retaliation; many victims fear that if they report a crime the perpetrators or others with similar views will retaliate against them (or their family, community). Victims may be unaware of the relevant legal provisions and the available procedures to access justice. In the case of the Lesbian, Gay, Bisexual and Trans-

30 ODIHR, Preventing and Responding to Hate Crimes, A Resource Guide for NGOs in the OSCE Region, 34, http://www.osce.org/odihr/39821?download=true, 27 January 2014.

31 'The EU-MIDIS survey results also show a pattern between general levels of trust in the police and perceptions of discriminatory police profiling. In the survey, respondents were asked a general question about their trust in the police prior to being asked questions about their experiences of police stops and whether they considered they were the victims of discriminatory police profiling. The results indicate that those respondents who tended to have lower levels of trust in the police also tended to perceive ethnic profiling more in their encounters with the police; for example: 50% of minority respondents who were stopped by the police and did not consider it to be a result of ethnic profiling said they generally trust the police, whereas only 27% of minority respondents who were stopped and did consider it to be a result of profiling tended to trust the police. Although it cannot be determined from the results whether heightened distrust in the police predated respondents' negative perceptions of police treatment, or whether negative perceptions of police profiling led to increased distrust in the police, the findings do point to the existence of a relationship that cannot be readily overlooked.' European Union Agency for Fundamental Rights (FRA), Towards More Effective Policing. Understanding and Preventing Discriminatory Ethnic Profiling. A Guide, Publications Office of the European Union, Luxembourg 2010, 43.

gender (LGBT) communities, victims may not want to report the crime because they would like to keep their sexual orientation or transgender identity private or because of any other personal reason.

Secondly, the lack of a comprehensive definition[32] and 'misqualification' may be also significant reasons that contribute to under-recording. Law enforcement agencies disregard the motivation during the investigation. Because the lack of knowledge of hate crime laws, police officers may not recognize the hate motivation which may derive from the low level of awareness (because of the lack of specialized training or guidelines). For instance, police officers in Hungary often identify incidents as vandalism instead of Art. 216 ('Violence against a member of a community'), thereby failing to recognize the hate motivation. Thus, the investigation is launched of an ordinary crime instead of a hate crime. It is vital that the police open the investigation of a hate crime instead of an ordinary crime, seeing as the qualification may determine the entire case from the phase of investigation through the prosecution up unto the tribunal phase. In the UK for instance, the police have adopted a policy that the investigation should start regarding a hate crime if the incident is perceived as such by the victim or by another person. Thus, the perception of the victim determines the qualification of the incident.[33]

As a consequence of underreporting and under-recording of hate offences, violence remains invisible for law enforcement authorities, for lawmakers, for public policy decision makers, and for the general public. Therefore, lack of data limits the ability to highlight the extent of this type of violence, while lack of information about where and when offences tend to take place restricts the possibility of preventing occurrences of hate violence. In addition, it makes it difficult to raise awareness among decision makers on the need to adopt laws to protect victims from hate violence.[34]

Cases and the Circumstances that May Confirm the Hate Motivation

There are factors that do not confirm that the incident was a hate offense but which may indicate the need for further investigation into motive, such as perceptions of the victim(s) and witnesses about the crime; the perpetrator's comments, gestures or written statements that reflect bias (e.g., graffiti or other symbols); similar incidents in the same town or neighborhood to determine whether a pattern

---

32 Because not all hate crimes fall under, *e.g.*, the provision of Art. 216. Criminal law does not create a specific category of offences based on motivation and does not require administrative agencies to collect special hate crime statistics. For instance in the case of homicide committed with malicious motive, there are no statistics for the number of hate crimes within the above mentioned aggravating circumstance.

33 Christine Loudes – Evelyne Paradis, Handbook on Monitoring and Reporting Homophobic and Transphobic Incidents, ILGA Europe (International Lesbian, Gay, Bisexual, Trans and Intersex Association Europe), 2008, 52, http://www.ilga-europe.org/home/issues/hate_crime_hate_speech/ilga_europe_reports, 26 January 2014.

34 Loudes – Paradis, Handbook, 10.

exists; whether the victim was engaged in activities promoting his/her group or community; whether the incident coincided with a holiday or date of particular significance; involvement of organized hate groups or their members; absence of any other motive such as economic gain.[35]

A. Austria

On 26 November 2006, a man broke into the Lauder Chabad School in Vienna, smashing windows and breaking other objects with a crowbar. The police arrested a man who was subsequently sentenced to 15 months in prison for vandalizing the school. During the trial, the man claimed that there were 'too many Jews in Austria'. His racist motivation was deemed as an aggravating circumstance by the court.[36] In the present case, vandalism was the ordinary crime and the anti-Semitic motivation constituted the bias motivation. The key indicators that indicated that a hate crime may have been committed: the perpetrator's comments, gesture, behavior, and statements during the procedure, and the place of the offence.

B. Hungary

In August 2012, Sz. N. contacted a homosexual man on a dating website, agreed with him on a date, planned the murder, took a knife, met him at the victim's apartment, and murdered him with more than twenty stabs. He stabbed several times to the chest and the back of the victim. He confessed that he wanted to kill more people following a homophobic motivation. The court sentenced him for life imprisonment for homicide, planned in advance, for base reason or purpose (the latter includes the hate motivation), with special cruelty etc. – several aggravating circumstances). In this case, homicide is the ordinary crime and the homophobic motivation constituted the bias motivation. The key indicators might be the perpetrator's comments, gesture, behavior, and statements during the procedure; and the absence of any other motive such as economic gain, for example.

Consequences

Adoption of adequate legislation to define and punish hate crimes is a key initial step in addressing the problem. Laws – especially criminal laws – are an expression of society's values. The extension of the legal framework may represent a sym-

35 The International Association of Chiefs of Police's (IACP) publication – Responding to Hate Crimes. A Police Officer's Guide to Investigation and Prevention – contains two training tools: a 12-page guidebook that covers major components of an effective response to an investigation of hate crimes and a smaller, detachable pocket guide outlining specific investigative procedures. IACP: Responding to Hate Crimes: A Police Officer's Guide to Investigation and Prevention, http://www.theiacp.org/ViewResult?SearchID=123, 3 September 2013.

36 ODIHR, Hate Crimes in the OSCE Region. Incident and Responses, Annual Report for 2006, 33. http://www.osce.org/odihr/26759, 5 February 2014.

bol for the victims of hate crimes. Hate crime laws both express the social value of equality and foster the development of values. However, the lack of specialized hate crime laws does not mean a lack of hate crime prosecution. Therefore, police officers and investigators have more important roles to play in responding to hate incidents and crimes. Police officers are usually the first professionals arriving to the scene of a hate crime, thus their actions significantly affect the outcome of the criminal investigation as well as the community's response to the incident. Law enforcement agencies have a special role in responding to, preventing, investigating, and prosecuting hate crimes.

Policing of hate crimes is a complex task. The police service is responsible for recording hate offences and for implementing related legislation. The police may influence the perception of hate crimes by the state and by the general public. The low level of trust towards the police by ethnic and sexual minorities and religious communities may be a special barrier.[37] To successfully carry out their tasks, police officers and prosecutors must receive training on recognition and investigation of potential hate crimes, have clear protocols on how to respond to hate violence, and develop innovative programs for preventing and responding to hate crimes.[38]

Proving the hate motivation may be difficult, because it is connected to the perpetrator's subjective mental status. Thus, law enforcement must investigate the additional aspects of the case (such as all of the personal circumstances, group membership, the perpetrator's comment) and find all of the possible evidence, which can confirm the hate motivation. Hate crime prosecution is important to both the individual victim and the affected community. It sends an important message to the society about the values of social cohesion.

The European Court of Human Rights (ECtHR) has ruled in a number of cases that states are obliged to 'unmask' the motivation behind crimes committed with bias motivation. If the criminal justice system overlooks the bias motivation behind a crime, then this amounts to a violation of Article 14 of the European Convention of Human Rights[39] (ECHR).[40] As the ECtHR pointed out in the case of *Secic v. Croatia* '[...] treating racially induced violence and brutality on

37 Neil Chakraborti – John Garland, Hate Crime. Impact, Causes and Responses, Los Angeles/London/New Delhi/Singapore/Washington 2009, 107.

38 U.S. Department of Justice – Office of Justice Programs – Bureau of Jusitce Agencies, Addressing Hate Crimes. Six Initiatives that Are Enhancing the Efforts of Criminal Justice Practioners, Washington, 2000, 7.

39 ECHR, Article 14, Prohibition of discrimination, http://www.echr.coe.int/Documents/Convention_ENG.pdf, 20 May 2014. 'The enjoyment of the rights and freedoms set forth in this Convention shall be secured without discrimination on any ground such as sex, race, colour, language, religion, political or other opinion, national or social origin, association with a national minority, property, birth or other status.'

40 FRA, Making Hate Crime Visible in the European Union: AcDone, I checked the footnotes and corrected the mistake. knowledging Victims' Rights, 7, http://fra.europa.eu/sites/default/files/fra-2012_hate-crime.pdf, 28 January 2014.

an equal footing with cases that have no racists overtones would be to turn a blind eye to the specific nature of acts that are particularly destructive of fundamental rights'.[41] In the case of *Nachova and Others v. Bulgaria* the Court declared for the first time that states have a positive duty, stemming from Article 14 of the ECHR, to investigate whether an act of violence was motivated by racial hatred. In the *Nachova* case, a military policeman shot two Roma men while he was trying to arrest them. According to the Bulgarian authorities, the act on police was compatible with the regulations on the use of firearms by the military police, leading to the authorities' refusal to prosecute the military police officer. The Court found that there had been a violation of Article 2 of the ECHR[42] regarding the two men's deaths and also because Bulgaria failed its obligation under Article 2 of the Convention to investigate the deprivation of life effectively. The Court found that the authorities failed in their duty under Article 14 of the ECHR taken in conjunction with Article 2 to take all possible steps to investigate whether or not discrimination may have played a role in the events. It follows that there had been a violation of Article 14 of the Convention taken in conjunction with Article 2 in its procedural aspect.[43]

States should consider persistent measures to ensure that law-enforcement officials, prosecutors, and judges are well equipped to prevent and respond effectively to hate crimes, by enforcing effectively the available hate crime laws. Professional training helps law-enforcement officers to identify, investigate and register bias motives, and ensures that prosecutors are trained how to present evidence of bias motivation. Education for service providers is a substantial component of long-term strategies aimed at reducing hate crimes reduction strategies, see, *e.g.*, a Canadian example, the 'City of Edmonton Hate and Bias Crime Investigation Online' training material.[44]

Cooperation with civil society is also a major factor. Civil society organizations may have the capacity and knowledge to supplement the law enforcement authorities' activities to address hate crime, especially through monitoring incidents and assisting victims. Several good practices are known in the field of encouraging reporting and increasing assess to support. A form of effective partnership engagement is cooperation with organizations with the capacity to introduce a third-party reporting system. Third-party reporting allows a victim (or any other person) to report the crime to a partner organization, which then forwards the report to the police. In London, the Metropolitan Police Service encourages members of all communities to report incidents to the police. Even if the incident

41 ODIHR, Prosectuing, 5.

42 ECHR, Article 2, Right to life.

43 Case of *Nachova and Others v. Bulgaria* (6 July 2005), HUDOC, European Court of Human Rights, http://hudoc.echr.coe.int/sites/eng/pages/search.aspx?i=001-69630#{"itemid":["001-69630"]}, 26 January 2014.

44 Canadian Police Knowledge Network, Course Catalogue, http://www.cpkn.ca/course_catalogue, 26 January 2014.

does not amount to a crime, the police will still record and investigate it. The police co-operate with independent civil society organizations with the aim of increasing the number of reported hate incidents. The victims of hate crimes within the LGBT community can report hate incidents to the police's partner organization Gay London Police Monitoring Group GALOP. The GALOP is an LGBT organization of volunteers who provide support and counseling to victims of homophobic and transphobic hate crimes.[45]

A Hungarian NGO coalition, 'Working Group against Hate Crimes' *('Gyűlölet-bűncselekmény Elleni Munkacsoport')*[46] has been working on hate crimes since 2012. The coalition issued recommendations for legislation and judicial practice on hate crimes and provided training sessions and seminars for police officers. The coalition also works on raising awareness among the target groups and conducts international research of investigation protocols, police structures, and adequate data collection. The working group's first initiative was to contribute to the codification process of the new Criminal Code of Hungary in 2012 by providing recommendations regarding the conceptualization of hate crimes. Some of the recommendations – *e.g.,* explicit mentioning of sexual orientation, gender identity, and disability among the protected characteristics – were integrated in the new Criminal Code. In March 2013, the working group participated in a hate crime seminar within the framework of a project delivered by the Police College. The coalition also regularly holds lectures and organizes conferences in cooperation with state institutions, university bodies and civil organizations. The member organizations of the coalition also provide services to victims, such as legal representation.

Besides the above-mentioned tools, community mobilization may also be an answer for hate activities. North America has the best practices with regard to community organizing, for instance, in Canada, the Alberta Hate Crimes Committee set up a toolkit collecting good practices in the field of community responses which helps to address hate as it arises in their community. It is designed to help community members to identify what hate is, what the relevant laws are, how to address hate crimes through community action, education, prevention and partnership, and how to protect groups and individuals targeted by hatred.[47]

The community-based movement called 'Not in Our Town' in the U.S. is aimed to guide, support and inspire people and communities to work together to

---

45 Metropolitan Police Service, Reporting Hate Crime Information, http://content.met.police.uk/cs/Satellite?blobcol=urldata&blobheadername1=Content-Type&blobheadername2=Content-Disposition&blobheadervalue1=application%2Fpdf&blobheadervalue2=inline%3B+filename%3D%22293%2F748%2Freporting_crime.pdf%22&blobkey=id&blobtable=MungoBlobs&blobwhere=1283591737823&ssbinary=true, 29 January 2014.

46 The author is a member of the Working Group Against Hate Crimes. http://gyuloletellen.hu/munkacsoportrol, 20 May 2014.

47 Alberta Hate Crime Community, Good practice: Canada Beyond Hate. A Resource Toolkit, Building a Community Response Plan to Counter Hate, February 2012, 7, http://www.beyondhate.ca/index.php/homepage/pdf-toolkit, 29 January 2014.

eliminate hate and build a safe, inclusive environment for all. The project's started twenty years ago, when a film crew went to Billings, Montana to document a story about community members who stood up for their neighbors when they were under attack by white supremacist, after attacks on a Native American woman's house, an African-American church, and a Jewish family's home.[48]

Another good example is the practice of employing liaison officers, merging the 'official system' and the community-based approach. Several countries have introduced liaison officers with specific responsibility for engaging with communities and providing support to victims and witnesses of hate crimes. In the UK over 150 police officers and support staff have trained as Gay Liaison Officers (GLOs), whose role it is to support LGBT people when they are victims of hate crime.[49]

Another critical area is data collection, as the above-mentioned differences between official and victim statistics demonstrated. There are numerous barriers to obtaining reliable data. The lack of accurate, comprehensive data on hate crimes undermines the ability of states to understand fully and to deal effectively with the problem of hate crime. Accurate monitoring of hate crimes is essential to give an overview of ongoing trends and enable appropriate preventive action in the form of support or referral to another agency (such as to ODIHR).[50]

According to the European Union Agency for Fundamental Rights (FRA)[51] report, official data collection mechanisms can be classified into three categories, based on their scope and transparency (amongst the 27 EU Member States): 'limited data', 'good data', and 'comprehensive data'. Countries in the 'limited data' category record few incidents and a narrow range of bias motivation; Hungary belongs to this category. Countries with 'good' data collection, such as Austria, record a range of bias motivations. Finally, countries with 'comprehensive' data collection record a range of bias motivation, types of crimes, and characteristics of incidents, such as in the United Kingdom.[52] In the UK in 2007, the members of the criminal justice system (police, Crown Prosecution Service, Prison Service, and other agencies) agreed on a common definition of monitored hate crime to cover five 'strands', in particular: disability, race, religion/faith, gender identity, and sexual orientation. Primarily, this was to ensure a consistent working definition to allow accurate recording and monitoring.[53]

---

48 Not In Our Town, About Not In Our Town, http://www.niot.org/about, 26 January 2014.

49 Loudes – Paradis, Handbook, 56.

50 Association of Chief Police Officers in Scotland (ACPOS), Hate Crime Guidance Manual 2010, Northern Constabulary, 2010, 29.

51 The FRA is one of the EU's decentralized agencies. These agencies are set up to provide expert advice to the institutions of the EU and the Member States on a range of issues. FRA helps to ensure that the fundamental rights of people living in the EU are protected, http://fra.europa.eu/en, 20 May 2014.

52 FRA, Hate, 8.

53 GOV.UK, Statistics. Hate Crimes. England and Wales 2011 to 2012, 13 September 2012, https://www.gov.uk/government/publications/hate-crimes-england-and-wales-2011-to-2012--2/hate-crimes-england-and-wales-2011-to-2012, 30 January 2014.

Unfortunately, the work in confronting bias, hate, prejudice, and violence is not over neither in Austria, nor in in Hungary. Hate crimes present a challenge to states to create effective legal frameworks, to law enforcement bodies to design mechanisms and systems for responding to the divisive and destructive impact of hate violence and to civil society organizations and communities to address and combat hate as it arises in local communities. However, it has to be acknowledged that Austria and Hungary have already taken effective steps to improve the hate crimes legislation. Nevertheless, they could strengthen hate crimes laws to protect historically oppressed groups against violence motivated by bias and intolerance, implement public awareness campaigns to include law enforcement officials and organize training for police officers, prosecutors and judges in order to ensure that they can recognize, investigate and prosecute hate crimes. As the differences between the official and victim statistics show both countries may consider to strengthen the implementation of hate crime legislation by continuing to monitor incidents. Finally, ensuring that victims of hate crimes have access to assistance and protection, including counseling and legal assistance, may help making hate crimes visible. Fortunately, several good practices are available for both Austria and Hungary to combat hate violence in all the significant fields.

IV. Shaping Mind and Memory

Paz Zvick

A Puzzle of Reality: Why are Extreme-Right Parties Successful in Hungary but not in Poland? A Comparative Research on the Rise of Extreme-Right Parties in Post-Communist Countries in Central and Eastern Europe

Hebrew University of Jerusalem

Introduction

The collapse of the Communist Bloc in the last decade of the twentieth century drastically changed the European continent, the global system, and, some might say, history as a whole. Among its many impacts, this process led to a re-arrangement of Central and Eastern Europe into independent national entities, not only *de jure*, but also *de facto*. These states were no longer a part of a totalitarian system led by common ideology, centralized governments, and planned economy[1], and the West expected that they would now turn into liberal democracies, through a similar path of evolution.[2] Nevertheless, two decades after this tremendous revolution, we are witnessing some very significant differences between these countries. My research wishes to address one of these differences, namely that extreme-right parties have gained electoral success in some post-communist countries but not in others. The question that stands in the core of this research is why extreme-right parties succeed today in post-communist Hungary but not in post-communist Poland? From this examination, my research tries to suggest what the causes are that allow or promote the electoral success of extreme-right parties in post-communist countries in Central and Eastern Europe. This question is examined in reference to the communist past of those countries and their unique characteristics today (partly stemming from their communist past) and in light of the variety of aspects of political life.

1 See Grzegorz Ekiert – Stephen E. Hanson, Introduction, in: Grzegorz Ekiert – Stephen E. Hanson (Eds.), Capitalism and Democracy in Central and Eastern Europe. Assessing the Legacy of Communist Rule, Cambridge 2003, 1–11.

2 See Edward D. Mansfield – Jack Snyder, Democratic Transitions, Institutional Strength and War, in: International Organization 56/2, Cambridge 2002, 297–337.

The research presents a holistic perspective, seeing political life as a puzzle that creates reality, based on the philosophy of Aristotle.[3] His philosophy sees political life and political organizations as composed of different elements, combined together to create the state ('[…] but the state is a composite, like any other whole made up of many parts'). Indeed Aristotle saw the citizens as the united elements, which create the states but this research seeks to paraphrase his apprehension onto the various fields of the political life (*i.e* politics, economy, society, institutions, and so forth, which together create the modern state). Therefore, my research argues that the rise of extreme-right parties in post-communist countries in Central and Eastern Europe is caused by a combination of different factors from diverse aspects of the political life (which mentioned above). This approach aims to provide a comprehensive, deep, and multi-level explanation of this phenomenon. This is also the reason why the theoretical framework of this research comprises nine different theories. In order to simplify this framework, I have divided the theories into four categories: political and economic, institutional, cultural and social, and regional theories (which relate to the European Union's Eastern enlargement and the rise of extreme-right parties in post-communist countries in Central and Eastern Europe). Since the research cannot present all of the existing theories in each category, I chose theories, which, in my opinion, strongly represent the explanatory power of each theoretical aspect. The categorization of the theories aims to simplify the theoretical framework and the empirical analysis of the research, as well as to illustrate the complexity of the political reality.

Three research assumptions stand at the core of this research: First, there is no single explanation for the rise of extreme-right parties in post-communist countries in Central and Eastern Europe. Second, my explanation is composed of a number of factors from diverse aspects of political life. Third, regional explanations *per se* cannot explain this phenomenon. The research focuses on two case studies – Poland and Hungary. Based on the conclusions drawn from the case studies, I will attempt to present broader realizations regarding the causes of the electoral success of extreme-right parties in post-communist countries in Central and Eastern Europe. The research proceeds as follows: The first part will define the variables, which assemble the research, *i.e.* the dependent and independent variables. The second part will discuss the choice of the case studies, in an attempt to establish a solid ground for the comparison between them. Subsequently, I will focus on the empirical aspect of the research. Thus, I will present in brief the different theories this research examines and apply each of them to the chosen case studies (due to limitations of space, I believe it is more important to emphasize the empirical analysis and not the theoretical framework). In the fourth part, I will draw my conclusions regarding the way in which different factors from the diverse aspects of political life influenced the electoral success of extreme-right parties in post-communist countries in Central and Eastern Europe, while at the

3 Benjamin Jowett, The Politics of Aristotle, Oxford 1885, lii.

same time aspiring to thereby argue my three research assumptions. In general, the research has found that internal factors have greater influence on the electoral success of extreme-right parties in post-communist countries in Central and Eastern Europe than regional factors. In addition, it found that all aspects of political life have certain influences on this phenomenon.

The Variables

The dependent variable of this research, *i.e.* the electoral success of extreme-right parties in post-communist countries in Central and Eastern Europe, is comprised of a few different terms. The term 'success' relates to electoral achievements, measured by crossing the fixed votes threshold and election into the national parliaments[4] (the research does not focus on regional-level parties, ex-parliamentary movements or sporadic organizations). The term 'parties' refers to those groups, to which the voters chose to deliver the authority for the decision-making process in the political institutions. These groups are depicted by Strøm and Müller (1999) as 'the most important organizations in modern politics'[5]. The terms 'extreme-right parties' refers to a certain group of political right parties, which are distinct from the 'mainstream right parties'. The first are usually called the 'new' extreme-right parties, in order to differentiate them from the 'old' extreme-right parties, *i.e.* the Nazi and fascist parties that evolved in Europe in the period between the two World Wars and during the Second World War.[6] Betz and Mudde recognize an ideological core in these parties. Betz argues that these parties are called 'extreme-right' parties since they reject individual and social equality, object to the integration of minorities and marginal groups and present xenophobic ideas. Mudde adds that the ideology of these parties consists of a cultural aspect of nativism[7], which relates to the state and the nation in a racial perception[8], stemming from the interpretation of ethnic differences as an eternal, permanent and unchangeable factor. He claims that these parties cannot be treated as 'mainstream' right parties since they use radical discourse (which mainstream parties avoid) and might object to some of the core liberal values of the democratic system, such as pluralism, equality, civil rights, protection of minorities, and checks on the ex-

4 See Cas Mudde, The War of Words. Defining the Extreme Right Party Family, in: West European Politics 19/2, London 1996, 225–248.

5 Kaare Strøm – Wolfgang C. Müller, Political Parties and Hard Choices, in: Kaare Strøm – Wolfgang C. Müller (Eds.), Policy, Office or Vote? How Political Parties in Western Europe Make Hard Decisions, Cambridge 1999, 1–35, here 1.

6 See Matt Golder, Explaining Variation in the Success of Extreme Right Parties in Western Europe, in: Comparative Political Studies 36/4, Thousand Oaks 2003, 432–466.

7 See David Art, Inside the Radical Right. The Development of Anti-Immigrant Parties in Western Europe, New York 2011, 10–12.

8 See John E. Richardson – Ruth Wodak, Recontextualising Fascist Ideologies of the Past. Right-Wing Discourses on Employment and Nativism in Austria and the United Kingdom, in: Critical Discourse Studies 6/4, London 2009, 251–267.

ecutive branch.[9] This definition is consistent with the fact that many of these 'extreme-right' parties ask to protect their states from globalization and European integration that seem to undermine the state's power and control[10] and that clash with their vision of the state as solely responsible for the citizens' well-being.[11] The term 'post-communist countries in Central and Eastern Europe' refers to the group of states that were a part of the communist conglomerate until the beginning of the 1990s. These states were separated into sovereign national entities after the collapse of the communist bloc and have gone through processes of democratization and liberalization ever since.[12] The common past these countries share and the similar processes that they have undergone in the last twenty-five years are the basis of the attempt of this research to relate to the unique post-communist characteristics and the current political evolutions we are witnessing today.

The independent variable of this research is a variety of causes from the different fields that compose political life, in other words politics, economy, institutions, culture, society and so on, as well as regional causes. Since almost all of the post-communist countries in Central and Eastern Europe are a part of the European Union, or at least the European integration process, I believe regional causes should also be taken into consideration while examining the internal developments in these countries today. Moreover, the fact that most, if not all, of these states are affected by the European integration process makes the conclusions of this research much more valid and feasible.

The Case Studies

Why Poland and Hungary? Both countries have undergone similar historical developments during and after the communist regime, which gives us a reason to believe that they will follow similar paths of evolution in the future as well. The first salient similarity between the two is active resistance to communist rule. In Hungary, this resistance came to the surface on 23 October 1956, the day the Hungarian Revolution broke out.[13] In Poland, which is considered to have a long history of resistance movements, various reformist movements were active from the beginning of communist rule, but only the emergence of the 'Solidarity' move-

9 See Art, Right, 10–12.

10 See *ibid.*

11 See Anna Grzymala-Busse – Abby Innes, Great Expectations. The EU and Domestic Political Competition in East Central Europe, in: East European Politics and Societies 17/1, Thousand Oaks 2003, 64–73.

12 See Miroslav Mareš, The Extreme Right in Eastern Europe and Territorial Issues, in: Central European Political Studies Review 11/2–3, Brno/Frankfurt am Main 2009, 82–106.

13 See Dorothee Bohle, East European Transformations and the Paradoxes of Transnationalization, in: EUI Working Papers SPS 2010/01, Florence 2010, http://cadmus.eui.eu/bitstream/handle/1814/13346/SPS_2010_01.pdf?sequence=1, 11 July 2013.

ment at the beginning of the 1980s changed the existing balance of power.[14] The 'Round Table' talks in April 1989, with the participation of representatives of the communist party, the 'Solidarity' movement and the Polish Catholic Church, indicated the end of the communist rule in Poland. The immediate result of these talks was the first free parliamentary elections in Poland (as an outcome of the legalization of the 'Solidarity' movement, the re-establishment of the Presidency and the Senate, a new electoral law and several amendments aimed to generate a checks-and-balance system in the country).[15] In fact, the Polish 'Round Table' talks symbolized the beginning of the collapse of the entire communist bloc from Berlin to Wladiwostok.[16] Later that year, the model was implemented in Hungary and led to the creation of an organizational framework in which all three branches of government are active and balanced. The fact that Hungarian Communism came to an end with 'Round Table' talks following the Polish model[17] is the second similarity between the two states.

The third is the similar path of transformation to democracy and a market economy. Both countries began the processes of democratization and liberalization more or less at the same time: the transition processes were driven to a large extent by multilateral institutions and by the desire of the local elites to be a part of the prestigious 'clubs' of the European Union and NATO[18] and both went through similar crises during the first years of the transition period. These crises were mainly a result of the failed economic reforms of the elected right-wing governments (the 'Shock Therapy' strategy of the 'Sacks-Balcerowicz Plan' in Poland[19] and privatization and strict budget limitations in Hungary[20]) and one of their most important consequences was the return of left-wing parties to the forefront of the political sphere in the mid-1990s. These parties, which were almost completely rejected by the voters at the first democratic elections after the fall of the Communism gained their power back as a consequence of the civilians' disappointment from the results of the drastic economic reforms of the chosen right-

14 See Marcia A.Weigle – Jim Butterfield, Civil Society in Reforming Communist Regimes. The Logic of Emergence, in: Comparative Politics 25/1, New York 1992, 1–23.

15 See Krzystof Jasiewich, Dead Ends and New Beginnings. The Quest for Procedural Republic in Poland, in: Communist and Post-Communist Studies 33, Amsterdam 2000, 101–122.

16 See Andres Aslund, How Capitalism Was Built. The Transformation of Central and Eastern Europe, Russia and Central Asia, Cambridge 2007, 1–3.

17 See John W. Schiemann, Hungary. The Emergence of Chancellor Democracy, in: The Journal of Legislative Studies 10/2, London 2004, 128–141.

18 See Mitchell A. Orenstein, The Political Economy of the Financial Crisis in Central and Eastern Europe. Poland and Hungary Compared, Draft Paper, Johns Hopkins University SAIS, Washington/Bologna/Nanjing 2010.

19 See Mitchell A. Orenstein, Out of the Red. Building Capitalism and Democracy in Postcommunist Europe, Ann Arbor 2001, 25–60.

20 See Dóra Győrffy, Structural Change without Trust. Reform Cycles in Hungary and Slovakia, in: Transformation, Integration and Globalization Economic Research (TIGER) Working Paper 112, Warsaw 2008, http://tiger.edu.pl/publikacje/TWPNo112a.pdf, 11 July 2013.

wing governments.[21] Today, the partisan systems in both countries function more or less like the ones in established democracies and their quantitative indicators (*i.e.* seats share of the opposition and coalition parties, the number of parties competing in the national elections, etc.) are also quite similar[22], and this is the fourth tangible similarity between them.

Nonetheless, despite these similarities, the partisan situation today in both countries is very different – while Poland has a quite solid, non-polarized partisan system[23], Hungary is not only led by a highly criticized right-wing government, but also the third largest party in its national parliament is a party which can easily be defined as an 'extreme-right' party.[24] This party, Jobbik (Jobbik Magyarországért Mozgalom [Movement for a Better Hungary]), openly stands against ethnic minorities in the country, presents populist rhetoric and resists the European Union and some of the most fundamental democratic values.[25]

In the next part of the research, the empirical analysis, I will try to ascertain the causes for this differentiation, based on a variety of theories that analyze the electoral success of extreme-right parties in reference to the particular characteristics of post-communist countries.

The Empirical Analysis

In order to illustrate the complexity of the political sphere and the fact that there is no single explanation to political developments, the distinct partisan situation in Poland and Hungary will be examined in light of different diverse aspects of political life. The first set of theories I will discuss are political and economic theories, which claim that extreme-right parties use the political and economic circumstances that were created after the breakdown of the communist bloc and during the transition period in order to strengthen their electoral power and increase their presence in the national parliaments. The political theories focus mainly on the ethnic composition of the post-communist countries[26], whereas the economic theories deal mainly with the economic difficulties that evolved in these countries.[27] Hence, when discussing the influence of political and economic

21 See Orenstein, Economy.

22 See Sarah Birch, Elections, Electoral System and Party System in the Visegrad States, 2005–2006, in: Vit Hlousek – Roman Chytilek (Eds.), Parliamentary Elections and Party Landscape in the Visegrad Group Countries, Brno 2007, 11–22.

23 See Krzysztof Jasiewicz, Poland. Nations in Transit 2012, http://www.freedomhouse.org/report/nations-transit/2012/poland, 11 July 2013.

24 See Balázs Áron Kovács, Hungary. Nations in Transit 2012, http://www.freedomhouse.org/report/nations-transit/2012/hungary, 11 July 2013.

25 See Jobbik Party. Official Website, http://www.jobbik.com/, 16 July 2013.

26 See Lenka Bustikova – Herbert Kitschelt, The Radical Right in Post-Communist Europe. Comparative Perspectives on Legacies and Party Competition, in: Communist and Post-Communist Studies 42, Amsterdam 2009, 459–483.

27 See Orenstein, Economy.

factors on the electoral success of extreme-right parties in post-communist countries in Central and Eastern Europe, it is important to notice that both in Poland and in Hungary since 1989, the governing parties have changed in almost every national election. Most of the times, the replacements of the ruling governments had a very strong connection to the country's economic performances. The failure of the economic program of the left-wing Hungarian government is one of the most significant reasons for the electoral success of both Jobbik and the ruling party, FIDESZ (Fiatal Demokraták Szövetsége [Alliance of Young Democrats]), in the national elections in 2010[28] (a success that repeated itself in the national elections held in the country not long ago, in April 2014)[29]. Since the elections of 2010, we have been witnessing two very disturbing developments in the Hungarian political sphere: First, the adoption of a new constitution, which includes anti-democratic content and stands in opposition to some of Hungary's international commitments (such as its obligation to respect and promote the ban of death penalty and life imprisoned without parole, the prohibition of discrimination on the background of sexual orientation and the suspension or restriction of fundamental rights by means of special legal order). As a result, it constitutes a tangible threat for ethnic and other minority groups living in the country.[30] Second, since the last elections, Jobbik has received more and more public support: according to surveys from 2011, the party got about 20% of the electorate votes. As I mentioned before, the failed economic policies of the left-wing governments have had a great influence on the contemporary situation, since they have created a vicious circle of lack of economic growth, mistrust towards the political institutions (and some might say towards the democratic system as a whole), and political radicalization.[31] These difficulties were heightened due to the very complex ethnic composition of the country and the dispersing of the Hungarian people in Central and Eastern Europe (as a result of the geo-political changes that took place in the region from the beginning of the Twentieth Century – from the disintegration of the Austro-Hungarian Empire, to the Treaty of Trianon, the Nazi occupation during the Second World War, the ethnic cleansings of Stalin in the mid-40s and so on, which all caused major borders and population changes).[32] Unlike Poland, which is considered to be very ethnically homogenous, Hungary is composed, as a result of all the above, of a Hungarian majority (a little more than 50% of the population) and a mixture of minorities, including Roma, Bulgarians, Croats,

---

28 See Kovács, Hungary.

29 See Arch Puddington, Viktor Orbán and the State of Hungarian Democracy, http://www.freedomhouse.org/blog/viktor-orban-and-state-hungarian-democracy#.U4CRpnKSx8E, 24 May 2014.

30 See European Parliament Resolution of 5 July 2011 on the Revised Hungarian Constitution, http://www.europarl.europa.eu/sides/getDoc.do?pubRef=-//EP//TEXT+TA+P7-TA-2011 0315+0+DOC+XML+V0//EN, 12 July 2013.

31 See Győrffy, Change.

32 See Timothy Snyder, Bloodlands. Europe between Hitler and Stalin, New York 2010, 313.

Germans, Slovaks, Romanians, Jews, and others. The Roma are considered to be the most problematic and weakened minority group in the country (in terms of socio-economic development) and most of its members live in the poor regions in North-East Hungary.[33] Another significant result of those borders and population changes is that Hungary is dealing with the fact that great parts of the Hungarian people live outside the country's territory, in 'external homelands' in Slovakia, Romania, Slovenia, Austria, Ukraine, and other countries.[34]

This complicated economic and political situation in Hungary was used by Jobbik in order to achieve electoral support. The party leaders used the rage of the population in the regions that were mostly hurt by the failed economic reforms in order to turn the Roma minority into a 'scapegoat', the 'other'. That way, the electorate in these regions was captured by the promises for a better future that would be achieved through nationalistic actions.[35] In Poland, on the other hand, not only is there no large rejected minority group that can become some kind of a 'scapegoat', but the economic situation has also significantly improved during the last few years, despite the global and the European economic crises. Moreover, extreme-right parties have achieved electoral success in the country in the first few years of the millennium, when the country went through series of economic difficulties. However, since the last elections no such parties are represented in the national parliament. The Polish political system today is relatively stable and consensual, and the result is much more moderate politics, which allow crisis management and enable sensitive solutions to be found before, during and after various crises. One of the most significant pieces of evidence for this political development is the reelection of Donald Tusk for a second term in 2010. Tusk is the first Prime Minister in Poland to be reelected after the end of Communism and the establishment of the democratic system.[36]

When it comes to institutional factors that may influence the rise of extreme-right parties in post-communist countries, institutional theories focus on the structure of the partisan system and on the structure of the constituencies. The structure of the partisan system is formulated both by deliberate choices of the elites[37] and by the split between Europeanization and conservatism.[38] It seems that both in Poland and in Hungary, extreme-right parties gained electoral success when political elites deliberately decided to use the split of Europeanization versus

33 See Roma in Hungary. A Terrible Waste of Human Potential, http://www.economist.com/blogs/easternapproaches/2013/08/roma-hungary, 10 August 2013.

34 Timm Beichelt – Michael Minkenberg, Explaining the Radical Right in Transition: Theories of the Right-Wing Radicalism and Opportunity Structures in Post-Socialist Europe, APSA 97th Annual Meeting, San Francisco 2001.

35 See Kovács, Hungary.

36 See Jasiewicz, Poland.

37 See Herbert Kitschelt, Formation of Party Cleavages in Post-Communist Democracies. Theoretical Propositions, in: Party Politics 1/4, London 1995, 447–472.

38 See Attila Ágh, The Hungarian Party System and Party Theory in the Transition of Central Europe, in: Journal of Theoretical Politics 6/2, London 1994, 217–238.

conservatism in order to attract votes. In the Polish case, this strategy brought extreme-right parties to the forefront in the elections around the time of they joined the European Union. During that period, extreme-right parties, such as the LPR (Liga Polskich Rodzin [League of Polish Families]) and the SRP (Samoobrona Rzeczpospolitej Polskiej [Self Defence of the Republic of Poland]), used the controversial link to the European Union and suggested a Eurosceptic nationalistic alternative that was no longer relevant after the accession process was completed and its benefits began to surface.[39] In the Hungarian case, Jobbik used the frustration of the people who did not see the benefits of membership in the European Union and provided them with a nationalistic agenda, which depicted the European Union as an outside coercive force[40] and called to concentrate first and foremost on national Hungarian interests.[41] Again, this process succeeded especially in the regions that were mostly hurt by the failed economic reforms (which in turn were largely influenced by the requirements of the European Union's bureaucratic system).[42] That way, because of deliberate decisions of the elites, the political system was formulated around a split between integration with regional powers and nationalistic conservatism. This split has allowed extreme agendas to come to surface and mobilize the electorate.[43]

With regard to the structure of the constituencies, one of the theories claims that extreme-right parties can gain electoral success where there are relatively few constituencies, the district magnitude is relatively large and where there is a mixed electoral system (MMP – Mixed-members Proportional Representation).[44] This theory works in the Hungarian case, where the mixed electoral system allowed Jobbik to concentrate its activity in the regions where it is most likely to get a significant share of the votes cast. In the Polish case, on the other hand, the opposite is true. The mixed electoral system there was discarded in 2001, and instead there were several more constituencies.[45] Nevertheless, in the elections that took place the same year, extreme-right parties did enter, for the first time after the collapse of Communism, to the national parliament (LPR and SRP for example).[46] When we examine this anomaly, it is important to notice that this theory deals with democratic states as a whole, and not particularly post-communist democratic

---

39 See Radoslaw Markowski – Joshua A. Tucker, Euroscepticism and the Emergence of Political Parties in Poland, in: Party Politics 16/4, London 2010, 523–548.

40 See Raul De Arriba Bueno, Assessing Economic Transition in Eastern Europe after Twenty Years, in: Transformation in Business & Economic 9/2/20, Vilnius 2010, 42–63.

41 See Jobbik Party. Official Website, http://www.jobbik.com/, 16 July 2013.

42 See Arriba Bueno, Transition, 42–63.

43 See Beichelt – Minkenberg, Right.

44 See Golder, Variation, 432–466.

45 See Michal Kubát, Electoral Reforms in Poland after 1991 and their Political Consequences, in: Politics in Central and Eastern Europe 2, Prague 2006, 41–62.

46 See Markowski – Tucker, Euroscepticism, 523–548.

states.[47] This may be an explanation for the fact that the mentioned theory does not work perfectly in every single case in the post-communist world. It also reinforces one of the core beliefs of this research, *i.e.* that research that focuses on the post-communist world should take into consideration its unique characteristics.

Regarding cultural and social factors, it is first of all important to understand that many decades of communist totalitarian regime have left an inerasable mark on the post-communist societies and that it may take many years until they will fully understand and implement the transition to democracy.[48] In this context, two major causes affect the rise of extreme-right parties in post-communist countries: First, an active civil society, which allows citizens to raise their voices outside the political system and decreases the need to turn to radical political solutions. The problem is that the communist regimes in Central and Eastern Europe banned almost every civil society organization during their period of rule, which made it harder for civil society to evolve after the disintegration of Communism.[49] Second, the ability to adjust to the 'transition costs' (*i.e.* the prices that the individual in post-communist societies has to pay as a result of the transition processes and the fast socio-economic changes they bring about) without being threatened by the new reality.[50] With regard to the civic society, in both cases, as of 2006, a relatively small percent of the economically active population works in this sector – 1.1% in Hungary and 1.8% in Poland (in comparison to an average of 4.6% in the other countries that were examined).[51] Moreover, in Hungary, most of the civic society organizations act in a small-scale way, with insignificant budgets and under strict limitations. In addition, the current government restricts their activities through laws, regulations, tight supervision, and other measures.[52] Under these circumstances, it becomes quite clear why many voters choose to give their votes to radical solutions that are being offered by extreme-right parties, especially in times of crises. The civic society in the country does not appear to be a serious alternative. It seems that in both countries the communist past still has a significant influence on the contemporary social and cultural patterns and that the deep understanding of the democratic system has still to evolve.[53]

With regard to dealing with the 'transition costs', we witnessed a rise of extreme-right parties at the beginning of the former decade in Poland, when the

47 See Golder, Variation, 432–466.

48 See George Schopflin, Postcommunism. The Problems of Democratic Construction, in: Daedalus 123/3, Cambridge 1994, 127–141.

49 See Cas Mudde, Civil Society in Post-Communist Europe. Lessons from the 'Dark Side', in: Petr Kopecký – Cas Mudde (Eds.), Uncivil Society? Contentious Politics in Post-Communist Europe, London 2003, 157–159.

50 See Beichelt – Minkenberg, Right.

51 See Lester M. Salamon, Global Civil Society. An Overview, in: The Johns Hopkins Comparative Nonprofit Sector Project, Denmark 2006, 30f.

52 See Kovács, Hungary.

53 See Mudde, Society, 157–159.

socio-economic implications of the transition began to surface. Poland went through very radical transition strategies in the first decade of the transition to democracy and a market economy (the 'Sacks-Balcerowicz Plan' in 1991–93, the 'Strategy of Poland' in 1994–97[54] and the radical reforms of Buzek's government in 1997–2001), which all created very high 'transitional costs' for the Polish citizens.[55] By 2001, the Poles had already experienced several democratic elections, and could have implemented the democratic idea of expressing their dissatisfaction through the ballot box.[56] In Hungary, the transition process has also had heavy socio-economic costs. Since the beginning of the 1990s, the country has been dealing with high rates of unemployment, poverty, and growing gaps in salary, which all lead to increasing inequalities. This is a fertile ground for extreme-right parties, such as Jobbik, which offer a conservative, traditional, and anti-liberal alternative that aims to bring back the old, familiar, and 'safe' reality. The promise to revitalize the well-known framework of the past seems appealing especially to those who do not see the benefits of the present neo-liberal globalized atmosphere and feel threatened by it.[57]

When it comes to regional theories, which relate the rise of extreme-right parties in post-communist countries to the European Union's Eastern enlargement, we should focus on the disappointment with long-term ramifications of the liberal reforms. While Western European liberal economists and transition governments promised the citizens that growth would occur after a period of recession, it now seems that reality is more complicated than that, and that periods of recession and stagnation may last much longer than expected. We should not forget, in addition, that the current global economic crisis also makes it difficult for the economy to grow and develop, and worsens economic difficulties. This gap, between reality and the promises of Western economists and internal political elites[58], has created a significant mistrust towards the European Union and pushed the citizens to look for anti-European alternatives. This process is naturally heightened in times of crises (such as the one that surfaced in Poland at the beginning of the 2000s and the one which broke out in Hungary as a result of the last global economic crises).

The second aspect of the enlargement process relates to the difficulties that the post-communist countries had endured due to the European Union's 'One Size Fits All' policy. Because of this policy, post-communist countries were forced to adopt the constitutional and regulative norms of the European Union (*acquis*

---

54 See Grzegorz W. Kolodko, A Two-Third of Success: Poland's Post-Communist Transformation 1989–2009, in: Communist and Post-Communist Studies 42, Amsterdam 2009, 325–351.

55 See Orenstein, Economy.

56 See Kristi Raik, EU Accession of Central and Eastern European Countries. Democracy and Integration as Conflicting Logic, in: East European Politics and Societies 18/4, Thousand Oaks 2004, 567–594.

57 See Beichelt – Minkenberg, Right.

58 See Markowski – Tucker, Euroscepticism, 523–548.

communautaire), whether they suited their own unique characteristics or not. This incompatibility caused, and is still causing, many difficulties for post-communist countries, which began the accession process from a very different starting point than Western European democracies (unlike the well-established democracies of Western Europe, the post-communist countries in Central and Eastern Europe did not enjoy a long legacy of democratic regime, and had to establish this kind of polity alongside their preparation for the accession).[59] These difficulties, especially the economic ones, hurt the citizens and pushed them towards radical political solutions.[60] Some scholars also claim that voting for extreme-right parties is a counter-reaction to the reduction of the policy space that was caused as a result of the convergence of all political parties around the accession process (the necessity of joining the European Union relied on a consensus across the entire political spectrum both in Poland and in Hungary).[61]

The third regional theory claims that the rise of extreme-right parties in post-communist countries in Central and Eastern Europe is related to a much broader European phenomenon – the democratic deficit. According to this explanation, the coercive characteristic of the enlargement processes limited the democracy in the candidate states, since in fact, only a small group of elites had decided the way that the transition should be performed. Deep democratic processes were not a part of these practices, since the European Union rewarded efficient and fast work. The result was damage to the quality of the democracy and a creation of technocratic and elite-centered political behaviors. This, in turn, created a deficit both in the candidate states' democratic level and in the political culture of the European Union as a whole. The lack of well-established democratic regimes in the transition countries, alongside the deep disappointment from the accession process, raised the possibility of turning to radical political solutions, because of the public's frustration and misunderstanding of the benefits of democracy.[62] The electoral success of extreme-right parties in Poland around the time of the enlargement indeed supports this theory, but the Hungarian case is not that clear. Extreme-right parties have become a part of the Hungarian national parliament only a few years after the accession process was completed, what makes it harder to determine that their success was influenced by the character of the accession process.

Conclusions

Many unique processes are still taking place in the post-communist world. Moreover, it is still very hard to define or determine the exact characteristics of the

59 See Laszlo Bruszt – David Stark, Who Counts. Supranational Norms and Societal Needs, in: East European Politics and Societies 17/1, Thousand Oaks 2003, 74–82.

60 See Grzymala-Busse – Innes, Expectations, 64–73.

61 See Bruszt – Stark, Norms, 74–82.

62 See Raik, EU, 567–594.

countries that are included under the definition of 'post-communist countries'. Nevertheless, I believe we can already view the post-communist period in Central and Eastern Europe from a certain perspective and draw broad conclusions regarding the current developments in it.[63]

Hence, based on the analysis of the case studies of Poland and Hungary, it can be asserted that given the unique characteristics of post-communist countries in Central and Eastern Europe, several factors affect the electoral success of extreme-right parties: first, political and economic difficulties, *i.e.* ethnic minorities, 'external homelands' and economic crises. These are most influential when combined together, as in the case of the present situation in Hungary. These circumstances create a fertile ground for manipulation and politicization of extreme-right parties, who wish to depict someone as the 'other', the outsider, the one to blame in this unfortunate situation. In order to mobilize the votes against this 'scapegoat', extreme-right parties use populist, xenophobic, nationalist, and aggressive rhetoric, while taking advantage of the economic difficulties with which the population is dealing. The absence of a major ethnic minority and Polish 'external homelands', as well as the significant economic improvement in Poland, is one of the reasons why extreme-right parties have not achieved electoral success in the country in the last two elections. This might also explain the relative success of these parties during elections at the same time of the accession process, which allowed them to depict the European Union as a foreign coercive force, using the challenging economic situation in the country at that time. On the other hand, the existence of a major rejected ethnic minority, 'external homelands', and economic difficulties in Hungary today explains why extreme-right parties are so successful in mobilizing the cast votes and gain more and more political power in the country, while emphasizing the fight against the 'other' and their commitment to the reunification of the Hungarian nation under one state.[64]

The second factor that affects the electoral success of extreme-right parties in post-communist countries in Central and Eastern Europe is the formulation of the partisan system around the split between Europeanization and conservatism, stemming from a deliberate choice of the political elites. This factor can explain both the former success of extreme-right parties in Poland and the current success of Jobbik in Hungary. The fact that the other institutional factor that affects the electoral success of extreme-right parties, *i.e.* the structure of the constituencies, is feasible in only one of the case studies, may strengthen my claim that when examining the post-communist countries in Central and Eastern Europe, it is important to pay attention to their unique characteristics. Theories that do not take these characteristics into account may have less explanatory value when it comes to post-communist countries. Nevertheless, I believe that theories that

63 See Shlomo Avineri, After Communism. Travails of Democratization, in: Dissent 5/3, Philadelphia 2008, 16–21.

64 See Jobbik Party. Official Website, http://www.jobbik.com/, 16 July 2013.

examine democratic states in general may provide certain insights regarding the post-communist countries following their transition to democracy, and therefore they should not be excluded from the discussion on the post-communist world.

Third, cultural and social difficulties, which accompanied the transition to democracy and market economy, have a great impact on the electoral success of extreme-right parties as well. Based on the empirical analysis of the two case studies, it can be asserted that the weakness of the civil society and the high 'transition costs' significantly influenced the electoral success of extreme-right parties in post-communist countries in Central and Eastern Europe. Moreover, it can be determined that the communist legacy has a great influence in this field, because of the difficulties the citizens have undergone to adjust to the democratic system, absorb its advantages and function under much less planned and dictated (and thus much less expected) political rule. These difficulties cause the citizens to search for extreme answers inside the political sphere instead of trying to look for a moderate alternative outside of it. These extreme answers promise to bring back the familiar, safe, well-defined patterns of the nation and the state, and they take the form of the conservative nationalistic rhetoric of the extreme-right parties.

In relation to regional causes that affect the electoral success of extreme-right parties in post-communist countries in Central and Eastern Europe, it seems that they indeed affect this phenomenon but only when combined with internal factors. Despite the important role that the European Union played in the transition process, the practical and ideological break of Communism caused such a great political and economic turbulence in the post-communist world, regardless of the accession process, so that it is only reasonable to assume that it will bring about many difficulties.[65] No doubt the pressure that accompanied the accession process has added to these difficulties, but I believe it is logical to assert that extreme-right parties would have gained electoral success nonetheless, because of the countless difficulties that accompanied the fall of Communism and the transition to democracy and market economy. Moreover, the starting point from which the post-communist countries entered the accession process was in many ways different than the one from which the Western democracies had started. Given that fact, it is possible to assume that a better political, economic and social situation in the post-communist countries would have reduced the severe impact of the 'one size fits all' policy. I do not wish to argue that the 'one size fits all' policy had no significant influence on the electoral success of extreme-right parties, because indeed it had, but I want to argue that its influence was so enhanced because of the internal situation of the post-communist countries. Regarding the claim that electoral success of extreme-right parties in post-communist countries in Central and Eastern Europe is related to a broader European phenomenon of democratic deficit, this research proves not only that this argument is not always applicable, but also that its influence is strongly related to the absence of a well-established democracy

65 See Mansfield – Snyder, Transitions, 297–337.

in the post-communist countries. This reinforces my argument that the accession process itself cannot explain the electoral success of extreme-right parties in post-communist countries in Central and Eastern Europe, and that it impacts this phenomenon only when combined with internal factors.

To conclude, this research finds that the rise of extreme-right parties in post-communist countries in Central and Eastern Europe is affected by multiple causes from diverse aspects of the political life. In an attempt to provide a broad, comprehensive and multi-level conclusions, this research is not focusing on one aspect of the political life, but instead trying to draw as wide picture as possible on the variety of circumstances and factors that support the electoral success of extreme-right parties in this specific kind of countries. This is an attempt to move away from a single-perspective analysis into a more complex and more holistic analysis of current developments, aiming to depict the intricacy of reality. The implementation of this of analysis on two case studies allows us, in my opinion, to draw much wider and generalized conclusions. This research points out that first and foremost there is no single explanation to the rise of extreme-right parties in post-communist countries in Central and Eastern Europe. On the contrary, this phenomenon is affected by multiple causes and circumstances, which together create a fertile ground for the strengthening of extreme tendencies, including extreme-right parties. Then the research establishes the case that the electoral success of extreme-right parties in post-communist countries in Central and Eastern Europe has a tight connection to the communist past of these countries. Moreover, it shows that theories that do not pay specific attention to this communist past have less explanatory power than theories that take this characteristic into consideration. After that, the research indicates that internal factors, and not regional (external) factors, have the most significant influence on this phenomenon. This correlates directly to my conclusion regarding the importance of examine the communist past when researching current events in post-communist countries, as this past has a great influence on these countries, even 25 years after the dissolution of the communist bloc.

Hence, even though the attempt to draw conclusions out of two case studies must be done humbly and cautiously, especially when processes are still taking place, this research wishes to argue that generalizations can be made, despite these restrictions. More importantly, this research claims that the echoes of the collapse of the Communism in Central and Eastern Europe are still heard and felt these days in the region, and influence current developments in post-communist countries, including the electoral success of extreme-right parties. It is not to say that the Communist was not over, but that its impacts on present days in post-communist countries cannot be disregarded. This point is crucial to our understanding of the post-communist countries today.

Theresa Mairhofer

Approaching the Concept of Confidence in Students' Lived (Learning)-Experiences

University of New Orleans

Research Question

Trust is an important factor in the academic achievement of students.[1] This is not a new idea. In 2002, Finland scored high on the Pisa test. When looking back at the Pisa results in 2002, it is likely that the sense of self confidence within Finnish students is connected with their academic achievement.[2] As evidenced by the Pisa study, there is a connection between trust and positive learning results of students. Yet, educators seem to pay little attention to the meaning of trust in a pedagogical context and its impact on school achievement.[3] When looking at the Pisa results of 2002, however, it becomes clear that trust in students does have an impact on their learning.

There is significant literature describing the impact of trust for a school climate and for students' academic performance. Opinions differ, however, whether a trustworthy climate amongst school leaders, or between student and teacher, actually leads to better academic performances of students. In the Anglo-American context, scholars such as Bryk and Schneider or Forsyth and others have investigated the impact of a trustful school climate on students' school achievements. They have found that a trust-building school climate fosters students' academic performance. Among European researchers, Schweer found out that even though a trustworthy relationship to the teacher is important, because it fosters students' learning, it does not necessarily lead to higher academic performances of the stu-

1 This study (Trust – A Phenomenological Study of Educational Learning Experiences) is sponsored by a stipend of the University of Innsbruck, the 'Doktoratsstipendium aus der Nachwuchsförderung', and follows the methodology, which was developed in a grant-funded project at the University of Innsbruck, lead by Univ. Prof. Dr. Michael Schratz.

2 Sabine Etzold – Reinhard Kahl – Ulrich Schnabel – Martin Spiewak – Astrid Viciano, Zwischen Erfurt und Pisa. Der Thüringer Amoklauf ist ein Einzelfall – und stellt dennoch das selektive Schulsystem infrage [Between Erfurt and Pisa. The Thuringian Rampage is an Individual Case – and yet Questions the Selective School System], *Die Zeit online,* 2002 May 2nd, 2.

3 Martin Schweer (Ed.), Bildung und Vertrauen [Education and Confidence], Frankfurt am Main 2006, 73–89.

dent.[4] None of these studies focuses explicitly on the students and how they experience trust when learning. Thus, there is an identified lack of surveys focusing on how students experience trust in different didactical settings.[5] Tschannen-Moran mentions this lack of empirical research focusing on students' trust. For this study, which aims to explore trust experiences students make at school, this is an important finding. This study follows Schratz' definition of 'lernseits'[6], thus an attempt is made to see and understand learning from the perspective of the student.[7] Students' lived experiences are the starting point to investigate how students experience trust when they learn. In order to get to the very bottom of the phenomenon of trust in regards to learning, special attention is paid to five facets of trust: how to trust, sense of basic trust, confidence, distrust and trustworthiness. This article primarily focuses on the facet of confidence. To start with this paper describes the purpose of this study, followed by an introduction of the phenomenologically-orientated vignette research. Afterwards a description of the theoretical background of the facet of confidence is presented, before a vignette from one of the field visits is read under the particular angle of confidence. Finally, the conclusion of this paper sums up the most important findings concerning the facet of confidence in students' learning and mentions future research steps for this project.

Purpose of this study

This study focuses consequently on the perspective of the students and how they experience trust while learning. A phenomenological methodology is used, which enables the researcher to explore the lived experiences of students at school. Cozek writes 'phenomenology is well placed to bring us closer to the phenomena that intrigue or puzzle us, through challenging us to bracket our taken-for-granted assumptions and usual ways of doing things as we explore our practice anew'.[8]

Learning in this study is seen through a phenomenological perspective, which allows an insight into corners and moments of learning, which are often taken for granted. Thus, it is the very aim of this study to present and uncover moments and experiences of learning which are often taken-for-granted in the field of education. For example, how does it feel for a student to experience self-confidence and what does this mean for his/her learning? Phenomenology can offer new in-

4 Cf. *ibid.*

5 Megan Tschannen-Moran, Trust Matters. Leadership for Successful Schools, San Francisco 2004, 213.

6 'lernseits' is a German term, founded by Michael Schratz (2009), meaning [being mindful of learning].

7 Michael Schratz, 'Lernseits' von Unterricht. Alte Muster, neue Lebenswelten – was für Schulen? ['Being Mindful of Learning' from Education. Old Models, New Living Environments – What Kind of Schools?], in: Lernende Schule 12/46–47, Seelze 2009, 16–21, here 20.

8 Chris Cozek, Phenomenology. A Review of Gloria Dall'Alba's (Ed.) Diverse Approach, in: Phenomenology & Practice, 6/1, Alberta 2012, 95–105, here 104.

sights into the field of learning and therefore these findings should not be exclusive for researchers. However, the goal of this study is to explore and present trust experiences in students' learning so that educators become more sensitive about the process of students' learning and adjust their teaching methods accordingly. The insight into learning, which will be gained through a phenomenological inquiry in this study, can enhance teachers' existing practice. I agree with Cozek that 'phenomenology potentially has the greatest contribution to make to education, especially in a context, in which accountability measures and economic imperatives threaten to overshadow the pedagogical and transformative purpose of education for our contemporary world'.[9]

Exploring Students' Lived Experiences – Phenomenologically-orientated Vignette Research

This study explores the essence of the phenomenon of learning when capturing students' experiences at school, which are read under the particular perspective of the phenomenon of trust. Focusing on lived (learning)-experiences of students is a unique way to get closer to the phenomenon of learning, which, as Buck claims, is still one of the most unknown human performances.[10] This study choses a perspective 'lernseitig', consequently focusing on the lived experiences of students.[11] The question arises: how is it possible to capture these experiences of students? How can the researcher manage to see what is actually there, rather than to assume what is there? How is it possible to capture another person's experience, which is not the one from the researcher? Which research method is suitable for experiencing others' experiences? A phenomenological orientation was found to be the right approach for this present study since phenomenology manages to get to this very essence of the phenomenon of study, 'learning' in this case. Researching things as they appear, in their experience as lived, derives from Husserl's idea of 'to the things themselves'. Such a phenomenological method requires an open attitude of the researchers, setting aside judgments about the phenomenon. Moreover, phenomenology, located among qualitative methods, focuses on the human being, such as the student in this study.[12] The goal is to 'tactfully access and capture in writing the fundamentally inaccessible, the lived experiences of children at school'.[13] Lived experiences are the source and the subject from phenomenological

9 Cf. *ibid.*

10 Günter Buck, Lernen und Erfahrung [Learning and Experience], Darmstadt 1989, 7.

11 Schratz, Unterricht, 20.

12 Max van Manen, Researching Lived Experience. Human Science Research for an Action Sensitive Pedagogy, London 1990, 11.

13 Johanna Schwarz – Tanja Westfall-Greiter, Planning for the Unplannable. Responding to (Un) articulated Calls in the Classroom, in: Phenomenology & Practice 6/2, Alberta 2012, 121–135, here 122.

research.[14] This idea is supported by Merleau-Ponty, when he states that 'phenomenology tries to give a direct description of our experience as it is, without taking into account its psychological origin and the causal explanations which the scientist, the historian or the sociologist may be able to provide'.[15] Meyer-Drawe, an important project mentor, 'describes our discourse as one which springs forth from the things themselves rather than by our assumptions, theories and judgments about them'.[16]

The researcher co-experiences the lived experiences of students as they are happening *in medias res*, in a pedagogic situation. Unlike van Manen's anecdotes, which stem from recall, vignettes emerge in the midst of a situation at school. Vignettes do not focus on what precisely happens in the field. Instead, the delightful, impressing or disturbing aspects of a moment are shown in a way that the complexity and liveliness of such experiences are expressed, at least in imprints.[17]

The vignette 'points to' something, rather than offering any explanation or conclusion.[18] Alike experiences, vignettes are 'grounded in a surplus' and 'there is always more announcing itself than that which is explicitly there'.[19] As Waldenfels writes, '[what] we see in a particular situation means paradoxically that we always see more than that which we see'.[20]

Vignettes enable the researcher to co-experience students' lived experiences in the classroom, as they are happening *in media res*. Familiar points of view can be seen from a new perspective, which is impossible for teachers due to their pedagogical acting in the classroom. When co-experiencing, the researcher attempts to stay open to observe pathic elements such as atmosphere, tone of voice, or facial and bodily expression. These notes, set down in protocols, serve as springboards for writing vignettes. Both learner and researcher have to be affected in the midst of a pedagogical situation, in order to capture (learning)-experiences *in statu nascendi*.[21] To be affected goes back to Husserl's 'affiziert werden'.[22] Waldenfels de-

14 Van Manen, Experience, 53.

15 Maurice Merleau-Ponty, Phenomenology of Perception, London 1962, VII.

16 Schwarz – Westfall-Greiter, Planning, 122.

17 Michael Schratz – Johanna Schwarz – Tanja Westfall-Greiter, Lernen als bildende Erfahrung. Vignetten in der Praxisforschung [Learning as an Educational Experience. Vignettes in Practice Research], Innsbruck/Wien/Bozen 2012, 35.

18 Hans Georg Gadamer, Truth and Method, New York 1975, 68.

19 Schwarz – Westfall-Greiter, Planning, 123.

20 Bernhard Waldenfels, Bruchlinien der Erfahrung. Phänomenologie, Psychoanalyse, Phänomenotechnik [Break Lines of the Experience. Phenomenology, Psychoanalysis, Phenomenotechnique], Frankfurt am Main 2002, 70, 138, cited in cf. *Ibid.*

21 Michael Schratz – Johanna Schwarz – Tanja Westfall-Greiter, Beyond the Reach of Teaching Measurement.
Methodology and Initial Research Findings of the Innsbrucker Vignette Research, Paper for Icsei Conference 2013 in Santiago de Chile, 1–25, here 9.

22 Edmund Husserl, Experience and Judgement, USA 1973.

scribes 'affiziert werden' as a pain, a being frightened, or a positive surprise when we live through something.[23]

In order to co-experience students' lived experience and to be affected, the researcher has to be engaged in the situation. In this context, Schratz and others mention Bakhtin, who 'claims that an event "can be described only participatively" [when] [...] being engaged in or "unindifferent" to the event itself'.[24] Moreover, they write that 'this creates a dilemma for researchers, when the expectation of the scientific community is to maintain objectivity, often manifested as indifference, in order for research to be acknowledged as legitimate and sound science'.[25] Following Bakhtin's argumentation, however, objectification will not lead to the insights of what it means to be a learner, to actually act as a learner:

> 'neither theoretical cognition nor aesthetic intuition can provide an approach to the once-occurrent real Being of an event, for there is no unity and no interpenetration between the content/sense (a product) and the act (an actual historical performance) in consequence of the essential and fundamental abstracting-from-myself qua participant in the course of establishing meaning and seeing.'[26]

Vignettes aim to show rather than to tell. Therefore, according to Merlau-Ponty's suggestion, vignettes attempt to describe, rather than to analyze or to explain in order for the main goal to be achieved; namely, to get back to the things themselves, as they appear. To say it in Merleau-Ponty's words, 'it is a matter of describing, not of explaining or analyzing', thus describing rather than analyzing.[27] This aspiration, to describe rather than to explain, requires an 'aesthetic sensibility' of the researcher.[28] Van Manen expresses the challenge of writing vignettes when he says, 'language speaks the phenomena rather than of it'.[29] The researcher is confronted with the difficulty to describe accurately and concretely the lived experiences from students. Crafting vignettes requires a recreation of the lived experiences of students at school in narrative form, rather than to only reconstruct the information.[30] Thus, 'it is a delicate task to ensure that as much of the surplus of experience as possible is captured in writing'.[31] It is understood that much of students' learning, such as 'I got it!' is audible, however hard to verbalize. Vignettes attempt to convey non-verbal articulations, such as slouched shoulders, a head rested in arms or

23 Waldenfels, Bruchlinien, 99.

24 Bakhtin Mikhail Mikhailovich, Towards a Philosophy of the Act, Austin 1993, 32. Cit in: Schratz – Schwarz – Westfall-Greiter, Reach, 10.

25 Cf. *ibid.*

26 Mikhailovich, Philosophy, 18.

27 Cf. *ibid.*, 4.

28 Schwarz – Westfall-Greiter, Planning, 123.

29 Van Manen, Experience, 13.

30 Schratz – Schwarz – Westfall-Greiter, Reach, 12.

31 Cf. *ibid.*

a body full of tension. Thus vignettes do not only describe what happened in the field but also make an effort to convey this full experience, which lies beyond the verbal articulation.[32] The aim is to make the atmosphere, under which the vignette emerges, comprehensible for the reader. Therefore, 'to capture data in the field that will yield a vignette, researchers must take a stance that goes beyond mere observation so that the events can be described fully as experiences'.[33] Special attention is paid to corporal expression such as a facial or bodily expression in order to get to the very essence of things. According to Merleau-Ponty every gesture of a person has a meaning.[34] Thus, when crafting vignettes, an attempt is made to use verbs which manage to express the tone: is it whispering, speaking under one's breath, shouting, or just being quiet? Here, again Merleau-Ponty explains, 'it is a matter of describing, not of explaining or analyzing', thus describing rather than analyzing.[35] Therefore, it is asked what is shown and how it is shown to the researcher. It is the aim to show without interpreting and no final statement is given. Van Manen and Merleau-Ponty also represent this literary quality in vignettes and phenomenological texts. Van Manen describes anecdotes as being so personal that they can be hard to paraphrase or summarize, since the sense is so strongly embedded.[36] Merleau-Ponty compares phenomenological research to literature.[37]

Being in the field, capturing empirically one's own 'experience of the lived experiences of students being taught at school', implies the fact that the lived experience from students at school is never the researcher's experience but always the experience of the student.[38] The lived experience undergoes a second transition from the actual lived experience when described through language. This aspect might be problematic, however, as for this study there is no other way than language to describe students' lived experiences. Van Manen supports the necessity of using language to describe lived experiences; thus, he is convinced of the importance of language in phenomenological research, when he writes that language is the only way the pedagogic experience can be communicated in research.[39]

After vignettes are crafted, they are phenomenologically analyzed, referred to as vignette reading. The researcher becomes involved in the text, trying to 'sense her way through the experience', without categorizing or operationalizing what is revealed.[40] Any interpretation, analysis, final or general conclusion must

32 Cf. *ibid.*

33 Cf. *ibid.*, 10.

34 Merleau-Ponty, Phenomenology, 15.

35 Cf. *ibid.*, 4.

36 Phenomenology Online: A resource for phenomenological inquiry, http://www.phenomenologyonline.com/inquiry/methodology/, 1 May 2012. Cit. in: Schwarz – Westfall-Greiter, Planning, 124.

37 Cf. *ibid.*

38 Schratz – Schwarz – Westfall-Greiter, Reach, 11.

39 Van Manen, Experience, 111.

40 Schwarz – Westfall-Greiter, Planning, 124.

be avoided at all cost. Nor are definite and final explanations given. As Gadamer says, the researcher 'points to', rather than he/she 'points out'.[41] He/she points to the richness and spontaneity of experiences, shown in different facets of different readings. In this study, the readings of vignettes point to the facets of trust, such as distrust, trustworthiness, basic trust, or confidence- experiences of students. It goes unsaid that the researcher has to be 'mindful of and opening to the "more" of the experience', asking questions, such as, 'what is there what I haven't seen before? What do I see in a new light, after a second, third, fourth look?' This process is a 'peeling off and adding of layers'.[42]

Schwarz and Westfall-Greiter describe the process of the reading of a vignette as follows:

> 'As phenomenologically oriented researchers we are actively passive, purposefully refraining from explanations that are definite and final. Like Michelangelo's finger, a reading comprises profoundly human gestures pointing to something, be it a turn of phrase, a naming an association, an image, a metaphor, a question, a particular focus or a reference.'[43]

The vignettes for this study have their origin in field visits done in 2012/2013 in New Orleans, which were sponsored with the Nick-Müller fellowship, funded by Tyrol and the city of Innsbruck. Three of these visits were done in two high schools in New Orleans, Louisiana. The method of the research project, 'Personalized Learning in Diverse Communities' finds its beginnings in Europe, Innsbruck in 2009/2010 and expanded to the US in 2012/2013. The concept and the data instruments of the qualitative research approach are the same.

In order to capture tactfully and sensitively students' lived experiences in school, the researcher collected data at three field visits over one academic year in a 6th grade class. For each field visit, at least two days were spent in the field at different times during the year (October 2012, February 2013, May 2013) to gain data, focusing on two learners who were picked by their homeroom teacher. Due to a combination of different qualitative data collection instruments, a broader insight into students' lived experiences at school could be achieved: protocols of lived experiences[44] were drafted during classes, which helped to guide conversations with the two selected students and their teachers. Additionally, conversations with focus groups (five children from the same subject class), principals, parents, and legal guardians provided additional information. Further tracks of learning at school were demonstrated with photo documentation or documents, picked by students and teachers to demonstrate the students' learning.

---

41 Hans Georg Gadamer, The Relevance of the Beautiful and other Essays, Cambridge 1986, 68.

42 Schwarz – Westfall-Greiter, Planning, 124.

43 Cf. *ibid.*

44 Van Manen, Experience.

The Facet of Confidence – An Example

In this section, a theoretical background on confidence, self-confidence and belief in a pedagogical setting is presented, before a reading of a vignette of confidence is explained. This study explores students' trust experiences. Confidence, as a facet of trust, is shown to be a very important factor for successful learning.

Confidence relates to the natural abilities of a human being. When thinking about it, one can have confidence in another person's ability; one can trust that this person will perform well in a certain activity, or one can also have confidence in oneself. It could be assumed that teachers should have confidence in their students' abilities to fulfill certain tasks, whereas students should feel confident in their teachers' competence about teaching their subject. The concept of confidence, as will be shown, is tightly connected with belief. We cannot be confident in ourselves or in others, if we don't believe in our or their qualities and our/their capacities to fulfill a requirement, an assessment or ability successfully.

Bollnow distinguishes between trust and confidence. He argues that the concept of confidence is a simpler form of trust, a 'less complicated preform of real trust', which causes fewer problems.[45] According to him, confidence is one-sided and it does not have the intrinsic moral character of trust so far. Confidence relates to a natural human ability: we might be confident that a person is capable in doing something. Being confident in somebody, however, does not require any response or reaction to our confidence in him/her. Moreover a person we have confidence might not react at all, he/she might not even know that we feel confident in him/her. This implies that one can feel confident even in a complete stranger. The concept of trust, which is defined as a reciprocal relationship, works differently and when we trust somebody we demand a response.

Being confident in a person, believing in his/her abilities, leads to an encouragement and improvement of this person's particular ability, especially if the person is aware of other's people's confidence in him/her. The feeling of other people's confidence works like a confirmation and thus self-confidence increases. The person, in whom another person has confidence, will try to justify the confidence others have in him/her. I agree with Bollnow, who claims that showing confidence in people increases their self-confidence, which is of the utmost importance in education.[46] Bollnow calls confidence the 'prerequisite for any demand or task with which we are confronting [the children] in the family and school'.[47] Nothing is more discouraging for a child than being given the impression of not being able to do something. Such an attitude discourages the child and their achievements will not grow, but rather decline. Therefore, having confidence in children

45 Otto Friedrich Bollnow, The Pedagogical Atmosphere. The Perspective of the Educator, in: Phenomenology and Pedagogy 7, Alberta 1989, 37–63, here 38.

46 Cf. *ibid.*

47 Cf. *Ibid.*

can improve their development. It is a fact that children possess a natural urge to test their abilities to their own limits. They want to find out how far they can go and where their personal limits are. Thus, according to Bollnow, children need their educator to have high expectations of them, they want to fulfill these expectations, and they demand the educator's confidence in them to be able to follow these high expectations.[48]

Besides being confident about someone's ability, confidence can also refer to oneself, meaning that a person is able to do a certain task. The concept of being confident in someone's own abilities, which is tightly connected with self-confidence, will be looked at in more detail now, before a vignette reading is presented, showing a student's self-confidence in a school setting. Moreover, it is shown that inner self-confidence makes people more ready to trust. Luhmann writes that people are more willing to trust if they have inner security.[49] As soon as we trust, we have to face the risk that our expectations can be disappointed. If we have an inner security, a kind of inner self-confidence, we can handle disappointments of trust relationships much better. Self-confidence and the readiness to trust relate to each other. Luhmann calls this an equation: self-confidence = readiness to trust.[50] Accordingly, Luhmann writes that possessing this inner assurance, meaning that the trustor always knows a way out of a certain situation, serves as an inner resource, and is a foundation for the readiness of trust.[51] When we trust, we also present part of ourselves and we make ourselves vulnerable. The trustor presents himself as someone who is ready to bestow trust. If the trustor's expectations do not get fulfilled, but rather disappointed, he/she is exposed to an awkward situation of being naïve, ridiculous, and stupid in trusting a specific person or situation. A person will be more likely to trust if he/she can be sure that his self-presentation will not be affected in case of disappointment.[52]

The concept of confidence is tightly connected with belief. We can only be confident in ourselves if we believe in ourselves, and we can only be confident in others if we believe in them. A teacher, for example, can only be confident about a student's ability in something if he/she believes in this student. Thus, we can say that especially in a pedagogical setting, belief is an indispensable factor, even though there is little attention paid to. In his article 'The Pedagogical Atmosphere', Bollnow explains the notion of belief. According to him, believing in a person is when you expect positive qualities in that person.[53] Bollnow explains that a person becomes what the environment believes about him/her when he writes, 'the environment [...] can indeed change a human being, for good or for

48 Bollnow, Atmosphere, 39.
49 Niklas Luhmann, Trust and Power. Two Works by Niklas Luhmann, Chichester 1979, 78.
50 Cf. *ibid.*
51 Cf. *ibid.*, 82.
52 Cf. *ibid.*
53 Bollnow, Atmosphere, 40.

worse, depending on the nature of his or her belief'.[54] Especially the child, when being exposed to good or to bad influences of the educator, forms him/herself to this imposed picture. If a teacher has a good opinion about a student, if he sees a child's reliability, devotion and sincerity, then he can evoke these qualities in the child. The belief of the adult reinforces the positive skills, which he or she assumes in the child.

The opposite, however, is also possible when the educator suspects bad qualities in the child, such as laziness, failure, or lack of intelligence. Under these circumstances, it could happen that the child actually becomes just as lazy and stupid as the educator supposes the child to be. Thus, the educator's distrust can produce a bad child and hinder the child's free development.[55] As Bollnow writes, 'it is most often [...] the educator himself who makes a person, a child, a boy into a bad person, a bad child, a bad boy. It happens when one is supposing a vicious, bad, or at least crooked intention in everything that is done by the child or the boy in ignorance or without consideration.'[56]

Bollnow (1989) rites that educators have to be very careful with such impulses of distrust. He mentions Fröbel (1951), who writes[57],

> 'unfortunately there still are such calamitous individuals amongst educators; they always see little, nasty insidious, lurking evils in children and boys, where others at most perceive an overabundance of fun or the results of a somewhat unbridled joy of life. Such ill-fated individuals, especially when they are educators, turn other persons or children, whether they are totally innocent or not, into culprits, by putting thoughts and actions in to them which otherwise would be unknown to them.'

Fröbel's quote is harsh and one-sided, but it seems that he noticed this pedagogical dilemma. I agree with Bollnow that teachers should be mindful in their accusations against students and in their distrust towards several students. It is a fact that it matters to children what their teachers think of them. If the educator shows distrust and disbelief towards a student, this can have a harmful influence and it can hinder the child's free development. In this context, Bollnow points out the importance of educators' trust towards the child, despite all disappointments.[58] When taking the teacher's perspective into consideration, it can be argued that the educator is also exposed to a certain risk when trusting the child. The educator must face the fact that trust follows the inevitability of nature and he/she must accept the student's unpredictable freedom, too. Educators, like par-

54 *Ibid.*, 39.

55 Cf. *ibid.*, 40.

56 Cf. *ibid.*, 41.

57 Cf. *ibid.*, 40.

58 *Ibid.*, 42f.

ents, should develop a blind confidence in the child, in order to maintain trust in the child, which might be sometimes disappointed. Therefore, according to Bollnow, the true educator knows about the possible crisis and weaknesses of a child. After a child makes a mistake, the child can improve its behavior by having the educator to promise his/her honesty too. Children therefore cannot improve their behavior on their own, but need another person, like the educator, who believes in them.[59]

Reading Confidence

After the theoretical discussion of confidence, the reading of a vignette below aims to present the facet of confidence in a pedagogical setting. The awareness of the importance of confidence in an educational setting will be fostered when reading the vignette. In the reading of the following vignette, Adrian, a 6th grader demonstrates an example of being self-confident and of possessing a readiness to trust. He trusts in himself, in being right about the meaning of a specific word he and his classmates come upon during English class.

> The English lesson starts; the students file into their seats, open their folders and follow the instructions on the worksheet. It is an exercise based on spelling and dictionary meanings. Adrian opens his folder and starts working on the exercises, while moving on his chair and chewing on his pencil. He looks away from the worksheet and around in the classroom, while squinting his eyes and he takes a deep breath. He grabs his books and folders and goes straight to another table where three other students are sitting. He takes the free chair, opens his folder again and goes on with the spelling and translation exercise. Suddenly he looks up, his eyes wide open and he asks the other students sitting on the table, 'Do you know what lush means? Have you heard this expression before?' 'No, this is a weird word, I don't know it!' answers the girl sitting next to him with a condescending tone in her voice. The other two students shake their heads, 'No, we haven't come across this word!' 'I'm sure it does not even exist!' answers the girl again, this time even more determined. 'It does exist!' Adrian replies energetically, with wide eyes and waving his arms. 'It means something like rich!' He moves his chair back, walks straight to the bookshelf in the class and comes back with a dictionary. Adrian looks very closely at the dictionary, his head only inches away from the book. He runs his forefinger along the pages of the dictionary, while he is shaking his feet under the chair. 'Yeah, found it, found it!' Adrian shouts, raising his voice and waving his hands. 'I was right, it does exist, look here!' The other kids look at him, raising their eyebrows and nodding their heads.

59 Cf. *ibid.*

Adrian starts working on his exercise, which is about spelling and dictionary meaning. He knows what he has to do; he opens his folders and starts. While looking on his worksheet he moves on his chair and chews on his pencil. Is something distracting him? Or can he concentrate better when he moves on his chair and chews on his pencil? Suddenly his glance moves up from his worksheet. His glancing around in the classroom seems as if he is looking for something. His squinting eyes support this impression. Suddenly, he seems to have found what he is looking for and it seems as if he takes a sigh of relief. He grabs his folder and goes straight to the free chair on the table with three other students. His movements seem to be determined, it seems as if he was looking for this free chair so that he can share the table with the other kids. He goes on working on his worksheet again. All of a sudden, something striking seems to happen to Adrian while he is working on his translation exercise when he comes up with this new word lush. This incident appears to be so impressive and exciting, indicated by his wide-open eyes and he wants to share his discovery with the other kids on the table, he needs their attention. The kids, however, do not seem to share Adrian's interest. They even seem to look down on him, ridiculing him when telling him, 'that is a weird word!' or 'I'm sure it does not even exist!' Adrian, nonetheless, speaks against their opinion, claiming, 'It does exist!' He is determined, which is expressed by his wide eyes and waving hands. It seems as if he cannot understand why the other students will not believe him, why they seem not even to care much about it. They do not do anything to find out about the existence and the meaning of the word. And even though he is the only one who is sure about the existence of the word 'lush', he keeps claiming that it does exist. He does not follow the other's opinion, he is confident in his own knowledge, more than he is confident in the other kids' knowledge about the existence of words. One could say that Adrian exposes himself of being made ridiculous by the other kids. He is not sure if he can prove the existence of the word to the others. The fact that he accepts this risk, of making a fool of himself, shows his self-confidence. Through his inner assurance, Adrian is ready to stand the fact that the kids try to make him feel ridiculous and he is ready to trust in his own abilities and knowledge. Luhmann's 'equation' should be mentioned at this point which describes that self-confidence and the readiness to trust relate to each other.[60] Adrian is forced to prove that he is right to the answers and he knows how to do that. There is a tension going on within Adrian, when looking through the pages of the dictionary. He knows what he is looking for when his forefinger runs purposefully along the pages. It appears as if he cannot wait to find the word, he is shaking his feet under the chair. Is he nervous that his friends were right and the word does not exist? Or do his shaking feet indicate that he cannot wait to tell his friends that he was right? Whatever way he feels, finally, the words explode out of his mouth, 'Yeah, I found it, found it!' His rising voice and his waving hands reinforce the feeling, his victory. Adrian

60 Luhmann, Trust, 78.

found proof of the existence of the word, and he is confident that he knows better than the other kids. Before looking up the word in the dictionary he does not know if he is going to be a fool in his assumption or not. He appears to be able to take this risk since he believes in himself and possesses an inner assurance. He is self-confident that he will be right. In this lesson, Adrian did not only learn the meaning of a new word, moreover he noticed that he can be sure about his confidence and that he can stand the other children's doubts towards him.

Conclusion

This paper gave an overview of the planned research project, which aims to approach students' lived-experiences at school, read under the particular angle of trust, rather than to present a finished product or to impact research and practice. After explaining the theoretical background and the method this study is based on, the facet of confidence was presented, as an example. Theoretical background knowledge as well as a reading of a vignette served to illuminate this facet of trust. As shown, confidence has a positive effect in the learning experience of children, illustrated in Adrian's example. Adrian is self-confident and ready to trust his own abilities when he is sure about the existence of the new word 'lush', which he explores during English class. Trusting in himself is important in this particular learning experience. This makes him feel like a king after a victory, when he can prove that he is right, and the other kids, who are suspicious and try to make a fool of him, are wrong. This vignette shows that confidence experiences children make at school can be beneficial to their learning. Thus, Adrian could stand the other kids' doubt about his discovery about the word lush and he could prove to them that he is right which is a very pleasant moment for Adrian. Having this in mind, it should not be said anymore that the facet of confidence does not have an impact on students' learning experiences at school. Thus, confidence should be defined as a vital facet in a pedagogical setting.

Besides the facet of confidence, the dissertation points out further facets of trust, such as basic trust, distrust, trustworthiness, or how to trust in regards to students' learning experiences. Further vignettes are read to deepen the insight into how students experience trust when they learn. As mentioned in the beginning, there is a lack of research, which focuses on the learner explicitly and how he/she experiences trust when learning. Focusing on the learner, thus taking a perspective 'lernseitig', while investigating students' lived (learning)-experiences at school, is a surplus of this study and gives new insights into how students experience trust, when they learn. This study aims to foster the awareness of the importance of trust in an educational setting, which can contribute to a better understanding of students' learning.

About the authors

Martina Bartečková Nováková is an external Ph.D. student at the Department of German Studies at the Philosophical Faculty of Palacký University in Olomouc. In her research she mainly focuses on the phenomenon of exile (exile between the World Wars in Czechoslovakia, German authors from Czechoslovakia in Latin America) and on cultural history.

Markus P. Beham is a Ph.D. fellow at the Department of Legal Philosophy, Law of Religion and Culture at the University of Vienna. His research work has focused on public international law, in particular philosophy of international relations and sources theory. He is currently on sabbatical to pursue an LL. M. degree at Columbia Law School. He holds degrees in law and history from the University of Vienna as well as the Aristotle University Thessaloniki.

Henriett Éva Dinók is a Ph.D. candidate at the Doctoral School of Law and Political Sciences at the University of Szeged. She is currently Research Assistant at the Wirth Institute for Austrian and Central European Studies in Edmonton, Canada. After graduating from Law School, following a short legal practice, she joined the Institute for Legal Studies of the Hungarian Academy of Sciences Centre for Social Sciences in Budapest, as a Junior Research Fellow. Her doctoral project focuses on bias-motivated crimes. She has also been active in working with human rights NGOs and Roma community organizations.

Maria Bianca Fanta is a Ph.D. candidate at the doctoral school of Central European Studies at Andrássy University Budapest. She studied Journalism in Graz and Paris. Her research interests are media history, communication studies, and historical communication research.

Dominik Hofmann-Wellenhoff studied German and Physical Education at Karl Franzens University Graz. He has studied abroad at the Hendrix College in Conway, Arkansas, the University of Las Palmas in Gran Canaria, Spain, and the University of New Orleans, where he finished his doctoral thesis. Since December 2013 he is employed at the Bischöfliches Gymnasium Graz as a teacher.

Patrick Jajko is a Ph.D. student at the Ph.D. programme of the Andrássy Gyula German-speaking University Budapest and is currently under a scholarship of the doctoral programme of the Faculty for Central European Studies. He holds degrees in European and Central European History from the University of Technology Chemnitz and the Andrássy Gyula German-speaking University Budapest. His personal research interests are in the history of Central Europe during the 19th and 20th century in general, in particular commemorative toponymy, as well as food culture.

Theresa Mairhofer is a Ph.D. fellow at Innsbruck University. She holds a Master degree in teaching English, Psychology, and Philosophy, and a further Master degree in education, with a special focus on counseling. In her dissertation she explores which trust experiences students undergo in different didactical settings. Research interests include teacher education, phenomenology, learning as experience, and trust as a matter of learning.

Thomas Rohringer is a Ph.D. fellow at the TU Berlin and the Max Planck Institute for Human Development. He holds a degree in History from the University of Vienna. His personal research interests include history of the Habsburg Empire and its successor states in the 19th and 20th century, gender studies, and history of emotions.

Ofer Waldman is a Ph.D. candidate at the Center for German Studies at the Hebrew University in Jerusalem, Israel, currently residing as a guest Ph.D. candidate at the Freie Universität, Berlin. He holds an Orchestral Musician Diploma from the University of the Arts of Berlin, and an MA in German Studies from the Hebrew University of Jerusalem. Ofer's research focuses on both the Czech-German encounter in the 20th century through the prism of memory studies as well as the linkage between memory and identity in East-German literature.

Paz Zvick is a graduate of the European Forum at the Hebrew University of Jerusalem. She holds an MA in European Studies, and a BA in Political Science and International Relations, both from the Hebrew University of Jerusalem. Her research areas focus on post-communist countries in Central and Eastern Europe, as well as extreme right parties in Europe and their effect on nationalism, minorities, and the European integration process.